International

This book is due for return on or before the last date shown below.

International Perspectives on English Language Teaching

Forthcoming titles in the series:

Sarah Rich (*editor*)
INTERNATIONAL PERSPECTIVES IN TEACHING ENGLISH TO YOUNG LEARNERS

Sue Garton and Kathleen Graves (*editors*)
INTERNATIONAL PERSPECTIVES IN ELT MATERIALS

International Perspectives on Motivation

Language Learning and Professional Challenges

Edited by

Ema Ushioda
University of Warwick, UK

palgrave
macmillan

First published 2013 by
PALGRAVE MACMILLAN

Palgrave Macmillan in the UK is an imprint of Macmillan Publishers Limited,
registered in England, company number 785998, of Houndmills, Basingstoke,
Hampshire RG21 6XS.

Palgrave Macmillan in the US is a division of St Martin's Press LLC,
175 Fifth Avenue, New York, NY 10010.

Palgrave Macmillan is the global academic imprint of the above companies
and has companies and representatives throughout the world.

Palgrave® and Macmillan® are registered trademarks in the United States,
the United Kingdom, Europe and other countries.

ISBN: 978–1–137–00086–6 hardback
ISBN: 978–1–137–00089–7 paperback

This book is printed on paper suitable for recycling and made from fully
managed and sustained forest sources. Logging, pulping and manufacturing
processes are expected to conform to the environmental regulations of the
country of origin.

A catalogue record for this book is available from the British Library.

A catalog record for this book is available from the Library of Congress.

Contents

List of Illustrations

Figure

Tables

Notes on Contributors

Pamela Aboshiha is Senior Lecturer at Canterbury Christ Church University, U.K. Her research and teaching interests are pre- and in-service teacher education, especially the needs of non-native speaker teachers. Her article 'Diverse changes to practice after an INSET programme' (NATECLA *Language Issues*) was published in 2012.

Darío Luis Banegas works as a secondary school teacher, adviser, and curriculum planner at Ministerio de Educación del Chubut, Argentina. He is an e-tutor at a distance pre-service programme and leads a research project on helping novice primary school teachers through action research. He is involved in projects together with the British Council in Argentina and Uruguay. His interests are materials development, CLIL and action research.

Budiyanto is Principal of Junior High School 7, Jambi, Indonesia. He is also an experienced English language teacher and holds an MA in educational management.

Xuesong (Andy) Gao is Associate Professor in the Faculty of Education, the University of Hong Kong. He publishes on language learner autonomy and teacher development. He is an associate editor for the *Asia Pacific Education Researcher* (Springer) and serves on the Editorial and Advisory Board for *TESOL Quarterly* (2011–13).

Alastair Henry teaches English and language education at University West, Sweden. His research interests include motivation to learn foreign languages additional to English and gender differences in language learning motivation.

Lane Igoudin is Assistant Professor at Los Angeles City College, where he teaches ESL and linguistics. He also serves as chair of the ESL Committee for Los Angeles Community College District. His research interests focus on the role of social identity in L2 acquisition, code choice and language learning motivation, as well as the use of the arts in TESL. His upcoming published works include a chapter in *Multilingual Identities: New Global Perspectives* and a paper in *Plurilingualism and Pluriculturalism in a Globalised World: Which Pedagogy?*

Kuchah Kuchah is Teaching Fellow at the University of Sheffield, U.K. He is completing PhD research at the University of Warwick. His research interests include context-appropriate ELT methodology, teaching and researching young learners, teaching and researching large and multi-grade classes, learner autonomy as well as teacher training and development.

Martin Lamb is Senior Lecturer in TESOL at the University of Leeds, U.K., where he teaches undergraduate and postgraduate courses in the areas of language teaching methodology, assessment, and global English. His main research interest is language learner motivation and its relationship with achievement in different social contexts.

Diane Malcolm is English Unit Head at Arabian Gulf University, Bahrain. Her research interests include learner autonomy, self-directed language learning, English for medical purposes, and L2 academic reading. Recent publications in these areas have appeared in *System*, *Arab World English Journal* and *Studies in Self-Access Language Learning Journal*.

Glenn Stockwell is Professor in Applied Linguistics at Waseda University, Japan. His research interests include mobile learning, computer-mediated communication, and the role of technology in the language learning process. Recent publications include *CALL Dimensions* (co-authored by M. Levy, 2006) and *Computer-Assisted Language Learning: Diversity in Research and Practice* (2012).

Florentina Taylor is Lecturer in Education and MA TESOL Programme Leader at the University of York, U.K. Her recent research has focused on identity in foreign language learning and teaching, as well as the motivation of British pupils to study Modern Foreign Languages.

Ema Ushioda is Associate Professor in ELT and Applied Linguistics at the University of Warwick, U.K. Her research interests are language motivation, autonomy and socio-cultural theory. Recent publications include *Teaching and Researching Motivation* (co-authored with Z. Dörnyei, 2011) and *Motivation, Language Identity and the L2 Self* (co-edited with Z. Dörnyei, 2009).

Lindy Woodrow is Senior Lecturer in TESOL at the University of Sydney, Australia. Her research interests are English language learning motivation and academic writing. Her latest publications include 'College English writing affect: Self-efficacy and anxiety' in *System* (2011) and 'Goal orientations' in *Psychology for Language Learning* (edited by S. Mercer, S. Ryan and M. Williams, 2012).

Series Editors' Preface

As series editors we were delighted to find that in her introduction to this launch volume of 'International Perspectives on ELT' Ema Ushioda manages to capture so elegantly what makes the series both necessary and impossible. Because, while we are insistent that the series should be genuinely international in range and focus, we are also forced to recognise that as far as language learning is concerned what counts as local is inherently problematic. In a situation in which 'contexts of learning and using English in the globalised world are becoming fluid, flexible, mobile, transitory, borderless and less easily definable' (Chapter 1, p. 5), distinctions between international and local blur to indistinctness.

We see this series, however, not as a matter of constructing international perspectives out of local experiences, but of exploiting connectivities that are part of ELT's global presence. In rejecting the linear myth of steady progress towards a methodological ideal, and setting aside what Canagarajah characterises as 'the spectacles of approaches and techniques' (2006: 2), ELT has opened itself to new ways of seeing and to new configurations of understanding. In this world, privileging local over global (or vice versa) is as unproductive as insisting on the primacy of the native speaker.

In order to reflect the many dimensions of ELT, topics in the series will range widely, some focusing on specific groups of learners or settings, others exploring particular aspects of teaching and learning. We begin with motivation, a core element in the language learning process, and this will be followed by collections focusing on young learners, materials, and classroom interaction. Whatever the topic, editors are asked to invite contributions that have a strong local flavour but are internationally relevant, having something distinctively fresh or original to say that is likely to stimulate debate.

Bringing together in one volume contributors from a variety of contexts offers the prospect of multi-voiced engagement with shared themes and concerns, rooted in what Kumaravadivelu has called 'a pedagogy of particularity' (2001: 537), but having global resonance. In gathering contributions from six continents (lamentably, ELT in Antarctica remains unexplored), Ushioda has responded to this challenge with impressively diverse perspectives on motivation, woven together by common themes and concerns.

Settings in this collection range from a large urban ESL programme in Southern California (Igoudin) to English lessons in a junior high school in provincial Indonesia (Lamb and Budiyanto), and the contexts cover those in which English is such an integral part of the everyday lives of students that

English lessons are seen as a welcome opportunity for rest and recuperation (Henry) to those in which English has only recently started to gain prestige status (Kuchah). Contributors may approach motivation issues from different perspectives and with different concerns, but their engagement with these contributes to a deepening of our shared understanding of the nature of language teaching and learning.

As with other books in the series, all the papers in this collection draw on original research by the author, but all have practical relevance, speaking to language teachers and educators rather than to those interested only in research. Inevitably, what is practical or relevant in one context may be pie in the sky in another, but the aim of this series is not prescription; instead we invest in the power of local illumination to prompt new ways of thinking and acting.

In her penetrating state-of-the-art chapter, Ushioda demonstrates how changes in the ELT landscape have had a profound influence on the development of thinking in the area of motivation, calling into question some of the most fundamental assumptions about its nature and giving rise to new perspectives on how it can be understood. The motivational dissonances that Ushioda refers to in this discussion, and returns to as she looks ahead in the concluding chapter, represent protean challenges made more intractable by the interplay of identity and alignment within specific contexts. Solutions, she suggests, are not to be found in blanket prescriptions but in the form of understandings generated through local engagement. As ever, much is demanded of the teacher, but the weight of responsibility can be lightened by shared understanding.

The papers that follow wrestle with contemporary challenges in ELT, identify fresh opportunities and engage with old problems in new ways. Individually, they may address local concerns, but as the engagement priorities at the end of each paper demonstrate, the issues they raise resonate internationally. These issues also reflect a professional context in which it is no longer meaningful to think in terms of a 'centre' or 'periphery' – the dynamics have changed. In any field, knowledge appropriation by the centre establishes a centrifugal dynamic which not only pushes advice and prescription out towards the periphery but simultaneously blocks the flow of reciprocal insight. By establishing a global knowledge exchange environment we change this dynamic to one which accommodates opposing flows: a systolic/diastolic relationship that becomes the heartbeat of our profession.

References

Canagarajah, A. S. (2006). TESOL at forty: What are the issues? *TESOL Quarterly*, 40(1): 9–34.

Kumaravadivelu, B. (2001). Toward a postmethod pedagogy. *TESOL Quarterly*, 35(4): 537–60.

List of Abbreviations

AGU — Arabian Gulf University
AMTB — Attitude Motivation Test Battery
ASEAN — Association of Southeast Asian Nations
BBS — (electronic) bulletin board system
CALL — computer assisted language learning
CBI — content based instruction
CDE — California Department of Education
CEFR — Common European Framework of Reference
CELTA — Certificate in English Language Teaching
CLIL — content and language integrated learning
CLT — communicative language teaching
CMS — course management system
DELTA — Diploma in English Language Teaching
EAP — English for academic purposes
EFL — English as a foreign language
ELF — English as a lingua franca
ESL — English as a second language
ESOL — English for speakers of other languages
ELT — English language teaching
FCE — First Certificate in English
FPS — first person shooter (game)
GCC — Gulf Co-operation Council (Arab Gulf states of Saudi Arabia, Kuwait, Qatar, Bahrain, Oman and the United Arab Emirates)
IATEFL — International Association of Teachers of English as a Foreign Language
ICT — information and communication technologies
IELTS — International English Language Testing System
IMF — International Monetary Fund
IRC — Internet Relay Chat
L1 — first language
L2 — second language
MMORG — massively multiplayer online role-playing game
MOO — multi-user domain object oriented
MUVE — multi-user virtual environment
NPA — New Pedagogic Approach (in Cameroon)
PDA — personal digital assistant
SLA — second language acquisition

SMS	short message service
SNS	social networking site
TBL	task-based learning
TEFL	teaching English as a foreign language
TESOL	teaching English to speakers of other languages

1
Motivation and ELT: Global Issues and Local Concerns

Ema Ushioda

What is distinctive about this book: starting with local concerns

Motivation is widely recognised as a significant factor influencing success in second or foreign language (L2) learning, and is perhaps one of the key variables that distinguishes first language acquisition from second language acquisition. After all, while motivation is not really an issue in the case of infants acquiring their mother tongues, being motivated (or not) can make all the difference to how willingly and successfully people learn other languages later in life (Ushioda, 2010: 5). The study of language learning motivation has a long history, dating back to the early pioneering work of Gardner and Lambert (1959) in Canada, and has generated a large body of literature. On the whole, this literature has been driven by the pursuit of explanatory theoretical models of motivation and their empirical exploration in a variety of formal and informal learning contexts. This is reflected in the current push towards new analyses of L2 motivation in terms of concepts of self and identity and of complexity theory (see, for example, the collections of conceptual and empirical papers in Dörnyei & Ushioda, 2009; Murray, Gao & Lamb, 2011). Since the 1990s, it is true to say that the research literature has increasingly concerned itself with motivation issues and practices of relevance to teachers, leading to the development of pedagogical recommendations in areas such as motivational strategies (Dörnyei, 2001), group dynamics (Dörnyei & Murphey, 2003), or teachers' communicative style (Noels et al., 1999). Yet the relationship between motivation theory and practice tends to be of a top-down kind in the sense that it is from theory and research that implications for practice are distilled, often in rather generalised terms for a wide potential audience (i.e., not tied to specific settings or local concerns).

In contrast, what makes the current volume distinctive is that it takes the local teaching–learning context as the starting point for reflections on motivation. In doing so, it seeks to acknowledge and capture the recent remarkable growth of interest in motivation in the English language teaching field – an interest that is largely shaped by local educational and pedagogical objectives rather than by the broader pursuit of theory.

In an era in which globalisation, global English and associated critical issues are having a significant impact on educational policy, curriculum provision, language pedagogy and, of course, on student motivation, interest in motivation within the ELT field is driven by local practical concerns. At a superficial level, the global importance ascribed to English might lead us to assume that the need to learn English is unquestionable, and that therefore student motivation is not really a problem. After all, English is a global language, spoken by an estimated 1.5 billion people worldwide by the turn of the millennium (Crystal, 2003: 6), and increasingly regarded as a basic educational skill alongside literacy, numeracy and information and communication technology (ICT) skills (Graddol, 2006). Hence, the motivation for learning English does not seem to require justification or examination. In reality, however, local ELT experiences and practices indicate that this simple logic does not hold. Rather, it seems that issues of motivation are often high on the agenda despite – or perhaps because of – the significant status English has in local or national educational policy, curriculum provision, high stakes gatekeeping exams, the professional job market and society at large. Where learning English is concerned, these local exigencies reflecting global trends and pressures have an inescapable impact on the motivation of students and teachers. Moreover, the power and status accorded to English may have negative consequences for students' motivation to learn other foreign, national or local languages, or for the motivation of policy makers or education providers to promote a more diversified language curriculum. In addition, with the growth of immersion and bilingual education and English-medium subject teaching in many countries across the world, motivation issues relating to learning English often become inseparably linked to more general issues and problems of motivation in mainstream education.

This book brings together motivation-related practical concerns and debates from a wide range of international contexts and levels of education, and from the perspective of writers who are practitioners as well as researchers. As the various chapters will show, these contextually grounded and locally produced insights, questions and understandings can have wider global significance, resonating with the experiences and concerns of ELT practitioners in other contexts, and contributing also to current theoretical analyses of motivation.

Motivation, contexts and the changing global landscape of ELT

A key message in this volume is that, with the rise of global English and the changing global landscape of ELT, contexts of learning assume particular importance for discussions of motivation. While in one sense the global English phenomenon and associated growth and mainstreaming of English language education may suggest processes of convergence and homogenisation, in reality the changing global landscape of ELT reflects an increasing diversity of geographical, political, social, cultural, linguistic, educational, institutional and technological contexts in which learning English is situated. Such diversity of contexts reflects, in turn, further local diversities – for example, in curricula, models of teaching, target varieties of English, materials and resources, teacher background and training. This contextual diversification was already apparent in Kachru's (1985) depiction of the historical spread of English around the world from its native Anglophone 'inner circle' bases (e.g., the U.K., North America), through the 'outer circle' postcolonial territories (e.g., Nigeria, Singapore) where English fulfils key social and administrative functions and has developed indigenised varieties, to the 'expanding circle' of countries where English is studied as a foreign language (e.g., Italy, China). As several commentators have since noted (e.g., Crystal, 2003; McKay, 2002), the 'expanding circle' has now expanded and diversified to the extent that in many such contexts (e.g., the Nordic countries, the Netherlands), the so-called 'foreign language' of English has a pervasive presence in society with more fluent bilingual English speakers than in many 'outer circle' contexts in which English has official second language status. Moreover, there have been growing discussions in some 'expanding circle' countries about making English an official second language (e.g., South Korea, Taiwan, Japan – see Graddol, 2006), which would render it steadily more difficult to categorise contexts of learning.

Traditional analyses of ELT contexts and motivation

In short, the global landscape of ELT is rather more complex than its traditional binary analysis in terms of English as a second language (ESL) and English as a foreign language (EFL) contexts, distinguished broadly according to linguistic setting (i.e., whether or not English is used in the surrounding society). As Howatt (1984: 212) has noted, the ESL/EFL distinction became 'widespread' in the 1950s. This period happened to coincide with the beginning of research interest in language learning motivation, through the work of Gardner and Lambert (1959) in North America. While Gardners and

Lambert's initial programme of research focused more on learners of French than learners of English, what is relevant to the discussion here was their interest in comparing L2 motivation in bilingual and bicultural (i.e., second language learning) settings such as Quebec or Louisiana, with L2 motivation in monolingual and monocultural (i.e., foreign language learning) settings such as Maine or Connecticut (Gardner & Lambert, 1972). The nature of the setting and the potential (or not) for regular social contact and integration with speakers of the target language thus constituted key considerations in the analysis of L2 motivation. These considerations became crystallised in the well-known distinction between 'integrative' and 'instrumental' reasons for learning a language, the former reflecting a more socially oriented desire to interact with, and possibly integrate into, the target language community, and the latter reflecting the more pragmatic benefits of acquiring target language skills.

It is important to note that Gardner and his colleagues have been at pains to deny a simple association between integrative motivation and second language contexts on the one hand and instrumental motivation and foreign language contexts on the other, and they have marshalled meta-analytic research evidence to show that such an association does not hold (Masgoret & Gardner, 2003). Nevertheless, as reflected in Dörnyei's (1990) contention that integrative reasons will feature more strongly in second language rather than foreign language settings, the association has long had intuitive appeal and, as Bhaskaran Nayar commented critically in 1997, has led to the assumption that integration must be a primary motivation for ESL learners. In short, at a superficial level, there has been a temptation to map the traditional binary analysis of the ELT landscape (EFL/ESL) onto the traditional binary analysis of L2 motivation (instrumental/integrative).

Yet, as Bhaskaran Nayar observed back in 1997, a problem with this assumption is that ESL contexts differ markedly depending on whether they refer to English language education for immigrants in native Anglophone settings such as North America or Australia, or to learning and using English in postcolonial settings such as India or Malaysia. While integration may be an understandable (though not a necessary) motivation for learning English in the former ESL settings (see Igoudin, Chapter 11), the relevance of integrative motivation seems less clear in multilingual postcolonial settings in which English may serve certain administrative functions or be used in particular sectors of society, and where people are likely to possess complex linguistic repertoires (e.g., Sridhar, 1996). Thus, perhaps, it was no great surprise that instrumental rather than integrative orientations emerged more significantly in two early L2 motivation studies in postcolonial ESL settings – the Philippines (Gardner & Santos, 1970), and India (Lukmani, 1972). More recently, Coetzee-Van Rooy (2006) has strongly criticised the concept of integrative motivation as untenable in relation to learners and speakers of indigenised varieties of English (i.e., world Englishes) in postcolonial contexts, since the concept cannot account for the complex sociolinguistic realities of language learning and use in such settings in which multidimensional identities and pluralism (rather than integration) are the norm. As Coetzee-Van Rooy argues, with the global spread of English there is now a growing diversity of contexts in which English is learned and to which traditional concepts of L2 motivation cannot be uncritically applied.

In short, with the increasing diversity and complexity of the ELT landscape, the associations between context and motivation are also becoming ever more complex, as will be explored in the following sub-sections.

Motivation and the fluidity of today's learning contexts

At one level, complexity lies in the fact that, with the growth of migration and mobility and advances in communication technologies, contexts of learning and using English in the globalised world are becoming fluid, flexible, mobile, transitory, borderless and less easily definable. In relation to communication technologies, for example, students can interact with people across the world via the Internet, participate in discussion forums and webinars with other students and teachers in different locations, access learning materials and resources via their smartphone or tablet computer while on the move, or get feedback and comments on their blog-writing from a local or global audience (e.g., see Stockwell, Chapter 9). Communication technologies also mean that migrants, business travellers, international students and tourists can maintain daily contact with family, friends and colleagues they have left behind, or can access national news and television programmes from their own countries. Thus, they can maintain a strong virtual foothold in their home communities and in social or professional networks while living, studying or travelling abroad, and cheaper air travel also means that it is relatively easy to return in person or even to commute on a regular basis. In effect, the contexts within which people learn and use English are not so easily definable in geographical, physical, cultural, social or linguistic terms. Thus, the distinctions between learning English as a 'foreign' language and learning English as a 'second' language become increasingly difficult to sustain when immersion in an English-speaking community or the return to one's home community are readily possible, both virtually and physically. In particular, characterising learning settings on the basis of whether or not English is spoken in the surrounding environment is becoming less and less easy across the internationalised higher education sector. This is due to phenomena such as the globalisation of universities competing in the international academic marketplace, the spread of English-medium academic teaching in many countries (e.g., in the Middle East – see Malcolm, Chapter 6), the growth of international universities offering degree programmes taught in English (e.g., Maastricht University) and the setting up of transnational overseas campuses by a growing number of American, British and Australian universities (e.g., Monash University in Malaysia, Nottingham University in China, Temple University in Japan).

Hence, this complexity in defining what we mean by local learning contexts raises critical questions about how we can characterise people's motivation for learning English in a globalised world. As Pavlenko (2002) has argued, traditional categorisations of L2 motivation operate on the assumption that the world consists of largely stable homogeneous and monolingual cultures, of in-groups and out-groups in situations of inter-ethnic contact (e.g., Giles & Byrne, 1982), and of individuals from one ethnolinguistic community moving into another (e.g., Schumann, 1978). However, when there is such fluidity of movement as there is today, when multilingualism rather than monolingualism is the norm, and when people regularly traverse multiple social networks and communities locally, virtually and internationally, how can we possibly characterise the interactions between context and motivation for learning and using English?

Motivation and the growth of English in mainstream education contexts

At another level, on the other hand, the complexity of the associations between context and motivation lies in the unprecedented growth of English in mainstream education in many countries around the world. Here, the notion of context refers not just to geographical setting but also to curricular context. English is now dominating language curricula in more and more regions of the world, is moving down the curriculum from secondary to primary education, and is spreading across the curriculum to the teaching of other subjects. This mainstreaming of English language education has several repercussions for motivation. It constrains the curriculum by effectively eradicating choice for institutions, teachers, students and parents. Or, as noted earlier, it reduces students' interest in learning other foreign or local languages when the need to acquire English is prioritised. This is the case, for example, in the countries of Central and Eastern Europe where English has quickly outstripped traditional regional languages such as German or Russian in the mainstream curriculum (e.g., Dörnyei et al., 2006; for overall statistics see Eurydice, 2005). It is similarly the case in Scandinavia where students' interest in learning second foreign languages (other than English) is increasingly under threat (see Henry & Apelgren, 2008; Trebbi, 2003). Even in bilingual education contexts in which there is a choice of language or of medium of instruction, it seems that there are social and economic pressures to opt for English, as Kuchah (Chapter 4) explores in his analysis of the motivation of Francophone parents and children for English medium schooling in Cameroon.

Across the world, the mainstreaming of English language education is also creating downward pressures at primary school level where non-specialist teachers may yet lack the language skills, training and, indeed, the motivation to teach English let alone teach through English as may be increasingly expected of them. The motivational risk for primary school children is that, with poor quality learning experiences, they may develop an early dislike of English which can have damaging consequences for long-term motivation (on the impact of initial learning experiences on subsequent motivational trajectories, see for example Carpenter et al., 2009). On the other hand, for children who are motivated by early experiences of learning English through play and fun activities in primary school (e.g., see Pinter, 2006), the transition to the more cognitively demanding challenges of formal language study in secondary school may quickly turn that motivation sour. Whatever the target language of study, research on global changes in L2 motivation in formal learning contexts typically points to patterns of motivational decline as students progress through the upper years of schooling (e.g., Chambers, 1999; Tachibana et al., 1996; Williams et al., 2002). Unless the transition from primary to secondary English is managed very carefully, a major concern is that the onset of this motivational decline may simply happen earlier.

In many contexts, moreover, the mainstreaming of English language education also has repercussions for students' engagement with other subjects of study across the school curriculum. As Banegas (Chapter 5) reports, there are now well-established traditions of content-based instruction (CBI) or content and language integrated learning (CLIL) in many parts of the world, where students study curriculum subjects (e.g., history or science) or associated topics through the medium of L2 English (for recent overviews, see Coyle et al., 2010; Crandall, 2012; Dalton-Puffer, 2011). Of course, one can readily appreciate the motivational benefits of engaging students of English with subject matter content that has real learning value and curriculum relevance (e.g., Huang, 2011; Lasagabaster, 2011). At the same time, it is clear that integrating content and language presents pedagogical and motivational challenges for teachers who may not be subject specialists or language specialists or who may need to engage in collaborative teaching with language or subject specialist colleagues. Integrating language and content may also present motivational challenges for linguistically weaker students who lack the English skills needed to deal with cognitively demanding subject matter and learning materials. As Malcolm (Chapter 6) reports in the context of Gulf Arab students studying medicine through English in Bahrain, the pressures of having to develop adequate proficiency in English to cope with high-level academic study can have seriously deleterious effects on students' motivation and self-esteem.

Returning to the earlier discussions about the fluidity of contexts across which English is now learned and used, the mainstreaming of English language education can create a further set of motivational challenges for students and teachers – specifically, motivational dissonances between in-class and out-of-class contexts of English learning and use. As Banegas (Chapter 5) comments in relation to his local teaching context in Argentina, many students attend private language institutes as well as mainstream state education and thus may be well ahead of their classmates in terms of English proficiency or even ahead of the school syllabus. This dissonance between the English skills students have developed outside mainstream education and the English lessons they are obliged to attend in school can clearly have demotivating repercussions. It should be noted that the repercussions may affect not just the students who have developed more advanced English skills but also those in the class who have not had privileged access to private tuition. As McKay (2012) comments, in many parts of the world the burgeoning market in private after-school English classes and even English language kindergartens (e.g., in South Korea) is creating an economic divide and inequality of access to English language education since not all parents can afford to send their children for private lessons.

Motivational dissonances are explored, too, by Taylor (Chapter 3) in the rather different setting of state education in post-communist Romania, where she reports young teenagers' sense of boredom and frustration with school English lessons on the one hand, and on the other their intrinsically motivated engagement with English in their lives outside class through various entertainment media, online social networking and other personal pursuits. The need to bridge this authenticity gap between contexts of English use in popular youth culture and contexts of formal English learning in school is similarly highlighted by Henry (Chapter 8). He reflects on the situation in Sweden, where English has become such an integral part of young people's leisure activities outside the classroom that it is difficult to engage their interest in classroom-based activities for learning English. Henry proposes that one motivational approach may be to provide classroom opportunities for more creative, authentic and self-congruent interactions in English similar to those experienced in online digital gaming. At the same time, he warns against indiscriminate appropriation of youth culture content into the English language classroom, while Stockwell (Chapter 9; also 2008) likewise highlights the risk of encroaching too much on students' 'private' spaces (e.g., through mobile learning), and stresses the need to respect their motivation to keep 'private' spaces separate from 'studying' spaces.

In short, there is a delicate tension between how students engage with English inside and outside the classroom, which can create motivational dissonances if, on the one hand, they perceive the gap as too great or if, on the other hand, they perceive that their personal, social and virtual worlds are being appropriated by teachers for language learning purposes (see Levy,

2009). In order to address these motivational dissonances, what seems important is to nurture and support students' sense of personal ownership and autonomy in relation to learning and using English for their own purposes and needs (Ushioda, 2011a). This places a premium on understanding students' personal perceptions of what English and learning English mean for them, how they relate to this language, and to what extent they take ownership of English as an integral part of their desired social identity (see Igoudin, Chapter 11). It is to this important aspect of motivation for learning English that we now turn.

Motivation, identities and the role of English

As we have seen, with the spread of global English and the growth, complexity and fluidity of contexts across which English is now learned and used, it is becoming more and more difficult to explain people's motivation for learning English in terms of an interest in the target languages culture and community and a possible desire to integrate into this community. While in some contexts the concept of an integrative motivation may well still be meaningful for some learners of English, it is clearly rather difficult to apply to contexts in which people acquire English for the functional purpose of communicating in a lingua franca with others for whom English is also a second language. As statistical estimates show, such lingua franca communication encounters account for the vast proportion of English language use in the globalised world (Crystal, 2003; Graddol, 2006). In these kinds of 'international English' communication settings, the notion of a target language reference group or community (fundamental to the concept of integrative motivation) is difficult to conceptualise. One could argue, for example, that people are motivated to learn English as an international language of communication which will enable them to integrate in different ways with members of the global community – that is, we might describe their motivation as representing a generalised international orientation or outlook akin to what Yashima (2002) has termed 'international posture' in relation to Japanese learners of English. Yet, since people are also in principle members of this global community themselves, one might also argue that they are motivated to learn English to enhance their sense of cosmopolitan identity and connectedness as part of this imagined English-using global community. In other words, being an English user may be integral to how they wish to see themselves – that is, part of their desired identity or sense of self.

Reframing L2 motivation in relation to self and identity

This re-theorising of L2 motivation in relation to concepts of self and identity is now central to research in the field (e.g., Dörnyei & Ushioda, 2009;

Murray, Gao & Lamb, 2011). A particularly influential theoretical framework is Dörnyei's (2005; 2009) L2 Motivational Self System, which draws on the psychological theory of possible selves (Markus & Nurius, 1986). Possible selves are future-oriented dimensions of the self-concept and constitute potential future self-images which may be positive or not. Future self-representations that are highly desirable are likely to shape motivation, effort, persistence and growth, in contrast with future self-images that are less attractive or less personally valued or internalised. In Dörnyei's L2 Motivational Self System, possible future self-images as a proficient L2 user are categorised according to whether they are personally desired (ideal L2 self) or desired for us by significant others (ought-to L2 self).

While the notion of possible selves is grounded in psychological theories of the self-concept, related discussions in the L2 motivation field have drawn somewhat more loosely on theories of identity to characterise how motivation for learning a new language may shape – and be shaped by – processes of identity development and construction (e.g., Lamb, 2004; Lamb & Budiyanto, Chapter 2; Norton, 2000). These discussions mirror a much wider critical concern with issues of identity across the field of research on L2 learning and use, reflecting what Block (2007a) has characterised as 'the rise of identity in SLA research' in the early twenty-first century, as evidenced in several book-length publications around the theme (e.g., Block, 2007b; Jackson, 2008; Jenkins, 2007; Lin, 2007; Pavlenko & Blackledge, 2004). More broadly, identity-focused discussions of L2 motivation reflect a growing paradigm shift from achievement-oriented to identity-oriented theories of motivation in mainstream educational psychology (see Kaplan & Flum, 2009). These identity-oriented theories highlight how individual motivation is linked to the pursuit of identity goals that are personally valued and also socially formed. In the case of learning a new language, as van Lier (2007) explains, people engage in forging new identities and new ways of expressing and negotiating their identities through new words and in new worlds. The extent to which they are comfortable with developing these new identities and expanding their sense of self may connect profoundly with their motivation for language learning (see Ushioda, 2011b).

These themes of identity goals and possible selves permeate nearly all the chapters in this volume and, thus, clearly resonate with the experiences of learners and teachers across a range of contexts. A strong message seems to be that learners' English-related self and identity goals and possible engagement with globalisation processes are firmly shaped by and grounded in local contexts and practices, such as the development of supportive social networks and communities to help motivate and sustain efforts to learn and use English (see Gao, Chapter 10), or such as teachers' explicit promotion of identity work through classroom activities that stimulate and challenge learners' sense of self (see Lamb & Budiyanto, Chapter 2).

What English and learning English mean for students

Yet as Lamb and Budiyanto also comment (citing Block, 2007b), the degree to which learning English in school may necessarily engage (let alone transform) students' sense of self or identity, or indeed whether it should, is open to question. In many educational contexts, after all, English functions as a core curriculum subject and, as Graddol (2006) observes, its increasingly widespread introduction at primary school level (and even pre-school level) seems to reflect a growing perception that English is simply a basic educational skill alongside other basic skills such as literacy, numeracy and ICT skills. One may, therefore, reasonably ask whether motivation for studying English is qualitatively different from motivation for studying other curriculum subjects, and whether it necessarily entails some kind of self-transforming psychological investment or identity striving; or whether in many circumstances people's motivation for learning English can be better explained in terms of more general theories and concepts of motivation (for detailed discussion, see Ushioda, 2012). This latter question is taken up by Woodrow (Chapter 7) in her study of international EAP (English for academic purposes) students taking foundation courses and then progressing to undergraduate programmes in Australia. As she discusses, these students' motivation to develop their English skills and to study in English at an overseas university cannot be accounted for simply in terms of their motivation as language learners since it is clear that strong academic goals and needs come into play. Woodrow thus finds it useful to draw on theoretical perspectives relating to academic learning motivation (i.e., self-determination theory, mastery and performance goals) to analyse these EAP students' motivational aspirations and experiences through their foundation course studies and their transition to the first year of undergraduate studies.

In short, we may well question whether transformative self and identity goals are necessarily implicated in the motivation for learning English as a basic skill, a school subject or a medium for academic study. For many students in many contexts the external pressures to learn English are strong because of the critical role that English plays in gatekeeping tests at significant transitional stages of education and of entry into the world of work. This test-focused orientation to studying English may disconnect students from any sense of the personal communicative value of learning English, particularly where teachers struggle to integrate communicative language teaching with the form-focused instruction needed to enable students to pass exams or, in Sakui's (2004) words, struggle to wear two pairs of shoes at the same time. Thus, the extent to which learning English in school engages students' identities in a potentially transformative sense may be doubtful as long as they perceive English and learning English to mean little more than the business of mastering grammar and vocabulary and taking tests.

Furthermore, even where students recognise the pragmatic value of acquiring English for the purposes of communication and access to information, they may simply perceive English as a practical tool, skill or necessity (much like being able to use a computer or drive a car) that does not particularly implicate their self-concept or identity. Within the English language teaching (ELT) field, there is a developing view that motivation for learning English may be detached from any sense of investment of identity, given that English is an international communication code not bound by particular cultures, values, contexts or standards, although the extent to which it can be culture- and value-free is of course questionable (see, for example, Kirkpatrick, 2007; Sharifian, 2009). A somewhat contentious issue in this regard is whether the target variety of English to be taught should be modelled on an 'English Lingua Franca Core' as proposed by Jenkins (2000; 2007), in which the emphasis is on mutual intelligibility rather than proximity to native standards of accuracy, and on strategies for effective intercultural communication with other non-native English speakers (e.g., for discussion see Seidlhofer, 2004). Such a language curriculum policy would clearly have significant motivational repercussions for learners who, for whatever reason, may aspire to native speaker English models and standards and feel frustrated by the models and targets presented to them in the classroom.

Motivation, identities and implications for ELT teachers

More broadly, local and national policy decisions concerning varieties of English to be taught can also have motivational repercussions for teachers charged with the responsibility for providing target models and standards. With the changing global landscape of ELT and particularly the expansion of English teaching across mainstream education and downwards into primary level in many countries, the make-up of the ELT profession has also changed. In essence, the majority who teach English these days are locally trained teachers who share their students' linguistic and cultural background and have themselves learned English as an L2. While figures are hard to determine, a recent estimate (Braine, 2010: x) suggests that around 80 per cent of the ELT profession across the world are teachers in this category. A growing literature is now developing around the challenges and issues faced by so-called non-native speaker teachers in terms of their sense of status, linguistic and cultural competence and professional skills and identity (e.g., Kamhi-Stein, 2007; Moussu & Llurda, 2008). In this respect, while the specifically motivational dimension of non-native English-speaking teachers' experiences remains rather under-researched (although, see Kubanyiova, 2012), issues of motivation are clearly implicit in analyses of such teachers' sometimes self-perceived lack of English competence or their feelings of 'impostorhood' (Bernat, 2008) vis-à-vis the idealised native speaker model. Issues of motivation are implicit, too, in more critical discussions of how such teachers are negatively positioned in the ELT profession (e.g., Canagarajah, 1999; Inbar-Lourie, 2005).

At the same time, however, the changing global landscape of the ELT profession also has significant repercussions for native speaker teachers. They may, in Holliday's (2005) words, struggle to teach English as an international language as they try to navigate this changing landscape where their long-held linguistic and cultural capital and professional identities as native speaker teachers may be losing value. Such repercussions will depend on the extent to which native speaker teachers are motivated to engage with this changing professional landscape and associated academic discourses surrounding target varieties and standards of English, English as an international language, and native speaker versus non-native speaker models. As Aboshiha (Chapter 12) shows in her revealing and thought-provoking study, the motivation of some native speaker teachers to engage with these issues may in fact be rather limited and the position they adopt quite defensive.

In short, the changing global landscape of ELT clearly raises some critical challenges for the motivation and professional identities of all English language teaching practitioners, regardless of their linguistic and cultural background.

Concluding remarks on the structure of this book

Despite (or because of) the global importance ascribed to English, motivation is undoubtedly a significant concern for many students and teachers of English across the world and presents various language learning and professional challenges at a local level. The ensuing chapters discuss some of the motivational challenges faced by learners and teachers from a wide range of international settings and educational sectors. The chapters follow a loosely structured sequence that highlights some broad themes while traversing contexts from one continent to another:

- classroom practices (Lamb and Budiyanto on English lessons in provincial Indonesia, Chapter 2; Taylor on students' perceptions of English lessons in Romania, Chapter 3);
- English as a medium of learning (Kuchah on French versus English medium schooling in Cameroon, Chapter 4; Banegas on CLIL in Argentina, Chapter 5);
- English for academic and professional purposes (Malcolm on medical students in Bahrain, Chapter 6; Woodrow on EAP students in Australia, Chapter 7);

- youth culture and technology (Henry on digital gaming and ELT in Sweden, Chapter 8; Stockwell on technologies and ELT in a variety of contexts, Chapter 9);
- self and identity goals (Gao on learners of English in China, Chapter 10; Igoudin on ESL learners in the United States, Chapter 11);
- changing global landscape for teachers (Aboshiha on the perceptions of British native speaker teachers working in a variety of international settings, Chapter 12).

While grounded in different local contexts and concerns, the discussions in these chapters clearly have much wider significance as discussions that resonate with the experiences and concerns of students and teachers in other ELT settings, and which contribute to or, perhaps, interrogate, current theoretical analyses of L2 motivation. Each chapter concludes with a list of 'engagement priorities' which set out, in the form of questions and directions for exploration, the broader pedagogical or theoretical implications of the local issues under focus. The volume concludes with a brief chapter that highlights key issues emerging from the collection and draws out their wider implications for ELT practice and motivation theory and research.

References

Bernat, E. (2008). Towards a pedagogy of empowerment. The case of 'impostor syndrome' among pre-service non-native speaker teachers in TESOL. *English Language Teacher Education and Development Journal*, 11: 1–8.

Bhaskaran Nayar, P. (1997). ESL/EFL dichotomy today: language politics or pragmatics. *TESOL Quarterly*, 31(1): 9–37.

Block, D. (2007a). The rise of identity in SLA research, post Firth and Wagner (1997). *The Modern Language Journal*, 91(5): 863–76.

Block, D. (2007b). *Second Language Identities*. London: Continuum.

Braine, G. (2010). *Nonnative Speaker English Teachers: Research, Pedagogy and Professional Growth*. Oxford: Routledge.

Canagarajah, A. S. (1999). Interrogating the 'native speaker fallacy': non-linguistic roots, non-pedagogical results. In G. Braine (ed.) *Non-Native Educators in English Language Teaching*. Mahwah, NJ: Lawrence Erlbaum, 77–92.

Carpenter, C., Falout, J., Fukuda, T., Trovela, M. and Murphey, T. (2009). Helping students to repack for remotivation and agency. In A. M. Stoke (ed.) *JALT2008 Conference Proceedings*. Tokyo: JALT, 259–74.

Chambers, G. (1999). *Motivating Language Learners*. Clevedon: Multilingual Matters.

Coetzee-Van Rooy, S. (2006). Integrativeness: untenable for World Englishes learners? *World Englishes*, 25(3/4): 437–50.

Coyle, D., Hood, P. and Marsh, D. (2010). *CLIL: Content and Language Integrated Learning*. Cambridge: Cambridge University Press.

Crandall, J. A. (2012). Content-based instruction and content and language integrated learning. In A. Burns and J. C. Richards (eds) *The Cambridge Guide to Pedagogy and Practice in Second Language Teaching.* Cambridge: Cambridge University Press, 149–60.

Crystal, D. (2003). *English as a Global Language* (Second Edition). Cambridge: Cambridge University Press.

Dalton-Puffer, C. (2011). Content and language integrated learning: from practice to principle? *Annual Review of Applied Linguistics,* 31(1): 182–204.

Dörnyei, Z. (1990). Conceptualizing motivation in foreign-language learning. *Language Learning,* 40: 45–78.

Dörnyei, Z. (2001). *Motivational Strategies in the Language Classroom.* Cambridge: Cambridge University Press.

Dörnyei, Z. (2005). *The Psychology of the Language Learner: Individual Differences in Second Language Acquisition.* Mahwah, NJ: Lawrence Erlbaum.

Dörnyei, Z. (2009). The L2 Motivational Self System. In Z. Dörnyei and E. Ushioda (eds) *Motivation, Language Identity and the L2 Self.* Bristol: Multilingual Matters, 9–42.

Dörnyei, Z., Csizér, K. and Németh, N. (2006). *Motivation, Language Attitudes and Globalisation: A Hungarian Perspective.* Clevedon: Multilingual Matters.

Dörnyei, Z. and Murphey, T. (2003). *Group Dynamics in the Language Classroom.* Cambridge: Cambridge University Press.

Dörnyei, Z. and Ushioda, E. (eds) (2009). *Motivation, Language Identity and the L2 Self.* Bristol: Multilingual Matters.

Eurydice. (2005). *Key Data on Teaching Languages at School in Europe.* Brussels: Eurydice European Unit.

Gardner, R. C. and Lambert, W. E. (1959). Motivational variables in second language acquisition. *Canadian Journal of Psychology,* 13: 266–72.

Gardner, R. C. and Lambert, W. E. (1972). *Attitudes and Motivation in Second Language Learning.* Rowley, MA: Newbury House.

Gardner, R. C. and Santos, E. H. (1970). Motivational variables in second language acquisition: a Philippine investigation. *Research Bulletin No. 149.* London, Canada: University of Western Ontario, Department of Psychology.

Giles, H. and Byrne, J. L. (1982). An intergroup approach to second language acquisition. *Journal of Multilingual and Multicultural Development,* 3: 17–40.

Graddol, D. (2006). *English Next: Why Global English May Mean the End of 'English as a Foreign Language'.* London: British Council.

Henry, A., and Apelgren, B. M. (2008). Young learners and multilingualism: a study of learner attitudes before and after the introduction of a second foreign language to the curriculum. *System,* 36: 607–23.

Holliday, A. (2005). *The Struggle to Teach English as an International Language.* Oxford: Oxford University Press.

Howatt, A. P. R. (1984). *A History of English Language Teaching.* London: Oxford University Press.

Huang, K.-M. (2011). Motivating lessons: a classroom-oriented investigation of the effects of content-based instruction on EFL young learners' motivated behaviours and classroom verbal interaction. *System,* 39: 186–201.

Inbar-Lourie, O. (2005). Mind the gap: self and perceived native speaker identities of EFL teachers. In E. Llurda (ed.) *Non-Native Language Teachers.* New York: Springer, pp. 256–82.

Jackson, J. (2008). *Language, Identity and Study Abroad: Sociocultural Perspectives.* London: Equinox.

Jenkins, J. (2000). *The Phonology of English as an International Language.* Oxford: Oxford University Press.

Jenkins, J. (2007). *English as a Lingua Franca: Attitudes and Identity.* Oxford: Oxford University Press.

Kachru, B. B. (1985). Standards, codification and sociolinguistic realism: the English language in the outer circle. In R. Quirk and H. G. Widdowson (eds) *English in the World: Teaching and Learning the Language and Literatures.* Cambridge: Cambridge University Press, pp. 11–30.

Kamhi-Stein, L. D. (ed.) (2007). *Learning and Teaching from Experience: Perspectives on Non-Native English-Speaking Professionals.* Ann Arbor, MI: University of Michigan Press.

Kaplan, A. and Flum, H. (2009). Motivation and identity: the relations of action and development in educational contexts. An introduction to the special issue. *Educational Psychologist,* 44(2): 73–77.

Kirkpatrick, A. (2007). *World Englishes: Implications for International Communication and English Language Teaching.* Cambridge: Cambridge University Press.

Kubanyiova, M. (2012). *Teacher Development in Action: Understanding Language Teachers' Conceptual Change.* Basingstoke: Palgrave Macmillan.

Lamb, M. (2004). Integrative motivation in a globalizing world. *System,* 32: 3–19.

Lasagabaster, D. (2011). English achievement and student motivation in CLIL and EFL settings. *Innovation in Language Learning and Teaching,* 5(1): 3–18.

Levy, M. (2009). Technologies in use for second language learning. *Modern Language Journal,* 93: 769–82.

Lin, A. (ed.) (2007). *Problematizing Identity: Everyday Struggles in Language, Culture and Education.* Mahwah, NJ: Lawrence Erlbaum.

Lukmani, Y. M. (1972). Motivation to learn and language proficiency. *Language Learning,* 22: 261–73.

Markus, H. and Nurius, P. (1986). Possible selves. *American Psychologist,* 41: 954–69.

Masgoret, A.-M. and Gardner, R. C. (2003). Attitudes, motivation, and second language learning: a meta-analysis of studies conducted by Gardner and associates. *Language Learning,* 53(Supplement 1): 167–210.

McKay, S. L. (2002). *Teaching English as an International Language.* Oxford: Oxford University Press.

McKay, S. L. (2012). English as an international language. In A. Burns and J. C. Richards (eds) *The Cambridge Guide to Pedagogy and Practice in Second Language Teaching.* Cambridge: Cambridge University Press, pp. 15–22.

Moussu, L. and Llurda, E. (2008). Non-native English-speaking English language teachers: history and research. *Language Teaching,* 41: 315–48.

Murray, G., Gao, X. and Lamb, T. (eds) (2011). *Identity, Motivation and Autonomy in Language Learning.* Bristol: Multilingual Matters.

Noels, K. A., Clément, R. and Pelletier, L. G. (1999). Perceptions of teachers' communicative style and students' intrinsic and extrinsic motivation. *Modern Language Journal,* 83: 23–34.

Norton, B. (2000). *Identity and Language Learning: Gender, Ethnicity and Educational Change.* Harlow: Longman.

Pavlenko, A. (2002). Poststructuralist approaches to the study of social factors in second language learning and use. In V. Cook (ed.) *Portraits of the L2 User.* Clevedon: Multilingual Matters, pp. 277–302.

Pavlenko, A. and Blackledge, A. (eds) (2004). *Negotiation of Identities in Multilingual Contexts.* Clevedon: Multilingual Matters.

Pinter, A. (2006). *Teaching Young Language Learners.* Oxford: Oxford University Press.

Sakui, K. (2004). Wearing two pairs of shoes: language teaching in Japan. *ELT Journal*, 58(2): 155–63.

Schumann, J. H. (1978). The acculturation model for second language acquisition. In R. Gingras (ed.) *Second Language Acquisition and Foreign Language Teaching*. Arlington, VA: Center for Applied Linguistics, pp. 27–107.

Seidlhofer, B. (2004). Research perspectives on teaching English as a lingua franca. *Annual Review of Applied Linguistics*, 24: 209–39.

Sharifian, F. (ed.) (2009). *English as an International Language: Perspectives and Pedagogical Issues*. Bristol: Multilingual Matters.

Sridhar, K. K. (1996). Societal multilingualism. In S. L. McKay and N. H. Hornberger (eds) *Sociolinguistics and Language Teaching*. Cambridge: Cambridge University Press, pp. 47–71.

Stockwell, G. (2008). Investigating learner preparedness for and usage patterns of mobile learning. *ReCALL*, 20 (3): 253–70.

Tachibana, Y., Matsukawa, R. and Zhong, Q. X. (1996). Attitudes and motivation for learning English: a cross-national comparison of Japanese and English high school students. *Psychological Reports*, 79: 691–700.

Trebbi, T. (2003). Curriculum development and learner autonomy in the foreign language classroom: constraints and possibilities. In D. Little, J. Ridley and E. Ushioda (eds) *Learner Autonomy in the Foreign Language Classroom: Teacher, Learner, Curriculum and Assessment*. Dublin: Authentik, pp. 166–84.

Ushioda, E. (2010). Motivation and SLA. *EUROSLA Yearbook*, 10: 5–20.

Ushioda, E. (2011a). Language learning motivation, self and identity: current theoretical perspectives. *Computer Assisted Language Learning*, 24(3): 199–210.

Ushioda, E. (2011b). Motivating learners to speak as themselves. In G. Murray, X. Gao and T. Lamb (eds.), *Identity, Motivation and Autonomy in Language Learning*. Bristol: Multilingual Matters, pp. 11–24.

Ushioda, E. (2012). Motivation: L2 learning as a special case? In S. Mercer, S. Ryan and M. Williams (eds) *Psychology for Language Learning: Insights from Research, Theory and Practice*. Basingstoke: Palgrave Macmillan, pp. 58–73.

van Lier, L. (2007). Action-based teaching, autonomy and identity. *Innovation in Language Learning and Teaching*, 1(1): 46–65.

Williams, M., Burden, R. L. and Lanvers, U. (2002). 'French is the language of love and stuff': student perceptions of issues related to motivation in learning a foreign language. *British Educational Research Journal*, 28: 503–28.

Yashima, T. (2002). Willingness to communicate in a second language: the Japanese context. *Modern Language Journal*, 86(1): 54–66.

2
Cultural Challenges, Identity and Motivation in State School EFL

Martin Lamb and Budiyanto

Introduction

In the past decade or more, a consensus has formed in the applied linguistic community around the importance of identity in language learning. All learning, from a social perspective (e.g., Lave & Wenger, 1991), can be viewed as the construction of a new identity in relation to a certain community; for example, learning to play tennis involves gaining knowledge of the game and physical skills for participation, but it also implies 'becoming a tennis player' in one's own eyes and that of other players – feeling comfortable holding the racket, having the right shoes, speaking the jargon and so on. Similarly, 'learning an L2 involves a struggle to forge a new identity that is true to the self' (van Lier, 2004: 47) while being recognised by others as a competent user of the L2. In fact because language is so closely connected to our sense of selfhood, the path to proficiency is likely to be strewn with even more personal challenges than is learning other skills. The novice tennis player can assert his or her other more expert identities (as bank manager, chess player, mother) when chatting with other players, whereas individuals learning a second language in a foreign country are denied their most basic means of self-expression at the same time that they are challenged by aspects of the local culture. Their sense of self may be destabilised, and they may feel ambivalence towards their new community – 'feeling a part and feeling apart', as Block (2007: 864) neatly puts it. Such 'identity work' is just as much a part of successful language learning as grammar work or skill-acquisition. Eventually, if the process continues far enough, the successful learners regain a coherent sense of self, begin to feel comfortable using the L2 to communicate intentions and feelings and are increasingly recognised by others as competent to do so – they develop an 'L2 identity'.

Researchers have presented considerable evidence for such identity work being undertaken in naturalistic adult migrant settings in which immigrants struggle to gain a foothold in new L2 communities (e.g., Norton, 2000; Pavlenko & Blackledge, 2004), or in study-abroad contexts in which an extended sojourn in a foreign country can provide multiple challenges to young adult students (e.g., Pellegrino-Aveni, 2005; Jackson, 2008). But what about for those learning the second language in home-country institutions, perhaps distant from any actual community of L2 users, and whose main daily preoccupations may be doing well in class quizzes or getting to the end of the latest coursebook? Block has expressed deep scepticism about how far such learners are able to develop L2 identities: 'there is usually far too much first language-mediated baggage and interference for profound changes to occur in the individual's conceptual system and his/her sense of self' (2007: 144). In classrooms, the argument goes, the primary identity of learners is that of pupil, and while some change is possible within that role – for example, becoming recognised as a star pupil, or as a class rebel – too often their true selves are not engaged, and the L2 is just another subject on the school curriculum, quite divorced from the powerful resonances which it might have in the communities where it is used.

It has also been suggested that where English is being learned as a 'lingua franca' (ELF), as it is in most education systems worldwide, it has effectively lost its function as a 'language for identification' and can instead be categorised as a 'language for communication' (House, 2003). ELF is 'not a national language but a mere tool bereft of collective cultural capital' (p. 560), and identification is not involved in its learning or use because there is no clear community of ELF speakers. The appropriation of English on a personal or societal level becomes much less problematic when it is perceived as a 'post-identity language' (Lo Bianco, 2005).

Complicating the picture further is the issue of age. Early adolescence is typically considered a period of flux and uncertainty, when the individual questions the identities ascribed during childhood, experiments with new identities and struggles to achieve a coherent sense of self – a period that sometimes has the character of a crisis, and which in the modern world can extend well into one's twenties or even thirties (Côté, 2009). In her review of research on adolescent migrants in Anglophone communities, Harklau (2007) shows how ethnolinguistic identity is one such facet of the self which comes under critical questioning. The vast majority of the work done on adolescent identity, however, has been conducted in Western contexts, and we know much less about youth development in other international contexts. Arnett (2002) has argued that globalisation is having a profound effect on youth, at least in the wealthier urban segments of societies in which economic development means they share the extended period of 'identity explorations' and, indeed, the 'identity confusion' of Western youth. Further, he argues that 'most people in the world now develop a bicultural identity, in which part of their identity is rooted in local culture while another part stems from an awareness of their relation to global culture' (p. 777). Lu and Yang (2006) elaborate on the Chinese bicultural self, which they conceive as 'a dynamic process of constantly resolving conflicts and striving for a better adaptation when the individual is caught up in a transitional society with both traditional and modern cultural systems side by side' (p. 170); young Taiwanese, for example, seek to reconcile a local socially oriented self with a Western-influenced individualism. As the global lingua franca, we might expect English to be strongly associated with the modern self to which many young people aspire.

The rest of this chapter relates this debate to the preliminary stages of teaching English during early adolescence in a junior high school in provincial Indonesia. Although the data is drawn from one particular institution – set in a relatively prosperous area, aspiring to be the best state school in town and receptive to the inquiries of foreign researchers – it in many ways represents a ubiquitous context for the learning of language in the early twenty-first century. English is recognised by government and people as both a global and local lingua franca (it is the official language of the ASEAN trading association). It is an important and compulsory part of the curriculum, taught for four hours per week to fairly large classes (approximately 35 pupils) by low-paid and often overworked teachers using locally written textbooks. Their pupils are of mixed ability, most of whom may have learned some English in primary school or in private language schools, and have increasing exposure to English in the media and their physical environment but rarely have any direct contact with native speakers or other foreign users of the language. Therefore, we believe the issues raised may have some resonance for the very large numbers of educationalists working in such contexts.

This chapter does not report the results of a specific research project but instead draws on the experiences and reflections of the two authors. The second author has taught for 11 years in this school, which we shall call SMP X, and previously for seven years in other schools in more rural contexts in Indonesia. The first author has visited SMP X on numerous occasions during the past decade, including visits of three to four weeks in each of the years 2002–04 while conducting his doctoral research, and made shorter visits in subsequent years (2006, 2008, 2010 and 2012); during these visits he made formal observations of over 30 classes, taught scores of classes in years 7, 8 and 9 (ages 12–14), conducted formal and informal interviews with English teachers on numerous occasions and, thanks to the characteristically open architecture and welcoming nature of this particular school, was able to observe in a more casual way the teaching and learning going on inside (and outside) classrooms on a daily basis.

We begin by presenting three vignettes of English learning in the school. These are then discussed in relation to the literature on identity and L2 motivation. The chapter then presents further descriptions of language teaching practice in the school, while the final section offers practical recommendations for promoting identity work in the classroom, thereby helping to sustain learner motivation over these three crucial years.

Three vignettes from the Indonesian junior high school

Vignette No. 1

The English teacher has organised a debate in one of his 'elite' year 8 classes. The topic is: 'Do ghosts exist?' He starts the class by telling an anecdote about a family member's encounter with a ghost and elicits various comments, some gently mocking, others more serious enquiries. He directly asks the students whether they believe in ghosts or not. There is a roughly even split, with several 'not sure'. He then suggests the class debate the issue and arbitrarily divides the class into two groups, one to prepare arguments why ghosts do exist, the other to argue the opposite. He then leaves the class for about 30 minutes while the two groups cluster in different parts of the room and get on with the task of preparing their arguments. There is much animated discussion, mostly in Bahasa Indonesia, but students write out comments in English to prepare for the oral debate. Some students switch groups; a few sit on their own, apparently not engaged in the task or else preparing their own thoughts. When the teacher returns, he asks the group that believes in ghosts to present their arguments first. Several students make comments, mostly in the form of personal anecdotes or relating reports of local legends involving ghosts and spirits. The members of the other group respond in similar fashion, with two distinct lines of attack: some students argue that modern science has effectively disproved the existence of ghosts, others that Islam forbids its followers from believing in anything other than *jinns*, which are invisible to people. All class members listen with interest, sometimes making comments to the class or to each other; public comments are in English, private comments usually in Indonesian. Sometimes pupils ask the teacher how to express something in English. The teacher allows the debate to continue for over half an hour before eventually making some closing conciliatory comments of his own.

Vignette No. 2

The teacher has asked his year 8 class to write a diary at least once a week and in it reflect on meaningful events in their lives; only he would read it, he has promised, and it should be written in English so it would be 'secret' from parents/siblings who did not know the language. Some learners have produced long entries of a very personal nature, which they give to the teacher every week to read and comment upon. Here is one extract from a 13-year-old girl's diary:

> 14th February: Friday, maybe today every pair asserted their love to her/his darling with flowers, chocolate, or a present. That was mean, it was a special day for some of the people in the world but wasn't for me because according to my religion we might not celebrate it. I thought that didn't have a purpose or advantages. Forget about it!?!

On the following page is a beautifully designed Valentine's Day card.

Vignette No. 3

An English teacher has invited a British visitor to the school to meet her year 7 class and 'motivate them to speak English'. The teacher and visitor arrive at the classroom about ten minutes after the class was due to start; some students are inside doing gap-fill exercises in their textbook while others have to be summoned from various sites around the school; one group was sitting under a tree listening to a boy strumming his guitar. However, once they are seated at their appointed desks the class captain quickly calls them to order and they give a greeting in chorus: 'Good morning teacher!' The teacher introduces the native speaker and invites them to ask him questions. Since none are forthcoming, the native speaker introduces himself, giving his name and nationality and purpose for coming to the school. Recognising that the class has limited English, he tries to speak as clearly as possible and checks that they understand him – they all say that they do, so he invites them to ask him questions. Again, there is silence, and the class teacher urges them to take this opportunity to communicate with a native speaker. Eventually, after a lot of giggling and a nudge in the ribs from his neighbour, a boy at the back raises his hand. 'Yes!' says the native speaker with relief. 'How old are you, Mister?' asks the boy. The native speaker explains that this is not a question one normally asks in his culture, at least not of older people. The boy looks crestfallen, so the native speaker gives him an approximate answer, and now other questions start to come, mostly about his experiences of the school and town: e.g., 'Where do you stay?' 'What is your favourite food?' 'What do you think of Indonesian students?' One or two students venture questions about the United Kingdom: e.g., 'What is your football team?' 'Do you know Justin Bieber?' There is much laughter and much chattering among the students, and when the teacher finally calls a halt after about 30 minutes and the native speaker gets ready to leave, the students all rush to the front individually to take his hand and touch it to their foreheads. Some get snapshots of themselves posing with the native speaker on their BlackBerry phones.

Identity and the school English language learner

We shall argue here that in each of these vignettes, we are witnessing learners of English in a heightened state of emotional stimulation, and that this frisson is generated by the way the language is associated with challenging cultural values. In the first vignette, the topic excites debate because ghosts are a traditional feature of local belief systems, are associated with particular places in the neighbourhood and are an ingredient in many of the stories passed on by older family members; yet the learners will also be aware that those English speakers of Western societies who follow the tenets of materialist science would allow no role for ghosts outside of Hollywood horror movies. Perhaps the *imams*, or teachers, at their local mosque have also condemned the notion in the name of modern Islam. In other words, the topic naturally stimulates debate among these learners – and pushes them to produce English at the very limit of their capabilities – because it probes the tension within many of them between their current identities, as local citizens and dutiful sons and daughters, and imagined identities of the future as sophisticated English-speaking citizens of the world (Lamb, 2004; 2009).

This tension also manifests itself in the triple punctuation marks that end the girl's diary entry in Vignette No. 2. Valentine's Day is a recent cultural import from the West, taken up with special enthusiasm by the urban young but also regularly challenged as un-Islamic or contrary to national values (e.g., *The Jakarta Post,* 2012). The girl's diary entry reveals her ongoing struggle to reconcile her local self with this attractive ritual from the permissive West; she is aware that a future English-speaking self may gain access to some of the fruits of economic and cultural globalisation, but will also expose her to Western (or other) influences which could lead to alienation from the home community. The diary-writing exercise itself was extremely successful, motivating many of the learners to produce large amounts of written text in English – often reflections on issues of current personal concern – which was of great value to their linguistic development. We would argue its success lay in the way it allowed the learners to 'try out' their English-mediated identities in the sheltered context of a 'secret' diary.

The third vignette presents a scenario which has been repeated by the first author in dozens of classrooms in SMP X. The native speaker's appearance galvanised the pupils in a dramatic way; it returned them swiftly to their seats, riveted their attention on the person of the visitor, and struck them dumb. Only once the initial nerves were settled did they start to speak, and when those more forward individuals found that their English 'worked', they were keen to speak further. With minimal wit or personal ingenuity, the native speaker was able to induce a state of collective excitement that lasted beyond the day's class; local teachers claim that such visits boost the students' long-term motivation to learn English, and this belief underlies SMP X's current policy of inviting native speakers to visit English classrooms whenever such individuals are available, even when they are not qualified as teachers or, indeed, even when they are not native speakers (international English speakers are also welcome). Again, we would suggest that this motivational effect derives from the way learners are suddenly encouraged to perform an identity as a member of the global English-using community, with all its potentially threatening customs and values, which hitherto have only been imagined. The content of the interaction may appear mundane, but many of the self-referential questions (another example, certain to evoke great hilarity, is 'what do you think of *dangdut* music?') allow them to use the English-speaking outsider as a mirror, reflecting light on their own familiar world, and suddenly juxtaposing their local interests and values with those of the supposedly cosmopolitan Westerner.

Blommaert (2010: 133) argues that 'the homogenizing ring of a word such as "English" is the indexical trap of globalization'. Like all languages, English carries different connotations in different societies and, indeed, within particular niches within a single society. House (2003) may be right that ELF is regarded primarily as a 'language for communication' among the German university students she teaches and researches, but it is far from a neutral code for many Indonesian teenagers. Likewise, Block (2007) drew his conclusions about the lack of identity work going on in EFL classrooms largely from his observations of Spanish adult evening classes. Arguably, the cultural proximity of these European contexts of learning to Anglophone cultures makes the appropriation of the language unproblematic in identity terms, involving relatively little 'destabilisation of the self'. The more culturally 'distant' the context, the greater the potential challenge to individual learners' sense of identity, even for those mainly studying the basics of the language in school.

In contrast to Block, Kramsch (1993; 2010) has consistently highlighted the transformative potential of language learning. Many teenagers, she argues, are 'anxious to liberate themselves from the constraints of the one (monolingual) mother tongue' (2010: 206) and exhibit a powerful desire for the way a second language can open up new worlds and new means of expressing their feelings and aspirations:

> Seduced by the foreign sounds, rhythms and meanings, and by the 'coolness' of native speakers, many adolescent learners strive to enter new, exotic worlds where they can be, or at least pretend to be, someone else, where they too can become 'cool' and inhabit their bodies in more powerful ways. (Kramsch, 2010: 16)

Of course exposure to new languages and cultures may excite, but it will also challenge; learners may feel uncomfortable trying to express themselves in the foreign tongue; others may actively resist the identities that the language potentially imbues, as Canagarajah (1999) describes among Sri Lankan learners of English. Individuals in this Indonesian context, too, may objectively recognise the potential value of English yet remain personally detached and unwilling to invest effort in learning it – two examples are described in Lamb (2011).

For English as a lingua franca, there is legitimate debate about precisely with what communities and cultures the language is, or should be, associated. Canagarajah (2005) and Kumaravadivelu (2007), for example, have both recently discussed the way cultural globalisation has made the relationship more complex, with learners of English no longer necessarily looking to join Anglophone communities but, instead, using English to negotiate membership of hybrid and fluid communities within and beyond their own national contexts. As Baker (2009: 588) asks: '[i]f it is not possible to identify a clear language–culture relationship for lingua franca communication, then how are participants in ELF communication to be prepared for the wealth and complexity of cultural backgrounds and the associated communicative practices and forms they are likely to encounter?'. This is an important question with serious pedagogic implications but, at early stages of the language learning process, among school pupils with few immediate communicative needs, the more urgent concern is to recognise that 'language can never be culturally neutral' (Baker, 2009: 588), that in more 'distant' contexts this cultural content can bring an emotional charge through challenge to learner identity and that, as Miyahara (2011) has pointed out, the emotions generated by these identification processes can contribute significantly to learners' motivation to acquire the language.

More typical English language learning activities

We are emphatically not saying that these vignettes represent typical practice in SMP X. In fact, rather the reverse is true – they are all exceptional. English class debates are not a common pedagogic practice, particularly in junior high school, even if nationally organised English language debates serve to motivate elite students in senior high schools; no other English teachers in the school have used diary-writing as a means of motivating students to write; native speaker visits are rare events. Instead, the vast majority of English classes at SMP X involve practices that actually divest the English language of its cultural meanings. Lessons revolve around the textbook and the related 'exercise book', which all pupils bring to class. Central to each unit of the textbook, and so to each lesson, are certain aspects of language knowledge: structures, sets of lexis and, in more recent versions reflecting national curricular priorities, skills and sub-skills expressed as competencies. While lessons may begin with brief oral exchanges between the teacher and pupils in which the main topic is introduced, most lessons then become overwhelmingly focussed on written language: on the reading of texts, on answering comprehension questions based on the text, and completing follow-up grammar and vocabulary exercises. Punctuating this individual work are teacher explanations about the language and pupils' production of their written answers. Listening or speaking activities specified in the textbook are often ignored, as most classrooms lack devices for playing CDs, and many teachers lack both awareness of communicative teaching methodologies and confidence in their own oral abilities. Further, although some of the reading texts describe aspects of Western (usually Anglophone) culture, few of the teachers have any personal experience of such cultures and, as a result, these texts are rarely exploited to stimulate thought and discussion. Finally, as students move into the 9th grade the work becomes more oriented towards practice for the local and national exams; these include a listening component, but not speaking.

The huge emphasis on written forms of the language, and especially on grammatical and lexical knowledge, is a source of dissatisfaction for many learners. Survey results consistently indicate that pupils want to do more 'conversation' and 'dialogues' (Lamb, 2007). As one pupil said to the first author in 2008, 'in school it's just about grammar, grammar, grammar and grammar; I still learn about grammar since I was elementary school and this, I feel this thing'. Indeed, Lamb (2007) reports the general fall in learners' enjoyment of their English lessons over the first two years of study in this school, and on a recent visit to the school, one experienced teacher commented that by year 9 pupils 'think only about the final exam; they are not interested with the subject'. Of course this pattern of declining intrinsic motivation is not confined to Indonesia; Ryan (2009) for example describes the toll taken by a regimented exam-oriented language education system on Japanese school leavers' desire for English.

Promoting identity change in the classroom

To review our argument so far: the three vignettes demonstrate that even at a very early stage, and in a formal educational setting, the learning of English brings identity into play, and when it does so it appears to generate strong emotions, arguably because it triggers tensions between the young people's local selves as dutiful members of the local community and potential future identities as citizens of the world. However, in the normal course of events, this rarely happens; most of the time, English is taught and learned as a values-free body of knowledge conveyed via official textbooks and assessed in high-stakes exams. Two sorry outcomes of this are a diminution of learners' long-term motivation to learn the language and a failure to develop intercultural awareness.

Changing this state of affairs is inevitably complex, as it involves multiple factors at different levels of the education system (Wedell, 2009). Feeding the systemic inertia here are both teachers' and learners' avoidance of risk – teachers preferring to avoid both the unpredictability of speaking activities and the moral ambiguities of intercultural lesson content, and learners prioritising performance in their assessments. But the vignettes show that the seeds for change exist in the school. Here we will suggest some small steps that teachers can take to ensure that their lessons do involve 'identity work'. Our ideas are based on successful activities conducted by the second author, and the first author's observations and conversations with other teachers in the school. What is more, as we will explain, our ideas involve practices already familiar to the teachers and do not presume any familiarity with communicative teaching methodology.

Simple speaking activities – performing not communicating

In most classes at SMP X, there are only three situations in which pupils are encouraged to speak English. The most common by far is where learners give or read out answers to their written exercises. Another quite frequent occurrence is at the beginning of lessons, where teachers may introduce the topic of the class with some comments and questions in English, to which some learners might respond. The third type is also common, but only in classes whose teachers see value in giving learners opportunities to speak. In this activity, pupils work in pairs (in the fixed paired seating common in Indonesian schools, this will almost always be the person sitting next to them) to prepare a dialogue based on a situation in the textbook unit (e.g., giving directions, having a telephone conversation, explaining how to use a technical device); they then rehearse the conversation until it is memorised; then volunteers are invited to the front of the class to perform the dialogue, using whatever props are available.

The first author has observed this simple activity in other national contexts, and we would speculate that it is a ubiquitous form of speaking practice in the early stages of language learning, particularly in state education systems. Interestingly, there is a key difference between this activity and the activities recommended in contemporary teachers' guides (e.g., Hadfield & Hadfield, 1999): it is not communicative. There is no information gap between the role players, no spontaneous negotiation of meaning. Its popularity with teachers is probably in part because it requires no extra materials preparation and affords practice of language items targeted in the class textbook, but as the first author has observed and the second author has experienced, it is also an activity enjoyed by learners. We would suggest that the pleasure comes from the way the simple role play allows them to 'perform' the language, to enact imagined identities as English speakers in the sheltered environment of the classroom, in front of their friends and a supportive 'expert'. What is more, the imagined setting is also usually familiar: they are eating in an Indonesian restaurant, for example, or speaking on the phone to their own Indonesian friend. Without any international experience, these young adolescents would have difficulty imagining any other setting and, in fact, some of the humour generated by the activity comes from the discordance of using the international language, English, in local settings. This was evident in an activity observed by the first author in a year 8 class recently, in which the pupils constructed dialogues around bargaining for goods in a local marketplace; the dialogues were inauthentic in that they contained phrases (such as 'please give me a cheap price!') which would almost never be heard in an Anglophone cultural setting, and most of the gestures and behaviour of the pupils were slightly theatrical versions of themselves rather than attempts to mimic those of Western users – but the activity produced laughter and obvious enjoyment.

It could be argued further that in 'translating' the local communicative event into English the learners are becoming more aware of features of their social world, of how they may look to outsiders; and, therefore, the activity represents a very elementary form of intercultural learning. The second author has conducted similar speaking activities which, while again sometimes lacking a communicative element, encourage learners to represent their culture to English-speaking outsiders. A notable example is the writing of a prayer in English: pupils are encouraged to choose their favourite prayers and as a homework task to translate them into English; at the following class they read them out to their friends. A similar activity involves the translation and performance of Indonesian songs. A third example is the creation, in English, of a recipe for an Indonesian dish; in an unusually elaborate lesson, the pupils have the opportunity to explain the recipe while actually preparing the dish over a grill in the manner of a TV chef. These activities generate very high levels of involvement.

In many national education systems the representation of one's own culture to outsiders is recognised as a legitimate motive for the learning of English. Such activities could be said, therefore, to directly address this objective. However, they also have a more subtle motivational role in the way they bring into play the current and future elements in learners' potential bicultural selves; that is, in forcing them to 'perform' aspects of their current selves in English – as when reciting a favourite prayer in the language – they are being encouraged to see themselves in a new light, to question a habitus, to develop a new self-image that they may aspire towards. As we have argued in relation to the ghosts debate and Valentine's Day diary entry, such identification processes can be intrinsically motivating for language learning because the tensions involved produce emotions. In the longer term, they may also be an early-stage contribution towards the creation of an Ideal L2 self (cf., Hadfield & Dörnyei, in press). Claire Kramsch (2010: 205) writes:

> The challenge for teachers, as Vygotsky repeatedly stressed, is to teach to the potential adult, not just to the past or even the actual adolescent. This means giving the students the space to engage both the teenagers that they are and the adults they might become. The language classroom is precisely the place to explore with our students alternative ways of representing themselves...

Of course there is the possibility that tensions produce some discomfort, as well as excitement, and it is the teacher's role to judge the suitability of a particular task for a particular group. For example, such activities might fail to motivate a class of learners – perhaps in a rural setting less exposed to the forces of globalisation – for whom English is simply an alien code without any meaningful cultural associations. Alternatively an activity that confronted learners with too powerful a challenge to their local, traditional self may provoke a strong reaction against the language. To invoke Vygotsky again, educators have to work within their learners' cultural zones of proximal development. As learners become older and gain more knowledge of the outside world, such pedagogic activities should encourage learners to imagine interacting directly with international users of English (native speaker or otherwise), adapting both their verbal and body language accordingly. Baker's (2012) taxonomy of the features of intercultural awareness offers educationalists in Asia a helpful framework for sequencing classroom tasks.

A role for native speakers

In recent years it has almost become TESOL orthodoxy to downplay the value of native speaker teachers and advocate the strengths of non-native local teachers of English on the solid grounds that knowledge of the learners' home context and language gives them significant professional advantages (e.g., Medgyes, 1994; Holliday, 2005). Rivers (2011) goes even further in arguing that the consistent use of native speakers of English as models and interlocutors promotes a monolingual ethic and 'serves to train students in the development of less favourable attitudes toward English language speakers of other racial, national and ethnic backgrounds' (p. 843), and possibly even reinforces a 'heightened sense of anxiety and inferiority among the students' (p. 851).

These arguments tend to emerge in contexts in which native speaker teachers are plentiful, or are even in competition for jobs with non-native speaker teachers. In many areas of the contemporary world, however, the English language has spread in advance of actual human users, and probably the majority of school learners of the language have had no face-to-face contact with a native speaker. Such conditions should force a re-evaluation of the native speaker's possible role. In the market economy, scarce commodities will find their own price, so it is no surprise to find that in Indonesia, as elsewhere, private sector language institutes will pay relatively high salaries to attract native speaker teachers. Where that is not possible, they will encourage their pupils to seek out native speakers in the local environment, armed with questionnaires – a popular pedagogic activity known locally as 'hunting'. As stated above, SMP X is also actively looking to recruit short-term native speaker teachers, even unqualified ones, in the belief that they will help motivate pupils to learn to speak English. Their role would be primarily to serve as interactants in the language – their lack of explicit grammatical knowledge will not be a drawback, since L2 explanations can be confidently left to their Indonesian counterparts, and their lack of proficiency in the Indonesian language could even be construed as an advantage, in that it leaves English as the only possible medium of communication. But we would argue that their main legacy will lie in the learners' imaginations – intense experiences of successful interaction will make it easier for them over time to envision a modern English-using globally involved self. At the same time, in seeing their own lives and culture reflected in the voiced experience of the outsider, their intercultural awareness is enhanced.

Rivers (2011), Baker (2012) and others are right to stress the educational benefits of employing other international users of English, whether L1 users (e.g., from Singapore, Hong Kong or India) or L2, to encourage 'more pluralistic and dynamic conceptions of English use in Asia' (Baker, 2012: 26). The likelihood is that Indonesian youngsters will use English more with other Asians than with Westerners, and alternative linguistic models are available, just as alternative lifestyles and moral values are laid out as options for their personal futures. Nevertheless, teachers in this locality stress the motivational potential of native speakers for their learners. This could be because, as the research of Timmis (2002) and Jenkins (2007) has found, the teachers themselves view native speaker models as the prestigious professional variety, and learners pick up that message; another explanation, one more in tune with the arguments of this chapter, is that learners find difference exciting.

Conclusion

Riley (2006: 296) has pointed out how the very expression 'foreign language learning' should alert us to the fact 'that issues of identity are massively present', and it is also true that languages are likely to be perceived by learners as more or less 'foreign'. Our main contention in this chapter is that, based on our experience of EFL in one state school in provincial Indonesia, identity work is present in mainstream EFL, that it can be motivating for learners through the emotions it arouses, and that there is the potential for much more without the need for major methodological change on the part of teachers. Block (2007) may be right to argue that identity work is often absent, particularly in European settings in which English is simply less foreign and brings fewer challenging cultural associations. It is also probably true in other settings, such as here in Asia, where many teachers and pupils prefer to play safe by divesting the language of its cultural content and instead emphasising the linguistic content presented in detail in the class textbook. But this represents a major lost opportunity to engage young people in the process of foreign language learning.

Of course cultures are not monolithic entities. Adolescents with little personal experience of foreign cultures will likely base their identifications on stereotypes that need to be critiqued as they move through the school system, and we would support the kind of intercultural awareness-raising proposed by Baker (2012). Likewise we have to acknowledge the cultural distinctiveness of SMP X within Indonesian society. The majority of pupils now come from middle-class backgrounds and have access to role models (in family members or through the media) of interculturally competent, globally aware English-speaking Indonesians and, therefore, have had the chance by early adolescence to develop aspirations towards biculturality and ideal L2 selves (Lamb, 2012). This is precisely why they see the moral character and cultural behaviour of Westerners as potential challenges to their own future English-speaking identity, and they react emotionally. In other more remote Indonesian contexts in which children are less exposed to outside influences and their future identities are anchored in local traditional society, the English language may not arouse the same emotions, and might instead meet the same indifference as Latin did to most twentieth-century Britons.

Engagement priorities

We are suggesting that cultural identification processes are present in the early stages of mainstream school EFL in this particular Indonesian context, and that these processes do affect learners' short- and long-term motivation to learn the language. But how widespread is this phenomenon? Are there teachers or materials writers in similar contexts who are deliberately exploiting these cultural challenges in order to motivate learners and encourage positive identity change? As mentioned, most of the current evidence for identity work in language learning involves adult migrants and study-abroad participants, or older and more advanced EFL learners: see, for example, Yihong's (2009) useful summary of Chinese research demonstrating self-identity changes among undergraduate learners of English. Research evidence is lacking for school-age foreign language learners. Here are some questions that practitioners might usefully consider:

- Is it true in your context that adolescents tend to develop 'bicultural identities', with a local self and a global self? Where might you look for evidence of this?
- This chapter describes some simple speaking activities for elementary learners which encourage them to 'perform' L2 identities (e.g., reciting a prayer in English, describing a local recipe), while also becoming more aware of features of their own culture. Can you think of other examples of such activities, suitable for your own context?
- To what extent do you consider language teaching as also the teaching of culture? If you do, which culture do you find yourself teaching in the English-language classroom? To what extent do you agree with Baker (2012) that, since we cannot predict what cultures our learners will come into contact with in the future, we should aim to develop their general intercultural awareness rather than favouring particular Anglophone cultures?
- There is a widespread assumption that native speaker teachers *do* motivate students to learn the L2. How could we investigate the validity of this assumption? It would be important to know IF they motivate, and if so, WHY and HOW. Some further issues to consider:
  - What research methods would be most effective in addressing these questions?
  - What population of learners/teachers could you take as your sample?
  - How could you carry out such research in a practical and ethical way?

Suggested further reading

Arnett, J. J. (2002). The psychology of globalization. *American Psychologist*, 57(10): 774–83.

A very readable and persuasive article by an American authority on adolescent psychology.

Baker, W. (2012). Global cultures and identities: refocussing the aims of ELT in Asia through intercultural awareness. In T. Muller, S. Herder, J. Adamson and P. Shigeo Brown (eds) *Innovating EFL Teaching in Asia*. Basingstoke: Palgrave Macmillan, pp. 23–34.

Baker argues that as English increasingly becomes an 'Asian' language, serving local communicative needs, pedagogical goals should no longer be centred on Anglophone linguistic models, and in this chapter he proposes an alternative approach based on helping learners to become 'interculturally aware'.

Kramsch, C. (2010). *The Multilingual Subject*. Oxford: Oxford University Press.

Learning a second language may be literally an academic pursuit for many, involving hundreds of hours of enforced study leading to exam success or failure. This book shows how, by contrast, it can be personally transformative.

References

Arnett, J. J. (2002). The psychology of globalization. *American Psychologist*, 57(10): 774–83.

Baker, W. (2009). The cultures of English as a Lingua Franca. *TESOL Quarterly*, 43(4): 567–92.

Baker, W. (2012). Global cultures and identities: refocussing the aims of ELT in Asia through intercultural awareness. In T. Muller, S. Herder, J. Adamson and P. Shigeo Brown (eds) *Innovating EFL Teaching in Asia*. Basingstoke: Palgrave Macmillan, pp. 23–34.

Block, D. (2007). The rise of identity in SLA research, post Firth and Wagner (1997). *The Modern Language Journal*, 91(5): 863–76.

Blommaert, J. (2010). *The Sociolinguistics of Globalization*. Cambridge: Cambridge University Press.

Canagarajah, A. S. (1999). *Resisting Linguistic Imperialism in English Teaching*. Oxford: Oxford University Press.

Canagarajah, A. S. (ed.) (2005). *Reclaiming the Local in Language Policy and Practice*. Mahwah, NJ: Lawrence Erlbaum.

Côté, J. E. (2009). Identity formation and self-development in adolescence. In R. Lerner and L. Steinberg (eds) *Handbook of Adolescent Psychology* (Third Edition). Hoboken, NJ: John Wiley & Sons, pp. 266–304.

Hadfield, J. and Dörnyei, Z. (in press). *Theory into Practice: Motivation and the Ideal Self*. London: Longman.

Hadfield, J. and Hadfield, C. (1999). *Simple Speaking Activities*. Oxford: Oxford University Press.

Harklau, L. (2007). The adolescent English language learner: identities lost and found. In J. Cummins and C. Davison (eds) *Handbook of English Language Teaching*. Amsterdam: Kluwer Academic, pp. 639–53.

Holliday, A. (2005). *The Struggle to Teach English as an International Language*. Oxford: Oxford University Press.

House, J. (2003). English as a lingua franca: a threat to multilingualism? *Journal of Sociolinguistics*, 7(4): 556–78.

Jackson, J. (2008). *Language, Identity and Study Abroad*. London: Equinox.

Jenkins, J. (2007). *English as a Lingua Franca: Attitude and Identity*. Oxford: Oxford University Press.

Kramsch, C. (1993). *Language and Culture*. Oxford: Oxford University Press.

Kramsch, C. (2010). *The Multilingual Subject*. Oxford: Oxford University Press.

Kumaravadivelu, B. (2007). *Cultural Globalization and Language Education*. New Haven, CT: Yale University Press.

Lamb, M. (2004). Integrative motivation in a globalizing world. *System*, 72(1): 3–19.

Lamb, M. (2007). The impact of school on EFL learning motivation: an Indonesian case-study. *TESOL Quarterly*, 41(4): 757–80.

Lamb, M. (2009). Situating the L2 Self: two Indonesian school learners of English. In Z. Dörnyei and E. Ushioda (eds) *Motivation, Language Identity and the L2 Self.* Bristol: Multilingual Matters, pp. 229–47.

Lamb, M. (2011). Future selves, motivation and autonomy in long-term EFL learning trajectories. In G. Murray, T. Lamb and X. Gao (eds) *Identity, Motivation and Autonomy: Exploring their Links.* Bristol: Multilingual Matters, pp. 177–94.

Lamb, M. (2012). A self-system perspective on young adolescents' motivation to learn English in urban and rural settings. *Language Learning,* 62(4): 997–1023.

Lave, J. and Wenger, E. (1991). *Situated Learning: Legitimate Peripheral Participation.* Cambridge: Cambridge University Press.

LoBianco, J. (2005). No longer a (foreign) language: the rhetoric of English as a post-identity language. *Journal of Chinese Sociolinguistics,* 2: 17–40.

Lu, L. and Yang, K.-S. (2006). Emergence and composition of the traditional-modern bicultural self of people in contemporary Taiwanese society. *Asian Journal of Social Psychology,* 9: 167–75.

Medgyes, P. (1994). *The Non-Native Teacher.* Basingstoke: Macmillan.

Miyahara, M. (2011). *Identity Work in Mainstream EFL Learners.* Paper presented at AILA 2011: The 16th World Congress of Applied Linguistics, Beijing, China.

Norton, B. (2000). *Identity and Language Learning: Gender, Ethnicity and Educational Change.* London: Longman.

Pavlenko, A. and Blackledge, A. (eds) (2004). *Negotiation of Identities in Multilingual Settings.* Clevedon: Multilingual Matters.

Pellegrino-Aveni, V. (2005). *Study Abroad and Second Language Use: Constructing the Self.* Cambridge: Cambridge University Press.

Riley, P. (2006). Self-expression and the negotiation of identity in a foreign language. *International Journal of Applied Linguistics,* 16(3): 295–318.

Rivers, D. J. (2011). Evaluating the self and the other: imagined intercultural contact within a 'native speaker' dependent foreign language context. *International Journal of Intercultural Relations,* 35(6): 842–52.

Ryan, S. (2009). Ambivalence and commitment, liberation and challenge: investigating the attitudes of young Japanese people towards the learning of English. *Journal of Multilingual and Multicultural Development,* 30(5): 405–20.

The Jakarta Post (2012) *Hardliners Call for a Ban on Valentine's Day Celebrations in Sukabumi* 12 February. Available at http://www.thejakartapost.com/news/2012/02/12 /hardliners-call-a-ban-valentines-day-celebrations-sukabumi.html [Accessed 20 April 12].

Timmis, I. (2002). Native speaker norms and International English: a classroom view. *ELT Journal,* 56(3): 240–49.

vanLier, L. (2004). *The Ecology and Semiotics of Language Learning.* Dordrecht: Kluwer Academic Publishers.

Wedell, M. (2009). *Planning Educational Change: Putting People and their Contexts First.* London: Continuum.

Yihong, G. (2009). Language and identity: state of the art and a debate of legitimacy. In J. Lo Bianco, J. Orton and J. Yihong (eds) *China and English.* Bristol: Multilingual Matters, pp. 101–16.

3
Listening to Romanian Teenagers: Lessons in Motivation and ELT Methodology

Florentina Taylor

In recent decades, few educational concepts have inspired more publications than motivation, the field of language learning also benefitting from a number of noteworthy volumes on the topic (Chambers, 1999; Dörnyei & Ushioda, 2011; Murray et al., 2011; Ushioda, 1996). This very volume is a clear indication that not only is motivation in language learning and teaching still generating very lively discussions, but also that these discussions have now reached a clearly global status.

In our perpetual search for ways in which to motivate our students, however, we may sometimes forget a simple fact, expressed clearly by the outspoken advocate of progressive education, Alfie Kohn (1993: 198–99):

> [...] children do not need to be motivated. From the beginning they are hungry to make sense of their world. Given an environment in which they don't feel controlled and in which they are encouraged to think about what they are doing (rather than how well they are doing it), students of any age will generally exhibit an abundance of motivation and a healthy appetite for challenge.

Not only may motivation be a natural attribute of a child, given the appropriate environment, but there are also suggestions that other factors may be more helpful in explaining student achievement. In Hattie's (2009) synthesis of 800 meta-analyses of factors contributing to educational achievement, motivation is ranked as 51st out of 138 domains, below many relational factors such as peer influences (41st), home environment (31st) and teacher–student relationships (11th). Crucially, the single best predictor of academic achievement in this meta-analysis of meta-analyses is students' estimation of their own performance. Interpreting this result, Hattie (2009) comments that, on the one hand, this may indicate that students are not always encouraged to exceed their own and others' expectations; on the other hand, students' own remarkable understanding of classroom achievement casts doubts on assessment-driven educational systems aiming to find answers that students already have.

These two insights – that students are naturally motivated, and that they can show remarkable understanding of classroom achievement – constitute the premises of the present chapter, which aims to show that students can and do have a voice that deserves to be listened to, valued and taken into account.

Why listen to students?

In an era of diversity and equity, it is perhaps surprising that including students in educational decision making is still rare in mainstream schooling. The persistent calls that marked the end of the last century (Corbett & Wilson, 1995; Kozol, 1992; Levin, 2000; Rudduck & Flutter, 2000) have clearly made a difference to student voice, at least in the English-speaking countries (Cook-Sather, 2006; Kidd & Czerniawski, 2011). Nevertheless, 'the most informed ... witnesses of schooling' are still marginalised in most educational contexts (Smyth, 2006: 279). Schools as places of genuine dialogue, in which the voices of the most important stakeholders – pupils – are specifically sought after and valued, are still rare (Leitch & Mitchell, 2007; Zhao, 2011).

Student perspective occupies a central position in social constructivist approaches to education (Brooks & Brooks, 2000; Larochelle et al., 2009), which have in common a Piagetian sociocognitive conflict and a Vygotskian sociocultural view of learning (Palincsar, 1998). According to the former, learning occurs when a child's level of understanding is challenged by new experiences in the social context, while the latter regards learning as an essentially social process in which a child advances along the developmental continuum through interaction with more advanced peers or adults, this interaction being realised via language and other symbolic means (Palincsar, 1998). In both situations, children have an active role in the process, as they learn by constantly comparing new and old information in their attempt to create meaning and make sense of the world around them (Larochelle et al., 2009). In educational contexts, as Lincoln (1995) explains, learning as meaning-making is only possible by giving students a legitimate voice in the classroom and allowing them to appropriate new information in a way that makes sense to them as individuals. Students have repeatedly been shown to prefer constructive to overly didactic learning environments (Kinchin, 2004; McIntyre et al., 2005), and constructivist instruction has been shown to positively predict deep processing strategies, self-efficacy, task value and achievement in large cohort studies (Nie & Lau, 2010).

Given that language is considered one of the main vehicles by which learning occurs (Vygotsky, 1992), it is not surprising that social constructivism has been adopted in the language learning literature, either explicitly (e.g., Kaufman, 2004; Williams & Burden, 1997), or implicitly, in various theoretical and methodological areas that emphasise a learner-centred approach, in particular task-based and problem-based language learning (e.g., Bygate et al., 2001; Ellis, 2003) and sociocultural approaches to language education (e.g., Lantolf & Poehner, 2008; Swain et al., 2010). Giving students a voice and an individualised approach to education have also been advocated by, for example, proponents of autonomy, who emphasise the learner's need to develop as a reflective self-directed individual in the social context (e.g., Cotterall & Crabbe, 2008; Little, 2007; Ushioda, 2009; 2011; van Lier, 1996); the learner-centred curriculum, which regards the language curriculum as the result of democratic teacher/student collaboration (Clarke, 1991; Nunan, 1988); and the Dogme approach to language teaching, which relies on student needs and interests as the sole basis for language teaching (Meddings & Thornbury, 2009).

While these developments have become mainstream in the international private ELT sector, in local state education contexts they are still rare. Romania is a case in point, in which constructivism and learner-centred education are hardly ever mentioned in the literature. In fact, as the pressure to publish and undertake research is still in its very early stages in the country, the amount of publicly available educational research is very limited indeed. Virtasalo (2008) explains the situation through the country's continued struggle to adapt to the new democratic structures after several decades of communism in which most research and development activities were limited to tightly controlled state institutes and were virtually absent from universities and industry.

Among the few authors who have explored the student's perspective in Romanian education and made their results available are Badea and Cuciureanu (2007), who investigated children's rights and responsibilities in school. One of their conclusions after interviewing 165 teachers and surveying 1637 pupils is quite telling: there is a balance between students' rights and responsibilities in Romania: teachers believe that pupils have too many rights, and pupils believe they have too many responsibilities. Other findings are that Romanian students tend to perceive learning as something they do 'for the teachers' rather than for their own lifelong benefit, that academic motivation is in clear decline; that students believe they have very little say in their own education; and that Romanian schools do not prepare students for taking responsibility in real life.

A more pupil-centred project initiated by the British Council, called Student Voice (Istrate & Velea, 2006) explored and encouraged the expression of students' views on education and schooling via an online platform, with over 700 participants from five Romanian and three British secondary schools. One of the insights gleaned from the asynchronous debates was the perception that teachers are extremely influential in determining students' attitudes and values, and that Romanian teenagers appear to cherish personal qualities in an educator more than subject knowledge.

Istrate and Velea (2006) maintain that projects like Student Voice can promote bottom-up educational change in Romania by giving adolescents opportunities to develop and practise decision making and responsibility, by making their voices heard and by giving them a platform for learning through interaction and democratic debate. While such scaffolded interventions are clearly beneficial and necessary in Romania, teachers themselves could also start their own educational reform in their own classrooms by routinely taking into account their pupils' perspectives (Taylor, 2009; 2010a). After an overview of learning English as a foreign language in Romania, two examples of more formalised research that continued my own informal classroom investigations as a teacher of English in Romania are reported in this chapter as examples of the motivational and methodological insights that Romanian adolescents have and are happy to share, if we are prepared to listen.

Learning English as a foreign language in Romania

A republic situated in south-eastern Europe, Romania is one of the latest two countries to join the European Union in January 2007 (the other being Bulgaria). Romania's long journey to democracy began in December 1989 with the elimination of the communist dictator Nicolae Ceausescu, which left the country's economy on the verge of collapse. The following year marked the beginning of a lengthy and difficult transition from a totalitarian regime with a deeply inbred and corrupt system to a democratic society and open-market economy (Light & Phinnemore, 2001).

As in most European countries, Romanian schools have no autonomy in deciding the content of the compulsory curriculum, but they do have the freedom to decide what teaching methods to use, with monitoring mechanisms in place (European Commission, 2008a). In theory, students are assessed through formative and summative methods including oral questioning, written papers, practical activities, projects and portfolios, according to standardised curricular descriptors approved by the Ministry of Education (European Commission, 2008b). In practice, however, oral questioning is prevalent, and marks are often 'based more on teacher's experience and perception rather than clean, relevant and unitary criteria' (Mihai, 2003: 69). In some contexts, bad marks are given for bad behaviour – leading to further bad behaviour, which in turn leads to more bad marks.[1]

Foreign language education has always been a high priority in Eastern Europe. While the Soviet bloc imposed the teaching of Russian as the only compulsory foreign language in most communist countries, the Romanian dictator opted for a colder relationship with Moscow in favour of a peculiar personality cult. In the 1970s, Russian was prevalent but not obligatory, French, German and English being also taught in Romanian schools and universities. Despite a historical preference for French as a fellow Romance language, it has been argued that in Romania an interest in Anglo-American culture and civilisation acted as a spontaneous form of opposition to communist indoctrination (Constantinescu et al., 2002). However, whilst all links with the West were severed under threat of imprisonment for all but the secret police and their all-pervasive informers, learning foreign languages in school had the sole purpose of getting satisfactory marks, with no link to authentic communication (Fodor & Peluau, 2003; Medgyes, 1997). Foreign language films, books and music were completely inaccessible, except for propaganda materials originating in other communist countries.

After 1990, the political-economic environment in Europe brought English to the fore, with the European Union and the need for a regional lingua franca playing an unquestionable role (Medgyes, 1997). The World Bank, Peace Corps and the British Council have also shaped the importance that English would have in the Romanian educational system in the future (Mihai, 2003). In 1990, a governmental decree made the teaching of a foreign language mandatory from the age of eight in all Romanian state schools. A second foreign language would be introduced at the age of ten. Unlike several other European countries, in Romania there is no compulsory foreign language, but English is clearly prevalent: 96 per cent of students opt for it in secondary schools – compared to an EU average of 84 per cent – and 39 per cent in primary schools (Eurostat, 2009). Since 1999, of the two foreign languages studied by every secondary school student in Romania, at least one must also be part of the final examination, the baccalaureate.

The combination of strong international influences and developments, on the one hand, and a controversial political atmosphere with changes of government triggering changes in educational policy every four years, on the other hand, has taken Romanian education through a perpetual cycle of reforms and structural changes in recent years (European Commission, 2008b; Mihai, 2003). Admittedly, monochrome Stalinist textbooks have been replaced by glossy materials featuring age-relevant issues; students watch English language films in class and may be assessed on project work more than on proficiency in literary translation, but the extent to which these recent developments have truly been appropriated by Romanian English language teaching is debatable. As Andrei (2006: 774) puts it, 'there still is a nostalgia for the past certainties, for more stable and more predictable curricula'. Although syllabi are allegedly based on a functional–communicative model of learning and teaching (National Curriculum Council, 2007a, 2007b), in practice, teaching is still heavily driven by grammar–translation methodology, and the structure of the final examination – which for most pupils still represents the main reason for studying – has long contradicted the theoretical principles stated in the official documents (Mihai, 2003).

Paradoxically, many Romanian adolescents are actually proficient speakers of English. Their intrinsically driven competence, however, may sometimes have little to do with their classroom activities. Many of them learn the language from films, music, computer applications and online social networks where they use English for authentic communication about personally relevant issues (Emmerson, 2009).

Listening to Romanian teenagers: some qualitative insights

Romanian teenagers' motivation to learn English and other associated processes have been explored recently in two mixed-method research projects – Taylor (2008) and Taylor (2010b) – whose key qualitative findings will be reported briefly in this section. More details about the participants[2] in the qualitative components of the two studies can be found in Table 3.1.

While the semi-structured interview schedules focused on identity processes, there were also questions on perceived relevance, motivation, perceptions of the English class and suggestions for possible improvement. The findings reported in this chapter are based on these questions.

The interviews, conducted in Romanian, were transcribed integrally, coded and analysed with the QSR NVivo 8 software package and translated selectively, for citation purposes. The qualitative data were analysed inductively, through thematic content analysis (Miles & Huberman, 1994). The findings discussed in this chapter do not claim to represent trends or generalisable results, which are not aims of qualitative research. While qualitative findings from one

Table 3.1   Participant details

	Methods	Number of interviewees	Gender distribution	Age range and mean	Number of schools	School specialisms
Taylor (2008)	Group interviews	53	20 M	15–19	3	Theoretical Various
	Focus groups		33 F	16.94		Various
Taylor (2010a)	one-to-one interviews	32	16 M 16 F	14–19 16.47	4	Economics, Tourism & Administration Computer science Music Modern languages

research context are often not transferable to other contexts, comparing results from different settings leads to a deeper understanding of the research problem (Richards, 2003).

The qualitative findings of the two projects will be discussed in an aggregated manner, in two main subsections. The former analyses the perceived direct proportionality between teacher motivation and student motivation, while the latter gives examples of students' intuitive understanding of English language teaching methodology and assessment.

From motivated teachers to motivated students

The literature describing the influence of the teacher in the classroom is abundant, both in general education (Birch & Ladd, 1996; Harter, 1996) and in foreign/second language learning (Noels et al., 1999; Papi & Abdollahzadeh, 2012; Ushioda, 2011). This influence was confirmed by the interviews conducted on the two research projects. One of the main motivational factors that student participants identified was the teachers' own motivation, engagement and interest – both with regards to the subject and to their students. Many participants explained that their motivation in the English class depended clearly on the teacher's attitude. Asked about his level of engagement and willingness to work hard in class, a participant explained:

> *It depends on the teacher.* If it's a good teacher, who knows how to approach the students, who also jokes with them and knows what to do…then I am really pleased to answer correctly, to work hard and all that. But if the teacher's not like that – umm, not really. [emphasis added] (M, 15)[3]

Similar comparisons were made by a 14-year-old female student, whose admiration for her English teacher is perhaps a little surprising given that she also considered she was constantly marked down in class. When asked to explain her perceptions, the student explained that, although the teacher was 'a very, very kind person', she also knew when it was necessary to be strict, so the girl trusted her wisdom:

> She's always known how to be both nice and useful. She's always known how to get involved where she needed to. Where she thought it unnecessary, she didn't, and it was very good what she did. [...] *We're not the same with all the teachers*, but when we see that she shows us this…enormous respect, then we like to do the same. [emphasis added]

Another girl, 15 years old, who admired her English teacher for starting her first class by asking students about their personal likes and dislikes so she would know what to emphasise in her lessons, thought this had an important effect on the students' motivation. A less interested attitude of the teacher, she felt, would result in students thinking: 'If the teacher's not bothered about what I want, why would I care about what she wants?' She felt that when the teacher was interested, students too were interested.

However, many participants had less positive experiences to share. A 16-year-old boy contrasted his present teacher to his previous one, commenting on the influence that the teacher's attitude had on his level of engagement:

> Our English teacher in elementary school took great interest in me. [...] She gave me extra work to do and all that. Here, the teacher is not very demanding. [...] Other teachers get us to work hard even if their subjects are not important for our specialism, but English is like... well, let's just do a little thing or two... [...] I love discovering things, but we can't discover much in the English class, because the teacher is not really bothered.

The teacher's apparent indifference can even engender aversion for the subject itself, which was also one of the findings that Istrate and Velea (2006) commented on:

> There's a class that I literally hate. [...] He teaches the subject and we look at him and... we literally see him like a... robot. It's mechanic, everything he teaches... he looks through you, really, it's not like he's talking to you... He looks right through you, he doesn't care that you... you can sit there and eat or... or I don't know what. He doesn't care! He just looks through you and he drives me up the wall! I really hate this, I really do! (F, 19)

The risk that negative perceptions of teachers may lead to negative perceptions of the subject they teach was also pointed out by one of the youngest participants in the second study:

> We don't learn the lesson from the classroom, which is very bad! [...] You go home to learn a lesson which maybe you're sick of, because maybe you're sick of the teacher... That's what usually happens: when you don't like a teacher, you don't like the subject they teach either. (F, 14)

The implications are dramatic: If the teacher is genuinely interested in the students, this increases the students' interest and engagement too. If, however, the teacher has not managed to bond with the students for one reason or another, this may diminish the students' interest and affective propensities for the subject itself. The beginning of this quotation is also essential, as the student makes a direct link between failure to learn in the classroom and not liking the teacher, therefore not liking the subject. The need for student autonomy could not be greater here. It is obvious that not every teacher will be liked by every student at all times, but if students are autonomous and understand that they are learning for themselves, not 'for the teacher' (Badea & Cuciureanu, 2007), then the relationship between not liking the teacher and not liking the subject would surely be weaker.

> For many others, a recurrent theme was contagious boredom:
> Teachers are bored and pass their boredom on to us. (M, 17)
> Classes bore me especially when I don't understand and the teachers don't know how to explain and can't show you how beautiful a subject is – so all you can do is sit there and nod off; and the teacher doesn't make any effort. (M, 17)
> There are few teachers who are really passionate about what they do. Many of them do it just because they've got to do it. [...] They no longer feel like it, they just come because they've got to come and to retire and to finish with it all. (M, 19)

This participant's words echo almost literally those of the student cited by Knesting and Waldron (2006: 607) in their analysis of factors contributing to student disengagement: '...many of the teachers don't care; obviously don't care about their jobs. They're just here to do what they do then get paid and go home'. Very similar perceptions were also reported by Phelan et al. (1992).

Several interviewees attributed the teachers' indifference to the generation gap and also to a 'mentality gap'. It was rather interesting to see that these teenagers, the oldest of whom had been born four years after the fall of communism, believed they could not communicate with their teachers because the latter were 'communist'. An 18-year-old felt he could not express his honest point of view in class because the teacher was communist. Having been born in democracy, he maintained, he respected people's right to a free opinion, but she did not.

Another participant believed similar differences were the origin of a 'wall' that prevented genuine communication between teachers and students:

> There's a wall between the student and the teacher. You can't really reach the student. [...] they've both created this wall, both the teachers and the students, I think. [Why?] Because...I suppose every generation brings a change. Maybe an improvement to the previous generation, or just a change. And if you, as a teacher, can't understand this and try to manipulate the students [...] or to introduce them into the system that you're familiar with, of course you get this rift. And students don't agree with this and you've lost them. I suppose this may lead to defiance...[...] Or simply that can't-be-bothered attitude...(M, 18)

Palmer (1997) discusses classroom interactions in similar metaphors. Teachers and students 'collaborate' with 'structures of separation', he believes, because they fear 'live encounters' (genuine person-to-person communication, being themselves in class). In order to avoid these encounters, Palmer explains, students hide behind their notebooks and their silence, while teachers hide behind their lecterns and their authority. The reason for this behaviour (Palmer, 1997: 37) maintains, is fear:

> We collaborate with the structures of separation because they promise to protect us against one of the deepest fears at the heart of being human – the fear of having a live encounter with alien 'otherness', whether the other is a student, a colleague, a subject, or a self-dissenting voice within. We fear encounters in which the other is free to be itself, to speak its own truth, to tell us what we may not wish to hear. We want those encounters on our own terms, so that we can control their outcomes…

Perhaps the fear of 'live encounters' and a desire to maintain control could also explain the perceived behaviourist teaching methodology that most participants described when talking about their usual English classes. There is evidence to show that psychologically controlling teachers, who pressurise students into acting and thinking in a particular way, may do so as a result of a pressuring school environment and because of their own low autonomy as teachers (Reeve et al., 2004; Soenens et al., 2012). Their autonomy and intrinsic joy of teaching can be stifled both 'from above', through curriculum constraints, performance standards, challenging colleagues, and 'from below', through disruptive and demotivated students (Pelletier et al., 2002). The argument that student autonomy depends on teacher autonomy has also been made in relation to language learning. Little (1995), for example, explained that the nature of the student/ teacher dialogue will always be more important in nurturing self-directed learners than strategy training. However, apart from being a crucial determinant of student autonomy, the nature of student/ teacher dialogue may itself be the key to the teachers' own comparatively low autonomy in such contexts. As recent research indicates (Klassen et al., 2012), relatedness with students is a more important factor in determining the level of engagement and positive emotions in teachers than other work-related relationships.

From behaviourist teaching to constructivist learning?

In the 2008 study, participants were asked to comment on their perceptions of English language lessons, teaching and school, in general. Their open answers are summarised in Table 3.2.

The summary indicates that these students appreciate fair teachers who help them experience and learn a subject that will be of use to them in real life.

Table 3.2   Student perceptions of English lessons, teaching and school

Students do not like	Students (would) like
Teachers who	Teachers who
– do not care about students as individuals: are not interested in their personal opinions; do not notice/care if they have lost the students' attention – lack enthusiasm and interest in the subject they teach – are unfair and take revenge by giving low marks – punish the whole group for one person – are arrogant and sarcastic, labelling and mocking students – answer their own questions, without giving students a chance – cannot control the class and maintain discipline	– are friendly and treat students as their friends – are competent in their subject and passionate about teaching it – show logical connections between subjects and their relevance for life – are able to summarise the subject matter without burdening the students with too much information – are fair, understanding and patient, explaining for as many times as necessary ('without shouting') – can maintain discipline in class
Class/Teaching style	Class/Teaching style
– too much textbook-driven grammar, too little communicative practice – too much to learn: students feel they cannot cope – no differentiation: students either get bored because the explanations are too easy, or disengage because they do not understand the activities (especially students who have only started studying English) – no choice: students have to do what is imposed on them	– varied, interesting and interactive classes with audio-video support – relaxed and encouraging atmosphere, so that students are not afraid to express themselves and talk about their interests and passions – the opportunity to learn about the real/practical use of English in the world – the possibility to apply theory in practice
Classmates who	School
– are noisy and rude, disturbing the teacher and the other students – call you a 'nerd' if you do well, or laugh at your mistakes – get into little factions that tease and gossip about the others	– longer breaks, with relaxing music; classes to start later – colourful rooms, with relevant teaching materials, plants and flowers – sports, projects and extracurricular activities – support in finding one's 'gift'/talent and pursuing it

Source: Taylor (2008: 70).

They want a nurturing and disciplined environment in which they have a voice that is valued and respected. In their comparison of 'traditional class-rooms' and 'constructivist classrooms', Brooks and Brooks (2000) list several aspects that the Romanian participants appeared to understand instinctively. A summarised and adapted version of this list can be seen in Table 3.3.

Table 3.3   A comparison of traditional classrooms and constructivist classrooms

	Traditional classrooms	Constructivist classrooms
Curriculum	Presented part to whole, with emphasis on basic skills	Presented whole to part, with emphasis on big concepts
	Strictly adhered to	Acts as a guide in pursuing highly valued student questions
	Relies heavily on textbooks and workbooks	Relies heavily on primary sources of data
Students	Blank slates onto which information is etched by teachers	Thinkers with emergent views about the world
	Tend to work alone	Tend to work in groups
Teachers	Didactic manner	Interactive manner
	Disseminate information to students	Mediate knowledge construction
	Seek the correct answer in order to validate learning	Seek the students' points of view in order to incorporate them in future lessons
	Keep assessment separate from teaching	Interweave assessment with usual teaching activities
	Assess mainly through tests	Assess mainly by observing students at work and evaluating work portfolios

Source: Based on Brooks and Brooks (2000: 17).

It is perhaps surprising that the participants in both studies reported here appeared to have such an accurate view of constructivist teaching and learning, given that apparently not many of them had experienced what they described as their ideal learning environment.

What the numerous theories of constructivism have in common is a view of learning as a meaning-making process. As Richardson (1997) explains, individuals create their own constructivist understandings based on the interaction of what they already know and believe with the phenomena or ideas they encounter. This is in contrast to traditional behaviourist pedagogy, which leaves no room for reflection and subjectivity – either in determining the learning content or in how information is used, interpreted or understood (Boghossian, 2006). Discussing measures of success in traditional educational settings, Boghossian (2006: 716) goes on to explain:

> In the traditional behaviorist model, learners undergo some form of conditioning. [...] The behaviorist would interpret, for example, a student's correct answer to a question as a sign of successful conditioning, and then continue to reinforce correct responses behaviorally by assigning good grades. [...] In a behaviorist paradigm, the student is engaged in the educational process only in that she displays the appropriate verbal behavior (e.g. checking the correct box on a multiple choice test).

Analysing Table 3.3 in the light of this very brief comparison, it does appear that, in the context of this research, English language teaching is perceived as predominantly behaviouristic, whereas the learning that the participants declare they long for shows signs of intuitive constructivist inclinations. These insights will be discussed below in further detail, with reference to teaching methodology, assessment and feedback, and valuing students as individuals.

Teaching methodology

The 'communication wall' mentioned earlier appeared to manifest itself in many of the participant groups through physical distance, which many teachers allegedly preferred and students appeared to dislike:

> The teacher sits at the front and the students at the back: everybody just listening like we're at a congress. (M, 17)
>
> [If I were a teacher], I'd be close to [my students], to see what they want, what they like and don't like – that's how you know them and can help them. (F, 18)

This physical distance was associated with teacher-centred instruction that appeared to favour a lecturing model of teaching and reduced opportunities for student fluency practice:

> Some sit at their desk and dictate and we write stuff for 50 minutes without a break. [...] Generally, we don't get a chance to speak in the English class – maybe we'll say a word or so in an hour. It's the teacher who talks, talks, talks, and we just sit there... I mean, if we could speak too, if we could show that we know... Or even if we don't know, at least we learn, as long as we can speak... (F, 14)

The 14-year-old cited here shows an apparent inclination towards a 'growth mindset' (Dweck, 2007; Mercer & Ryan, 2010), being aware that practice would help her and her peers develop even when making mistakes. She is not afraid to take risks, if this means her ability would expand.

Other students hinted at similar repetitive lecturing practice and a literal, non-differentiated application of the cyclical syllabus (Dubin & Olshtain, 1986):

> ...a notebook written four years ago looks almost the same as a recent one. (M,19)
>
> Nothing new. We've got bored hearing the same things all over again for eight years. (M, 18)

Apart from the perception that teachers adopted a lecturing style in the teaching of English (some actually lecturing in Romanian, according to several participants), many of these students felt too much emphasis on grammar left too little time for communicative practice.

> I'd make classes more interactive and interesting – not just teaching modal verbs and stuff. (M, 18)
>
> More emphasis on communication, talking more, that's what we need; even if we can write well, we find it very difficult to express ourselves when speaking. (F, 18)
>
> My idea of a perfect English lesson? I can't really describe it, because we've hardly ever had one. I guess one in which we speak freely, in which we express our views of things. Certainly not a class in which we write exercises on the board! (M, 18)
>
> I'd shorten the time given to grammar; I'd introduce much more speaking, just about ordinary things and then we'd also learn tenses and everything else. (F, 15)

Although very young, and without much apparent experience of communicative language teaching, these adolescents demonstrate keen insight into the principles of authentic communication tasks (Nunan, 2004). They understand that, if language tasks were *meaningful* and *purposeful* (Williams, 1998), students would also acquire grammatical knowledge in the process of genuine communication about issues of personal importance to them or simply about 'ordinary things'.

Some had clearly experienced such English classes and their perception of the lesson and of the teacher was very positive, as testified by this 16-year-old boy:

> I really do think that our teacher's style is a very good one. [...] Because we don't limit ourselves to solving exercises from the book and writing...I don't know what English word equals I don't know what Romanian translation. And having vocabulary lists in your notebook and homework and that's it. No! We do a lot of essays, so there's room for artistic expression, for imagination, for developing your vocabulary – because we're always looking for new words and then using them in front of the class and speaking freely, and that's how they stick and we learn them.

Or a similar, more orally focussed description of a perfect English class:

> Desks in a circle, teacher in the middle...and fun! [What sort of fun?] Say we've had to do some reading in English – a book, a story, anything. And the teacher asks: What can you tell us about this? Everything would be relaxed, not tense or stressful. I'd do things differently, I mean I'd have diversity, if

you wish. Not just...every lesson: writing on the board, exercises, reading, full stop. I'd bring games and things, people would get involved, team-work... (M, 15)

It is easy to recognise in the teenager's description the main elements of constructivist classrooms (Brooks & Brooks, 2000) that we saw above in Table 3.3.

Assessment and feedback

The perceived need for more interactive learning was also linked to assessment:

I'd love something more interactive. I mean, not the teacher sitting at her desk, reading the question, and you answering from your desk. Right, [mark] 10^4 for one answer! Or for some ticks! That's how we'd develop our oral skills too, which we don't really [develop much]. ... (F, 17)

A younger pupil, who confessed that, to him, marks were the only thing that mattered, also claimed that he only had high marks in English because they were informed in advance what they would be tested on, so they could prepare:

This way, I can study, but I only study that chapter, or that lesson that I need, and that's why I get a high mark. If she were to assess me on the whole syllabus, it would be a disaster. (M, 15)

The practices that these teenagers are referring to reflect clear behaviourist reinforcement of a preconditioned response (Boghossian, 2006; Ormrod, 2011). Such 'recitation script' practices have been discussed, for instance, by Gutierrez and Larson (1994) in terms of 'border reinforcement' and 'teacher hegemony' in the classroom, as their sole purpose is to display a reinforced behaviour that is controlled by an authoritative teacher.

Many participants believed it was always safer to be on the teacher's side, to create the right impression, to do their 'duty' as students and to avoid conflicts, as it was the teacher who gave their marks. Some students thought it was typical of 'the System' for teachers to bear grudges and take revenge by giving bad marks if one got into trouble with them. Fear of retaliation some-times prevented hard-working students from making the most of their English class. A 14-year-old confessed that she and her classmates were sometimes frightened to put their hands up and ask a question or confess they had not understood something. In turn, a 17-year-old girl told of a situation when she got scolded really badly by her teacher for making a mistake in a lesson when they were practising a newly taught concept. The student concluded: 'That's what makes people look up the answers at the back and fill them in before the lesson – and what have you done with that?' These are indications that testing and marking were used as expressions of power and control, as well as disciplinary tools, with little apparent awareness of the effects on test takers or any significance of such practices in the real world (Shohamy, 2001).

These strategies appeared to be clear to some students, who felt there was no connection between learning and assessment, and marks were used as an instrument of control, with little connection to the life outside the classroom:

> She wasn't really interested. Whether we learnt anything or not was our business. She was only there to evaluate us, that's all. (F, 19)
>
> You'll never find the way to your students if you keep that attitude of 'I'm a teacher and give bad marks – you're a student so you've got to do what I say'; marks shouldn't come out of fear; you should learn for life, not for these marks. (M, 17)

These students appeared to understand that such an approach to assessment 'promotes neither the interaction between prior and new knowledge nor the conversations that are necessary for internalisation and deep understanding' (Richardson, 1997: 3). On the contrary, whatever information is acquired from traditional teaching will normally only be elicited for assessment, and ignored at all other times, remaining unintegrated with the students' other knowledge, as Richardson (1997) explains.

Informal assessment, verbal feedback and other interactive cues were perceived as painful by many participants. A fairly common complaint was that they felt they were treated with arrogance and irony, labelled and ridiculed in class:

> We once had a term paper and I did a composition about winter, I think, and she started to read it aloud in class and to mock me and I felt really bad. (F, 19)
>
> When you see they're getting in and...they think you are stupid...and they are the best...I don't think that's normal. As long as they've come to teach you something, that's what they should do. (F, 19)
>
> I really loved English and was trying to learn more, but she would say to me: 'Oh, you're bound to get it wrong, I won't have you answer this question!'. [...] I used to feel like a real weirdo who didn't know anything and they knew everything. [Did you think you'd get it wrong when you put your hand up to answer?] I did, but I thought if I got it wrong then she'd correct me and I'd learn something new. But she didn't. [And you still put your hand up...] I did, and at some point she sent me to the board to write

it up and when she saw I'd got it right she said I'd cheated. I felt like a right crook then. Really left out I felt. (F, 15)

This is another example of a student who was willing to take risks, make mistakes and expose herself to ridicule in order to learn something new and develop her English language ability. These are the rare ingredients of a 'growth mindset' (Dweck, 2007; Mercer & Ryan, 2010), which many teachers would be grateful to see in more students. In this particular case, however, the teacher herself appeared to encourage a 'fixed mindset', whereby risk taking is avoided as it may reveal low ability that cannot be developed further. Given that students tend to perceive teacher responses as assessments of themselves as persons rather than of their abilities (Deci & Ryan, 1985; Dweck, 1999), it is little wonder that this experience had such a painful emotional impact on the pupil.

Such verbal cues are clear examples of controlling rather than informative feedback (Deci & Ryan, 1985), as they do not give the students any guidance on how they could improve their skills, or what their strengths and weaknesses are. Given such situations, it is perhaps not surprising that many participants reported having learnt to do their 'duty as students' in order to obtain passing marks. This is reminiscent of other reports of Romanian students learning 'for the teacher' (Badea & Cuciureanu, 2007) and may explain why English was perceived by many participants as an academic subject like any others rather than a real communication tool in class – a situation also reported in other educational contexts (e.g., Williams & Burden, 1999).

Valuing students as individuals

Doing one's 'duty' as a student – both in their interaction with an often impersonal and disengaged teacher, and in bidding for a passing mark – appeared as one of the strongest leitmotifs in both projects. In the former one (Taylor, 2008), this duty was perceived as putting in as little effort as possible to mislead the English teacher into thinking they were on task, while actually attending to numerous personally relevant activities with no connection to the lesson. In the latter project (Taylor, 2010b), one's duty as a student tended to consist in a complex display of socially imposed and often contradictory identities (e.g., that of a diligent student when interacting with the teacher versus that of an academically disaffected teenager when interacting with peers), whose main strategic goal was to keep the interlocutor on one's side (Juvonen & Murdock, 1993). These mechanisms were not without negative emotional consequences, however, as these two adolescents explain:

I've noticed it's best to agree with the teacher, although sometimes I've got a different opinion. Because she often clings on to her view and I can't convince her that this is my opinion and my choice. [...] I've tried, but I've realised it's not worth it. (F, 17)

I'll normally tell you straight all I've got to say, and it's a compromise for me having to hide the truth and to take roundabout routes. I hate this. But I've got to do it to avoid conflicts, especially with the teachers but also with my parents. (M, 17)

At the happier end of the spectrum, another student felt that the permission he had to be himself in class was a very useful pedagogic tool for his English teacher:

I've always tried to be very open and very honest in the English class. So my teacher knows all my good and bad sides. [...] She can be a better pedagogue through this. If she knows what motivates the pupil, she can use this as a weapon – in a good sense. [...] And I think that's what every teacher should do: try to know the pupil's personality and then try to...manipulate that personality in a very good direction...And I think this would motivate any pupil. (M, 17)

Another young man thought this was the key to removing the 'communication wall' that he felt prevented students and teachers from genuine interaction:

[If I were a teacher] I'd try to remove that wall I was talking about. I'd try to understand...to find their desire...to see where it comes from. And maybe to channel it in a certain way. If you've got the desire you can change a lot of things. (M, 19)

According to another 19-year-old male student from a different town, this is the only thing that differentiates one teacher from another – the gift of seeing each individual student's way of learning beyond any superficial defensive masks:

However rude [...] any student has a...side through which he can learn something. That's the...magic of a teacher...to find that way. [...] Because between teacher X and teacher Y, in terms of knowledge...often there's no difference, they're both equally capable as far as knowledge of the subject matter is concerned. But...this what-you-call-it...this teaching method-ology...[...] That's the secret. If he finds the way, then he's a very good teacher.

These students are clearly asking to be allowed to 'speak as themselves' in the language classroom (Ushioda, 2011). They want to have their right to a personal opinion acknowledged and valued (Rudduck & Flutter, 2000); they want to be treated with the respect for the individual that they are very happy to show to the teacher (Phelan et al., 1992). They also seem to have an intuitive understanding of what research has repeatedly shown: that discrepancies between what people believe is their true identity and an identity that is imposed on them from the outside act as barriers to academic engagement and well-being (Faircloth, 2009; Hatt, 2007; Phelan et al., 1993; Wortham, 2006).

Concluding remarks

Constructivist and learner-centred teaching approaches are not without criticism (e.g., Fox, 2001; Kirschner et al., 2006; Mayer, 2004), one of the main counterarguments being that students cannot learn without guidance – certainly not before they are advanced enough to provide their own support. This, however, is no different to what proponents of learner-centred approaches militate for: students' transition to a more active role in learning and society requires sustained training and support from adults (Corbett & Wilson, 1995); complex learning and problem solving necessitate robust scaffolding (Hmelo-Silver et al., 2007), and teachers are as indispensable as ever, both as pedagogues and as subject experts (Little, 2007). These conditions are also no different to the two basic principles of social constructivism discussed earlier: that learning occurs when a person's level of understanding is challenged by new experiences in the social context; and that learning represents progress along a developmental continuum through interaction with more advanced peers or adults (Palincsar, 1998).

As the numerous extracts above have demonstrated, these conditions are very similar to these Romanian adolescents' intuitive understanding and firm expectations of what teaching should represent. They were not asking to be left alone to discover their own way through to communicative competence and linguistic sophistication. In one powerful chorus, they were asking to be listened to, taken into account, included in their own education; to be treated like real people, who would love to bring their own real world into the language classroom and take the language out of the classroom into the real world.

Engagement priorities

However, putting such insights into practice is not a straightforward matter, as teachers' freedom in the classroom is often limited by assessment constraints and a duty to prepare students for high-stakes examinations. The question then arises as to how realistic these examinations are, how far they help prepare our students for using languages in the real world, for real communication, and whether assessment standards are not sometimes acting as a deterrent to language learning, particularly in contexts in which foreign language study is optional. Nevertheless, as teachers have been shown to have an important influence on students' motivation and engagement, they may be in the best position to help students overcome many perceived barriers to language study. Perhaps a good place to start would be for each of us to think of what stimulated our own interest in languages and motivated us to study them. Our students may well be motivated by similar factors.

I would like, therefore, to invite my fellow classroom practitioners and researchers in Romania and elsewhere to join me in exploring and reflecting on the following engagement priorities:

1. How can the students' methodological preferences be reconciled with formal assessment constraints?
2. How realistic are our assessment practices in language education?
3. How far are we still from language education as genuine communication between real individuals?
4. What would our students want to achieve in language learning if they knew nothing would stand in their way? How can we help them get there?
5. What motivated you to become interested in languages? Could something similar motivate your students too?

Notes

1. Statements that are not supported with references are based on anecdotal evidence and private communications, as well as on my own perception and experience as a student and teacher in the Romanian educational system.
2. One of the three institutions participating in the first study is the school where I worked as an English language teacher between September 2004 and February 2007. As a result, some of the participants in that school had been my students for up to 1 year before the data were collected (May 2008). All the participants in the other two schools in study 1 and all the participants in study 2 were unknown to me.
3. In order to protect the participants' anonymity, only their gender (M = male, F = female) and age are reported.
4. In the Romanian education system, marks are given on a 1–10 scale, 5 being the minimum pass mark.

Suggested further reading

Brooks, J. G., and Brooks, M. G. (2000). *In Search of Understanding: The Case for Constructivist Classrooms*. Alexandria, VA: Association for Supervision and Curriculum Development.

This is a highly accessible text written by two experienced practitioners with an interest in student-centred education. The book makes a persuasive case for constructivism in the classroom, discusses guiding principles of constructivist education and provides helpful advice on how these principles can be put into practice.Juvonen, J. and Wentzel, K. R. (eds) (1996). *Social Motivation: Understanding Children's School Adjustment.* Cambridge: Cambridge University Press.

This edited volume represents a classic collection of papers exploring pupil voice, success and failure, peer culture and teacher influence on pupils' learning and development. A landmark contribution to understanding children's motivation and achievement.

Kohn, A. (2011). *Feel-Bad Education: Contrarian Essays on Children and Schooling.* Boston: Beacon.

As an outspoken promoter of progressive education, Alfie Kohn advocates children's active role in their own education and the need for parents and teachers to treat them with respect and give them a voice. While each of Kohn's best-selling books transmits the same deeply humanistic message, this volume offers a good bite-size introduction to pupil learning and motivation, classroom climate and 'unconditional teaching'.

References

Andrei, L. (2006). Teaching English in post-modern Romanian education. *Journal of Organizational Change Management*, 19(6): 772–74.

Badea, D. and Cuciureanu, M. (2007). *Drepturile si Responsabilitatile Copilului in Context Scolar [Children's Rights and Responsibilities in the Educational Context].* Bucharest: Institutul de Stiinte ale Educatiei. Available at: http://www.ise.ro/LinkClick.aspx?filet icket=NY0xugdR8jE%3D&tabid=135&mid=474 [Accessed 03/01/12].

Birch, S. H. and Ladd, G. W. (1996). Interpersonal relations in the school environment and the children's early school adjustment: the role of teachers and peers. In J. Juvonen and K. R. Wentzel (eds) *Social Motivation: Understanding Children's School Adjustment.* Cambridge: Cambridge University Press, pp. 199–225.

Boghossian, P. (2006). Behaviorism, constructivism, and Socratic pedagogy. *Educational Philosophy and Theory*, 38(6): 713–22.

Brooks, J. G. and Brooks, M. G. (2000). *In Search of Understanding: The Case for Constructivist Classrooms.* Alexandria, VA: Association for Supervision and Curriculum Development.

Bygate, D. M., Skehan, P. and Swain, M. (eds) (2001). *Researching Pedagogic Tasks: Second Language Learning, Teaching and Testing.* Harlow: Longman.

Chambers, G. N. (1999). *Motivating Language Learners.* Clevedon: Multilingual Matters.

Clarke, D. F. (1991). The negotiated syllabus: what is it and how does it work? *Applied Linguistics*, 12(1): 13–28.

Constantinescu, I., Popovici, V. and Stefanescu, A. (2002). Romanian. In M. Görlach (ed.) *English in Europe.* Oxford: Oxford University Press, pp. 168–94.

Cook-Sather, A. (2006). Sound, presence, and power: 'Student Voice' in educational research and reform. *Curriculum Inquiry*, 36(4): 359–90.

Corbett, D. and Wilson, B. (1995). Make a difference with, not for, students: a plea to researchers and reformers. *Educational Researcher*, 24(5): 12–17.

Cotterall, S. and Crabbe, D. (2008). Learners talking: From problem to solution. In T. Lamb and H. Reinders (eds) *Learner and Teacher Autonomy: Concepts, Realities, and Responses.* Amsterdam: John Benjamins, pp. 125–40.

Deci, E. L. and Ryan, R. M. (1985). *Intrinsic Motivation and Self-Determination in Human Behavior.* New York: Plenum.

Dörnyei, Z. and Ushioda, E. (2011). *Teaching and Researching Motivation* (Second Edition). Harlow: Pearson.

Dubin, F. and Olshtain, E. (1986). *Course Design: Developing Programs and Materials for Language Learning.* Cambridge: Cambridge University Press.

Dweck, C. S. (1999). *Self-Theories: Their Role in Motivation, Personality and Development.* Hove: Psychology Press.

Dweck, C. S. (2007). *Mindset: The New Psychology of Success.* New York: Random House.

Ellis, R. (2003). *Task-Based Language Learning and Teaching.* Oxford: Oxford University Press.

Emmerson, D. (2009). *Lessons from Romania: The Learning English Video Project.* Available at: http://www.englishclub.com/esl-videos/lessons-from-romania/index.htm [Accessed 15/01/12].

European Commission (2008a). *Levels of Autonomy and Responsibilities of Teachers in Europe.* Brussels: EACEA, Eurydice Network. Available at: http://eacea.ec.europa.eu /education/eurydice/documents/thematic_reports/094EN.pdf [Accessed 20/12/11].

European Commission (2008b). *Organisation of the Education System in Romania.* Brussels: EACEA, Eurydice Network. Available at: http://eacea.ec.europa.eu/education/eurydice /documents/eurybase/eurybase_full_reports/RO_EN.pdf [Accessed 10/12/11].

Eurostat (2009). *Pupils Learning English: Upper Secondary General Education.* European Commission. Available at: http://epp.eurostat.ec.europa.eu/tgm/web/_download /Eurostat_Table_tps00057HTMLDesc.htm [Accessed 10/12/11].

Faircloth, B. S. (2009). Making the most of adolescence: harnessing the search for identity to understand classroom belonging. *Journal of Adolescent Research*, 24(3): 321–48.

Fodor, F. and Peluau, S. (2003). Language geostrategy in Eastern and Central Europe: assessment and perspectives. In J. Maurais and M. A. Morris (eds) *Languages in a Globalising World.* Cambridge: Cambridge University Press, pp. 85–98.

Fox, R. (2001). Constructivism examined. *Oxford Review of Education*, 27(1): 23–35.

Gutierrez, K. and Larson, J. (1994). Language borders: recitation as hegemonic discourse. *International Journal of Educational Reform*, 3(1): 22–36.

Harter, S. (1996). Teacher and classmate influences on scholastic motivation, self-esteem, and level of voice in adolescents. In J. Juvonen and K. R. Wentzel (eds) *Social Motivation: Understanding Children's School Adjustment.* Cambridge: Cambridge University Press, pp. 11–42.

Hatt, B. (2007). Street smarts vs. book smarts: the figured world of smartness in the lives of marginalized, urban youth. *The Urban Review*, 39(2): 145–66.

Hattie, J. (2009). *Visible Learning: A Synthesis of over 800 Meta-analyses Relating to Achievement.* London: Routledge.

Hmelo-Silver, C. E., Duncan, R. G. and Chinn, C. A. (2007). Scaffolding and achievement in problem-based and inquiry learning: a response to Kirschner, Sweller, and Clark (2006). *Educational Psychologist*, 42(2): 99–107.

Istrate, O. and Velea, L. S. (2006). *Student Voice Romania.* Bucharest: Centre for Development and Innovation in Education. Available at: http://www.tehne.ro/ resurse/TEHNE_SVR_Report_2006.pdf [Accessed 10/01/12].

Kirschner, P. A., Sweller, J. and Clark, R. E. (2006). Why minimal guidance during instruction does not work: an analysis of the failure of constructivist, discovery, problem-based, experiential, and inquiry-based teaching. *Educational Psychologist*, 41(2): 75–86.

Juvonen, J. and Murdock, T. B. (1993). How to promote social approval: effect of audience and outcome on publicly communicated attributions. *Journal of Educational Psychology*, 85(2): 365–76.

Kaufman, D. (2004). Constructivist issues in language learning and teaching. *Annual Review of Applied Linguistics*, 24: 303–19.

Kidd, W. and Czerniawski, G. (eds) (2011). *The Student Voice Handbook: Bridging the Academic/Practitioner Divide*. Bingley: Emerald.

Kinchin, I. (2004). Investigating students' beliefs about their preferred role as learners. *Educational Research*, 46(3): 301–12.

Klassen, R. M., Perry, N. E. and Frenzel, A. C. (2012). Teachers' relatedness with students: An underemphasized component of teachers' basic psychological needs. *Journal of Educational Psychology*, 104(1): 150–65.

Knesting, K. and Waldron, N. (2006). Willing to play the game: how at-risk students persist in school. *Psychology in the Schools*, 43(5): 599–611.

Kohn, A. (1993). *Punished by Rewards: The Trouble with Gold Stars, Incentive Plans, A's, Praise and Other Bribes*. Boston: Houghton Mifflin.

Kozol, J. (1992). *Savage Inequalities: Children in America's Schools*. New York: Harper Perennial.

Lantolf, J. P. and Poehner, M. E. (eds) (2008). *Sociocultural Theory and the Teaching of Second Languages*. Sheffield: Equinox.

Larochelle, M., Bednarz, N. and Garrison, J. (2009). *Constructivism and Education*. Cambridge: Cambridge University Press.

Leitch, R. and Mitchell, S. (2007). Caged birds and cloning machines: how student imagery 'speaks' to us about cultures of schooling and student participation. *Improving Schools*, 10(1): 53–71.

Levin, B. (2000). Putting students at the centre in educational reform. *Journal of Educational Change*, 1(2): 155–72.

Light, D. and Phinnemore, D. (eds) (2001). *Post-Communist Romania: Coming to Terms with Transition*. Basingstoke: Palgrave Macmillan.

Lincoln, Y. S. (1995). In search of students' voices. *Theory into Practice*, 34(2): 88–93.

Little, D. (1995). Learning as dialogue: the dependence of learner autonomy on teacher autonomy. *System*, 23(2): 175–81.

Little, D. (2007). Language learner autonomy: Some fundamental considerations revisited. *Innovation in Language Learning and Teaching*, 1(1): 14–29.

Mayer, R. E. (2004). Should there be a three-strikes rule against pure discovery learning? *American Psychologist*, 59(1): 14–19.

McIntyre, D., Pedder, D. and Rudduck, J. (2005). Pupil voice: comfortable and uncomfortable learnings for teachers. *Research Papers in Education*, 20(2): 149–68.

Meddings, L. and Scott, T. (2009). *Teaching Unplugged: Dogme in English Language Teaching*. Peaslake: Delta.

Medgyes, P. (1997). Innovative second language education in Central and Eastern Europe. In G. R. Tucker and D. Corson (eds) *Encyclopedia of Language Education* (vol. 4: Second language education). Dordrecht: Kluwer Academic, pp. 187–96.

Mercer, S. and Ryan, S. (2010). A mindset for EFL: learners' beliefs about the role of natural talent. *ELT Journal*, 64(4): 436–44.

Mihai, F. M. (2003). '*Reforming English as a Foreign Language (EFL) Curriculum in Romania: The Global and the Local Contexts*. Unpublished doctoral thesis. Florida State University, Tallahassee, FL.

Miles, M. B. and Huberman, M. (1994). *Qualitative Data Analysis: An Expanded Sourcebook* (Second Edition). London: Sage.

Murray, G., Gao, X. and Lamb, T. (eds) (2011). *Identity, Motivation and Autonomy in Language Learning*. Bristol: Multilingual Matters.

National Curriculum Council (2007a). *Programe Scolare Pentru Clasa a IX-a: Limba Engleza [Syllabi for Grade IX: English Language]*. Bucharest: Romanian Ministry of Education and Research.

National Curriculum Council (2007b). *Programe Scolare Pentru Clasele X-XII Limba Engleza [Syllabi for Grades X–XII: English Language]*. Bucharest: Romanian Ministry of Education and Research.

Nie, Y. and Lau, S. (2010). Differential relations of constructivist and didactic instruction to students' cognition, motivation, and achievement. *Learning and Instruction*, 20(5): 411–23.

Noels, K. A., Clément, R. and Pelletier, L. G. (1999). Perceptions of teachers' communicative style and students' intrinsic and extrinsic motivation. *Modern Language Journal*, 83(1): 23–34.

Nunan, D. (1988). *The Learner-Centred Curriculum: A Study in Second Language Teaching*. Cambridge: Cambridge University Press.

Nunan, D. (2004). *Task-Based Language Teaching*. Cambridge: Cambridge University Press.

Ormrod, J. E. (2011). *Human Learning* (Sixth Edition). London: Allyn & Bacon.

Palincsar, A. S. (1998). Social constructivist perspectives on teaching and learning. *Annual Review of Psychology*, 49(1): 345–75.

Palmer, P. J. (1997). *The Courage to Teach: Exploring the Inner Landscape of a Teacher's Life* (Tenth Edition). San Francisco, CA: Jossey Bass.

Papi, M. and Abdollahzadeh, E. (2012). Teacher motivational practice, student motivation, and possible L2 selves: an examination in the Iranian EFL context. *Language Learning*, 62(2): 571–94.

Pelletier, L. G., Séguin-Lévesque, C. and Legault, L. (2002). Pressure from above and pressure from below as determinants of teachers' motivation and teaching behaviors. *Journal of Educational Psychology*, 94(1): 186–96.

Phelan, P., Davidson, A. L. and Cao, H. T. (1992). Speaking up: students' perspectives on school. *Phi Delta Kappan*, 73(9): 695–704.

Phelan, P., Davidson, A. L. and Yu, H. C. (1993). Students' multiple worlds: navigating the borders of family, peer and school culture. In P. K. Phelan and A. L. Davidson (eds) *Renegotiating Cultural Diversity in American Schools*. New York: Teachers' College Press, pp. 52–88.

Reeve, J., Jang, H., Carrell, D., Jeon, S. and Barch, J. (2004). Enhancing students' engagement by increasing teachers' autonomy support. *Motivation and Emotion*, 28(2): 147–69.

Richards, K. (2003). *Qualitative Inquiry in TESOL*. Basingstoke: Palgrave Macmillan.

Richardson, V. (1997). Constructivist teaching and teacher education: theory and practice. In V. Richardson (ed.) *Constructivist Teacher Education: Building New Understandings*. London: Falmer, pp. 3–13.

Rudduck, J. and Flutter, J. (2000). Pupil participation and pupil perspective: carving a new order of experience. *Cambridge Journal of Education*, 30(1): 75–89.

Shohamy, E. (2001). *The Power of Tests: A Critical Perspective on the Uses of Language Tests*. Harlow: Longman.

Smyth, J. (ed.) (2006). Educational leadership that fosters 'student voice'. *International Journal of Leadership in Education*, 9(4): 279–84.

Soenens, B., Sierens, E., Vansteenkiste, M., Dochy, F. and Goossens, L. (2012). Psychologically controlling teaching: examining outcomes, antecedents, and mediators. *Journal of Educational Psychology*, 104(1): 108–20.

Swain, M., Kinnear, P. and Steinman, L. (2010). *Sociocultural Theory in Second Language Education: An Introduction through Narratives*. Bristol: Multilingual Matters.

Taylor, F. (2008). *Involvement Avoidance in the English Class: Romanian Insights*. Unpublished MA dissertation, School of Education and Lifelong Learning, University of Exeter.

Taylor, F. (2009). Some grim effects of a nationally imposed English curriculum in Romania. *Romanian Journal of English Studies*, 6: 417–27.

Taylor, F. (2010a). Surreptitious teacher development: Promoting change from within. *Romanian Journal of English Studies*, 7: 401–9.

Taylor, F. (2010b). *A Quadripolar Model of Identity in Adolescent Foreign Language Learners*. Unpublished doctoral thesis, School of English Studies, University of Nottingham.

Ushioda, E. (1996). *Learner Autonomy: The Role of Motivation*. Dublin: Authentik.

Ushioda, E. (2009). A person-in-context relational view of emergent motivation, self and identity. In Z. Dörnyei and E. Ushioda (eds) *Motivation, Language Identity and the L2 Self*. Bristol: Multilingual Matters, pp. 215–28.

Ushioda, E. (2011). Motivating learners to speak as themselves. In G. Murray, X. Gao and T. Lamb (eds) *Identity, Motivation and Autonomy in Language Learning*. Bristol: Multilingual Matters, pp. 11–24.

vanLier, L. (1996). *Interaction in the Language Curriculum: Awareness, Autonomy and Authenticity*. Harlow: Longman.

Virtasalo, I. (2008). *Status and Developments of Social Science Research in Central and Eastern Europe*. Strasbourg: European Science Foundation. Available at: http://uefiscdi.gov.ro/Upload/1843f6d4-87cb-4063-b984-2489402287fd.pdf [Accessed 19/01/13]

Vygotsky, L. S. (1992). *Thought and Language*. Cambridge, MA: Massachusetts Institute of Technology.

Williams, M. (1998). Teaching thinking through a foreign language. In R. Burden and M. Williams (eds) *Thinking Through the Curriculum*. Abingdon: Routledge, pp. 84–85.

Williams, M. and Burden, R. (1997). *Psychology for Language Teachers: A Social Constructivist Approach*. Cambridge: Cambridge University Press.

Williams, M. and Burden, R. (1999). Students' developing conceptions of themselves as language learners. *Modern Language Journal*, 83(2): 193–201.

Wortham, S. (2006). *Learning Identity: The Joint Emergence of Social Identification and Academic Learning*. Cambridge: Cambridge University Press.

Zhao, Y. (2011). Students as change partners: a proposal for educational change in the age of globalization. *Journal of Educational Change*, 12(2): 267–79.

4

From Bilingual Francophones to Bilingual Anglophones: The Role of Teachers in the Rising 'Equities' of English-Medium Education in Cameroon

Kuchah Kuchah

In this chapter, I attempt to explain why English-medium (Anglophone) education is fast becoming the coveted medium of education for many Francophone children in Cameroon in spite of the existence of complex language ideologies and attitudes that represent Anglophones and 'anglophonism' as second class in a country dominated by Francophones and a political system that is hugely borrowed from, and influenced by, France. I begin by exploring the historical foundations and linguistic heritage of the country, setting the pace for an understanding of the paradoxical shift in interest from French-medium education to English-medium education. Then I examine the literature on the role and importance of the English language today, as well as on language motivation and choice, followed by presenting and analysing data collected through school-based observations as well as interviews with Anglophone teachers and 'Francophone' children (and their parents) pursuing English-medium education.

Cameroon's dual colonial heritage, derived from its relationship with two former colonial powers, France and England, has placed this central African nation at the crossroads of political and linguistic controversy for a long time. The last two decades have seen an upsurge of tensions resulting in demands for a return to a federated state and, in some cases, for total secession of Anglophone Cameroon from Francophone Cameroon. These tensions, far from being resolved by the linguistic 'unification' that the adoption of French and English as 'neutral' languages at independence was meant to achieve, have instead been fuelled by both languages and the new identities associated with them.

Wolf (2001: 223) observes that 'the feeling of unity is so strong that "being Anglophone" [or Francophone] denotes a new ethnicity, transcending older ethnic ties'. Consequently, although multiculturalism in terms of ethnic diversity has hardly been a problem, 'ethnicity along the Francophone–Anglophone dichotomy is, and has whisked away attention such that it threatens national unity...more than anything else in the country' (Ayafor, 2005: 124). To better understand how this new ethnic hostility came about, it is important to return to the early beginnings of this nation.

Historical background and linguistic identification

The decision, in 1961, by Southern Cameroons (English protectorate) to join La République du Cameroun (French protectorate) led to a demographic dominance of Francophone Cameroonians over their Anglophone counterparts at all levels of public life, which has over the years explained the continuous presence of dissenting voices from the minority Anglophone community pointing to existing problems at various levels. These problems have been codified by various historians and sociologists as 'the Anglophone Problem' (Dicklitch, 2011; Konings & Nyamnjoh, 1997), an expression used to refer to an avalanche of grievances that have often been undermined by a heavily centralised and undemocratic bureaucracy dominated by Francophones. Political figures from Anglophone Cameroon (e.g., Ngwana, 2009) have accused their Francophone counterparts of using their political powers to marginalise the English language and Anglophones by relegating them to second-class citizens. One such instance of marginalisation was encapsulated in the 1984 constitution, which stated that 'This constitution shall be registered and published in the Official Gazette of the Republic of Cameroon in French and in English, *the French text being authentic*' (my emphasis), a legal provision that meant that English language, although one of the two official languages in the country, was not legally authentic. This constitutional provision created a situation wherein a poor translation into French, of an official document originally conceived in English, was considered more authentic than the original English version.

With the introduction of multiparty democracy in the early 1990s came a general atmosphere of distrust and threats of sectorial violence with the creation of groups like the Southern Cameroons National Council (SCNC); Southern Cameroons Youth League (SCYL) and its military wing, the Southern Cameroons Defence Force (SOCADEF); and the Southern Cameroons Independence Restoration Council (SCIRC) (Dicklitch, 2011; Konings & Nyamnjoh, 1997). Following nationwide post-election violence in 1992 and the enforcement of a state of emergency in the Anglophone northwest province, the provincial capital, Bamenda, became the icon of opposition with Anglophones and English being identified as agents of violence and disunity by Francophones, an image strengthened by references to Anglophones like 'les anglofoux' ('anglo-fools') and 'les enemies dans la maison' ('enemies in the house') by government ministers.

In the mid-1990s with continuous unrest and growing suspicion by Francophones and distrust and hatred by Anglophones, the government had become desperate to restore trust, especially amongst Anglophones. After two years of lobbying, Cameroon joined the Commonwealth of Nations in 1995, a move which in a sense helped to restore the status of the English language and Anglophones. In line with the country's new status as member of both the Francophonie and the Commonwealth, the constitution was extensively amended in 1996 and the English language ceased to be the 'unauthentic' language of previous constitutions, assuming *the same status* as French. The 1998 Education Law – which sought to redefine educational policies that would reflect the needs of a society both united and torn apart by identities built along the lines of two non-native languages – also pledged to protect the specificities of English-medium and French-medium subsystems of education. Desperate to restore 'national unity and integration', the state took a vague stand on bilingualism, institutionalising the implementation of English and French at all levels of French- and English-medium schools respectively, and allowing different forms of bilingual education to emerge: (a) French-medium schools in which English is a compulsory subject and vice versa; (b) English-medium schools with very large numbers of children from French-speaking homes; and (c) 'immersion' bilingual schools with children from French- and English-speaking homes studying school subjects in both languages and only deciding in the final year of primary education whether to pursue secondary educa-tion in English or French. This chapter examines the third form of bilingual education by exploring the role of English/Anglophone teachers in motivating the decision by Francophone children (and their parents) to pursue English-medium studies at the end of bilingual primary education. It is hoped that this study will highlight the important role that teachers play in language choices and raise the important issues of teacher quality for language motivation.

The rising demand for the English language in Cameroon

Dramatic interest in English-medium education by Francophones at the start of the last decade (Anchimbe, 2005; 2007; Kuchah, 2009; Mforteh, 2006) reveal that the English language is fast gaining a prestige status in a country where French is still the language of the ruling elite. Anchimbe (2005) provides statistics which reveal that in the 2001–02 academic year, 71.5 per cent of students on the MA programme in the Department of English of the University of Yaounde I were Francophones. The same study reveals that 54 per cent of 1782 children enrolled in three private English-medium primary schools in Yaounde were Francophones. Mforteh (2006) reports significant numbers of Francophone pupils in English-medium secondary schools based in the Anglophone part of Cameroon. In a recent study in three English-medium state primary schools in Yaounde (Kuchah, in progress), it was noted that 85 per cent of year 6 pupils in these schools were Francophones. In the case of the present study, 80.9 per cent of the 42 pupils in the English-medium final class were from Francophone homes. In a country like Cameroon where language and identity have become strongly interwoven icons of individual and group membership (Anchimbe, 2005), and where English and French have reinforced separate identities for Anglophones and Francophones respectively over years of mutual suspicion and hatred, one would ask what factors have motivated the sudden interest in English-medium education by Francophone Cameroonians.

Focho (2011) provides a summary of four important roles that English language plays in the international scene, and which could constitute motivating factors for learning the language. To her, English is a means to academic success, an added impetus for international employability, a medium for international communication and a catalyst for global education. In relation to academic success, Focho (2011) draws from studies that present English as the established language of science and technology (e.g., Hasman, 2004) and statistics which show that 45 per cent of the world's international students are in the United States, United Kingdom, Australia and Canada (Coleman, 2010), all of which are English-speaking countries; and she concludes that

> Students who seek to study in English medium universities despite language difficulties must be convinced of the potential gains. Proficiency in English seems to be an important gateway...to an education that is easily recognised and valued internationally (especially in the job market). (Focho, 2011: 139)

The phenomenon of migrant working arising from trends in globalisation in the new millennium (Coleman, 2010) has only helped reinforce the role of English as the language of the workplace for presentations, negotiations and international collaboration (Warschauer, 2000). Tembe and Norton (2011) explain that in a multilingual country like Uganda, English is perceived by parents as the language that offers wider opportunities for their children. This instrumental dimension (Gardner & Lambert, 1972) is well captured in a recent study (Pinon & Haydon, 2010) which reveals that in countries like Cameroon, Nigeria, Rwanda, Bangladesh and Pakistan, proficiency in English is fast becoming a precondition for jobs. The study argues that 'multinational corporations indirectly drive the development of English in Cameroon' (p. 31) since English-language skills are necessary for internal company communication with business partners based in English-speaking countries such as Nigeria, South Africa and the United States. This need for communication in English across countries underscores its importance for international communication, an importance that has been largely documented in the literature (e.g., Graddol, 2000; Hasman, 2004; Jenkins, 2006). An addition to this is an intra-national and intra-cultural dimension (Kuchah, 2009) which explains how English is also being used within the Francophone school system in Cameroon as a vehicle for the transmission of Anglophone cultural values in the hope that children will develop an understanding of, and a tolerance for, the immense cultural differences between Anglophone and Francophone Cameroonians. 'Such understanding fosters cross-cultural co-operation, tolerance and peace and helps minimise hatred, tribalism, racism and violence which inevitably lead to war' (Focho, 2011: 142). Encouraging such an understanding at national level is a basis for an international awareness and global education which Focho (2010) argues can better be transmitted through a global language like English.

However, to claim that the arguments raised above directly influence parents' and children's decisions for English-medium education will be difficult to sustain, given that with the multiplicity of English-language centres in Cameroon in recent years, and the institution of bilingualism at all levels of education, school leavers are now able to attain proficiency in the English language without necessarily undergoing English-medium education. To understand the factors that motivate the choice of English as a medium of education and lifelong identity therefore, we will need to look elsewhere.

Explaining the adoption of English-medium education: is L2 motivation theory enough?

Gardner and Lambert (1972: 3) establish a complementary relation between the integrative and instrumental orientations to second language learning, which add to the learner's attitude towards the second language speaking group to determine motivation to learn. In the case of Cameroon however, it can be argued (e.g., Ayafor, 2005) that the institutional approach to national integration takes an instrumental orientation, while linguistic integration takes an integrative orientation. This rift between instrumental and integrative orientations to bilingualism has been at the root of rising discontent in Cameroon. Anchimbe (2007) describes the phenomenon, identifiable amongst adults, of *identity opportunism*, a conscious process of linguistic/identity fluctuation motivated by the desire to reap benefits from different cultural and linguistic contexts. This is especially visible amongst descendants of Francophone Cameroonians who fled the 'Maquisard' armed resistance against the French colonialists in the 1950s and settled in the Southern Cameroons territories. This group has constantly fluctuated identities and allegiances between the two regions for personal gain (Mbuh, 2000). There are also numerous examples of Francophones who, after obtaining a bilingual degree from university, pursue further education in the medium of English and as such claim Anglophone identities when there is a political inclination, under the government's 'regional balance' policy, to offer opportunities to Anglophones. In a country where Anglophone–Francophone identities are still largely defined by territorial origins rather than linguistic and educational orientation, this instrumental penchant for an Anglophone identity has engendered several problems, making it imperative for the country to encourage an integrative policy in an otherwise fragmented and delicate political unity (Ayafor, 2005).

Studies by Anchimbe (2005; 2007), Kuchah (2009) and Mforteh (2006) show that recent years have witnessed an ever-rising interest in bilingualism by Francophone Cameroonians and, for some, this has taken the extreme form of embracing English-medium education. Although it is not evident that for most parents, English-medium education entails an identity mutation for their children – Anchimbe (2007) reports that 75 per cent of parents whose children pursue English-medium education refuse to identify their children as Anglophones – it is clear that for some parents (as we shall show later) and from the point of view of young learners themselves, English-medium education is transforming them into *linguabrids* – a term coined by Anchimbe (2007) to refer to children who are brought up between two linguistic and cultural identities and as a result, are not inclined to switching languages for opportunistic reasons, but for purely linguistic (and to some extent, integrative) reasons – distancing them from current in-group classifications that have often been exploited for cultural/linguistic victimisation and/or for personal gain. It is no surprise therefore that in Anchimbe's study only 7.5 per cent of parents associate their children's English-medium education with instrumental motives. It has been argued (e.g., Ushioda, 2008) that attitudes towards, and perceived status of particular languages, constitute a socio-cultural context which influences motivation to learn those languages. While this may not be the case with adult linguistic opportunists in Cameroon, it is arguably the case with Francophone children who, not having taken the decision to pursue English-medium education, eventually find, through interacting with peers and teachers, interest in English-medium education despite the added constraints of having to interact with siblings and parents at home in French.

The educational context within which learners operate has been identified as playing a motivating (or demotivating) role in their language learning experience. According to Gardner (2007), important motivating factors are the characteristics of the educational environment, such as policies, general environment of the school and, more directly, the language classroom environment which in a sense is determined by the teacher's attitude and the classroom culture he or she creates in their capacity as the main point of contact for the individual learner. Unfortunately, while much has been written about the ever-growing importance of English in Cameroon and the socio-political, economic and global factors that motivate Francophone Cameroonians to learn English, there seem to be very few published studies which focus on how teachers contribute to this phenomenon. Studies by Ebong (2004) and Focho (2011) explore strategies for motivating Francophone secondary school students learning English as a subject in the curriculum. In terms of the growing interest in English-medium education, there is yet no study, to the best of my knowledge, which examines how teachers influence the decisions of parents and pupils. This is partly because most linguists are more concerned with describing and explaining the phenomenon in the light of global trends and as such ignore the micro factors that are quintessential to individual choices. It is taken for granted that because of the global importance of English, Francophone parents will send their children to English-medium schools. Yet, it can be argued that these children go to school with no idea of what globalisation involves and as such could just as well perform very poorly in their first years in school, forcing their parents to move them back to French-medium schools. The important question still not answered regards what in English-medium schools motivates children to stay on and strive in contexts dominated by French.

Another reason for overlooking the role of teachers comes from the fact that the Cameroonian educational system has often been perceived only as consisting of two separate culture-based subsystems operating independently. Esch's (2012) study, which examines areas of convergence and divergence between English and French pedagogical cultures in Cameroonian primary schools, provides a sound basis for understanding how pedagogic cultures can influence pedagogic practices, but it does not explore how these practices can, in turn, influence learning and linguistic choices. This is simply because French-medium and English-medium schools have often been seen as separate entities, each developing learners who have only one option, that of pursuing education in a medium that has been selected for them by their parents. However, with the emergence of 'immersion' bilingual schools in which children are exposed to the curricula of both subsystems of education, there is a need to investigate those factors within the school environment which influence their decision as to which medium of education to adopt at the end of primary school.

Investigating the issues: considering the 'who', 'where' and 'how' of this study

This study explores the reported motivations of Francophone children and their parents and teachers regarding the influence of their Anglophone teachers on their decisions to pursue English-medium education. Data for this study was collected over a period of two academic years, from September 2007 to September 2009 and also during two other shorter visits to the school in 2010 and 2011. The main participants were upper primary (years 5 and 6) children from French-speaking homes. Year 5 pupils were still in an immersion class and were only to decide at the end of the year whether to proceed to an English-medium or French-medium final year class. On the other hand, year 6 pupils had already taken the decision to continue their education in English. Two groups of four pupils each were selected from each of the two classes, making a total of 16 pupil participants. To broaden the scope of insights into the situation discussed in this study, I have combined data collected through school/classroom observation, individual interviews with teachers and parents and focus group conversations with pupils. I use the word 'conversations' here to highlight the special considerations for interviewing children in friendship groups recommended in the existing literature (e.g., Lewis, 1992; Mayall, 2008), and the striving to dissipate power differentials between the adult interviewer and the child respondent through empowering interactional attitudes (Kuchah & Pinter, 2012).

The school referred to in this study (CamBil) was selected on the basis of its structural representativeness of an emerging model of bilingualism in primary education in Cameroon, as well as because of my particular connection and understanding, through several years of interaction with the school community, of the issues arising from the data. CamBil can be termed an 'immersion' bilingual school in the sense that although it recognised the inherent differences in the curricula of both subsystems of education, children in each class followed English-medium and French-medium education simultaneously. This meant that apart from final year classes, each class had both an Anglophone and a Francophone teacher who took turns to teach the subject content of their different curricula each day (see Table 4.1 in appendix for timetable of a bilingual class). However, extensive effort had been made to harmonise the content of different subject areas by drawing from subject content similarities across the two subsystems to design weekly schemes of work such that the children would be exposed to (nearly) similar content within each subject in both languages.

My relationship with CamBil began in January 2006 when, after a series of visits to the school (first on ministry assignment and later on a personal basis) to better understand how it functioned, I was later employed as resource person in the school (March 2006). My role was to act as mentor to both Francophone and Anglophone teachers. This included checking that their lesson plans were properly written, observing and commenting on their lessons, organising training sessions on particular areas of pedagogic relevance and offering advice on teaching and learning on a regular basis to teachers with particular difficulties. Through sustained interaction with the school community, therefore, I became grounded in the cross-cultural and cross-linguistic realities of the school and, as such, am able to interpret the discourses of all respondents. What is more, having worked with primary school pupils and teachers for over a decade, it was easy for me to frame my interview questions in the discourse of the children (Pinter, 2011) and, from a socio-semiotic perspective, to draw on my awareness of the linguistic and cultural factors that may be conveyed both in verbal and non-verbal communication (Ryen, 2001). While interviews with pupils and teachers were conducted in English, all interviews with parents were conducted in French and translated only by me into English.

Choosing English-medium education: where do teachers come in?

Four main themes explaining the motivational role of teachers in the decision for English-medium education emerged from the data collected for this study. These include the socio-affective influence of teachers, their peda-gogic practices, their role in ensuring success in final exams and their role in pupils' identity formation.

Socio-affective factors: relationship with teachers

The nature of the relationship between the pupils and their teachers emerged as a significant motivational factor. In the conversations, the pupils constantly referred to their Anglophone teachers as either Auntie or Uncle, but when they were talking about their Francophone teachers, they referred to them as either Mr (or Monsieur) or Mrs (or Madame). What is more, these 'titles' were followed, in the case of Anglophone teachers, by first names (e.g., Auntie Bridget), and by surnames (e.g., Madame Fotso) in the case of Francophone teachers. However, in class, the children addressed their Anglophone teachers as 'Sir' or 'Miss', in expressions like 'I have a question, Miss'. This was also the case when a Francophone teacher was teaching, except that while the children used 'Miss' for both married and unmarried female Anglophone teachers, they used 'Madame' (not Mademoiselle) when addressing both married and unmarried female Francophone teachers. This instance of formality/informality has also been documented in Esch (2012) as signifying a contrast in politeness between Anglophone and Francophone teachers. In this study, it emerged as an important influence on the children as can be drawn from the following conversation with year 5 children:

Kuchah: You said you will like to go to class 6 next year. Why do you prefer class 6 and not CM2?

Aisha: I prefer class 6 because Uncle Emmanuel is a very good teacher; he teach very well English and mathematics and everybody pass in common entrance [examinations to English-medium secondary school].

Kuchah: But I know that the CM2 teacher is also very good. Last year all your friends in CM2 passed the *concours d'entrer en sixième* [entrance exams to French-medium secondary schools].

Bini: Yes, is true but the CM2 teacher is very wild [aggressive].

Kuchah: Doesn't he have a name? Why do you call him the CM2 teacher?

Bini: Eeeeh, Monsieur Edou. He doesn't teach well maths, so I want to be scientist in future, he cannot help me. Also, Monsieur Edou is very serious; you cannot even play with him. But Uncle Emmanuel is behaving like our big brother, he play with us...

Aisha: But he can also punish

Manga: Yes, but not like Monsieur Edou, who is always serious, serious, serious [general laughter] and he is behaving like a soldier.

My own experience working with these teachers for over five years confirms this formal/informal relationship perpetrated by both groups of teachers. Francophone teachers generally addressed one another as Monsieur + surname while they addressed Anglophone teachers as Uncle or Auntie + first name. As the extract above shows, this impacted on the way pupils perceived their teachers and in a way inspired, despite visible language difficulties, an interest in English-medium education. From the perspectives of Anglophone teachers, the degree of informality in the relationship with learners is based on a cultural system that sees all learners as children. In an interview with the class 6 teacher referred to by the children above, it was revealed that he did not see his learners as pupils, but as 'children'. Constant reference to 'my children' in the interview point to a humanistic perspective that influences his relationship with them:

I do not treat them as pupils; they are my children in the sense that if anything happens to them while they are in school, it is my responsibility to protect them. Even if any of them runs into trouble in town and I am informed, I still have the responsibility to help. [...] In my culture, a child belongs to his mother only in the womb; once he is born, he belongs to the society. So I always consider these children as mine too. [...] It is not possible to be a teacher and not act like a parent, because these children have genuine needs and interests which we need to understand [...] when I teach, I consider that just like all the children from one father cannot behave in the same way, so too, my children cannot all behave in the same way. So I encourage them to be responsible and to take the right decisions and do the right things that can help them succeed in school and in life.

This assertion is in line with the humanistic perspective of learner-centredness which highlights a holistic approach to education in which learning is seen as an activity which involves learners as complex human beings, whose intellectual and affective resources can be drawn upon to enrich their experience of life (Tudor, 1993). The discourse of this teacher is further sustained by the following response from a Francophone parent:

> When I sent my second child to CamBil, I was not sure if she will survive in the Anglophone subjects. Today, I have two other children in CamBil; there is no doubt in my mind that they will all succeed. Zita [second child] has done very well; she is now in class 6 and I think even the other two will become Anglophones too. [...] I am sure it has to do with the way the Anglophone teachers behave towards the children. I have communicated with Zita's teachers very often. Her best teacher is called Auntie Prisca. When Zita fell sick last year, this woman was in hospital every day. That is Zita's second mother; there is no better way of bringing a child nearer to you than to show her that you care.

Clearly, therefore, Anglophone teachers demonstrate an alignment with social values that transcends professional expectations and embrace a more holistic perception of their role and responsibilities towards their learners. This alignment in a sense generates a socio-affective relationship which, for young learners, tends to dominate the learning experience (Kuchah & Pinter, 2012) and, as such, may constitute a motivating factor for both pupils and parents in choosing English-medium education at the end of a bilingual cycle of studies.

Pedagogic factors

A number of pedagogical practices were revealed as having an impact on learning outcomes and, consequently, on future choices. One of these was the teachers' pedagogical content knowledge (Shulman, 1986), that is, the way they make the knowledge accessible and understood to learners (Siraj-Blatchford et al., 2002). According to class 6 pupils, it was clear that their teacher invested a lot in encouraging classroom interaction in a way that empowered them to perform better, but also built their self-image and confidence. When asked how they felt being in an English-medium class and what in the teaching practices of their teachers had encouraged them to pursue English-medium education, the following responses were given:

> Mvogo: I am happy to be in class 6 because I am not afraid of English. Our teacher explains very well and give many examples, he makes us do many exercises and debates [...] when I was in the other classes, my

English teachers used many songs and poems to teach us English. They gave us much homework and always made us to ask them questions if we don't understand.

Berthe: I told my mother that I wanted to go to class 6 because I was better in the English subjects and French, but I prefer English subjects because my English teachers are good, especially Uncle Charles [...] he was my teacher in class 4. He teach very well...I could not read well in English in class 3, but he make me know to read; he make me to play games with sounds and he also make me to teach other children to read. I even teach my mother to read in English and I help my big sister who is in *Ecole publique* [French-medium primary school] how to read her English reader.

Arnaud: If I did not come to class 6, I will have cried until my father accepts!...You don't know how my Class 5 teacher made me to like English very well...I also love the other subjects in English because he always remind us of other things that we learn in other subjects when he is teaching one subject. Then I understand well, because he used many examples from our environment and even in history, he explained as if he was there when everything happened. He also told us many village stories when he teach English. It is very nice. [...] My French teacher does not explain very well like that; he just ask us to read and then he ask us questions and explain the answer if we don't understand.

A number of pedagogic practices are raised in the statements above, namely detailed explanations, extensive practice activities and homework, use of illustrative context-based examples, local stories, games, classroom debate, group/pair work and cross-curricula links. One teacher participant explained:

We understand that most of these children come from Francophone homes, so we put in a lot of effort to explain and demonstrate what we teach. In reading comprehension, for example, I spend a lot of time in brainstorming around their previous knowledge and make them act out different roles.[...] I also make them understand that all knowledge is related somehow, so I draw ideas from other subjects and other things they have learnt to make them understand me. [...] By the time we read the passage, they have already grasped the main ideas in it. We need to be patient with them.

And yet another teacher revealed that

I like to encourage pair and group work in my class and I take time to organise groups depending on how much progress each of them have made and how much support they can give their classmates. In English lessons, I mix up children from Anglophone homes with those from Francophone homes, so that they can help each other. Also, I try to bring in a lot of fun in the class to motivate them.

For these children, these are all motivating factors for loving their teachers and consequently for feeling comfortable in English-medium education. In the case of Arnaud for example, my imagination is not strong enough to ascertain the extent of his teacher's influence on his love for English language, and he recounts above how he was ready to impose his decision to pursue English-medium education on his parents.

From my own observation during the years I worked as resource person in CamBil, it was easier for Anglophone teachers to adopt a creative curriculum than it was for their Francophone colleagues. Francophone teachers specifically needed help on how to implement the stages of the 'New Pedagogic Approach' (NPA), a one-size-fits-all method (see Kuchah, in progress, for a critique of this approach) to teaching all subjects in primary schools recommended by the Ministry of Basic Education. This approach to teaching, consisting of six stages – observation, statement of hypotheses, research, verification of hypotheses, analysis and generalisation – had been designed to develop inferential thinking in mathematics and the sciences and was eventually codified in the *Head Teachers' Guide* (1999) as the standard method of teaching in Cameroonian schools. These teachers were, therefore, not willing to explore any methods that were not in line with the NPA for fear of disapproval by other pedagogic inspectors. On the other hand, it was much easier for Anglophone teachers to take on board creative activities which, although inconsistent with the specificities of the NPA, were considered useful in their classroom. While Francophone teachers felt comfortable that their pupils were mostly Francophones, or at least (in the case of Anglophone pupils) communicated with peers in French, it was the awareness of the Francophone background of their pupils which motivated Anglophone teachers to explore every resource available to them to help the pupils learn.

Sharing (pedagogic) responsibility for teaching: parental involvement

In an interview with one parent, it was revealed that there is an enabling working relationship between parents and Anglophone teachers which is in a sense pedagogic:

My daughter insists every day that I should listen to what she learnt in school and I have received letters from her teacher which she reads and explains to me. Her other sisters are in Francophone schools, so she is our English teacher. [...] She is very proud of herself for being our English teacher and I must say I am proud that she has progressed very well and is helping me learn a language that was my nightmare when I was a young student.

One of the teachers themselves asserted that involving parents in the education of their children by encouraging them to listen to their children was mutually beneficial to both parties:

We make it a duty to encourage children to share their learning with their parents. Most of our children are from Francophone homes and have difficulties in English when they first come here. One way to empower them is to encourage them to teach their parents everything they learn in school. [...] One parent, she told me that her child is very stubborn that he insists that she should learn English at her old age.[...] I told her that it is the only way they can help our work and also help themselves to understand what their children are going through in school.

Success in (final) exams

In a context like Cameroon where success in exams constitutes an important factor in determining good teaching/teachers (see Kuchah, in progress), there is no doubt that for children and parents, the possibility of passing high-stake exams like the entrance examination into secondary schools will be an important motivating factor for choosing medium of instruction. One pupil captures this very aptly when she says

I prefer class 6 because Uncle Emmanuel is a very good teacher; he teach very well English and mathematics and everybody pass in common entrance [examinations to English medium secondary school].

According to the *IMF Poverty Reduction Strategy Paper* for Cameroon (August 2010), low completion rates at primary schools as well as limited access to secondary education are problems which require a careful planning of action across both levels of education. The paper reveals that the failure rate of students taught entirely in English was lower than that of their French-taught peers (Pinon & Haydon, 2010: 20). This observation resonates with Aisha's perspective above, which lends credence to the reputation of the class 6 teacher in ensuring success in exams, a motivating factor in the context of the culture of certification that characterises Cameroon.

So far, I have shown how teachers' pedagogic practices can act as motivating factors for important decisions regarding the choice of medium of instruction.

It seems obvious from the perspectives expressed above that Anglophone teachers employ a variety of teaching strategies that both motivate and empower their learners to overcome their initial language difficulties. Also important is the connection they create between the home and the school and the mechanism through which they create and sustain the shared responsibilities between both environments.

Teacher's role in identity formation

A dominant part of the literature on bilingualism in Cameroon has been to explain how and why ethnological identities and language have been interwoven, and how this has led to language ideologies and attitudes that strengthen the Anglophone–Francophone divide in the country. In this study, it was revealed that teachers and the school environment can considerably dissipate or even transform such ideologies and attitudes to create new identities. The administrative set-up of CamBil did not define barriers between Francophones and Anglophones; parents attended the same meetings irrespective of their language backgrounds, and information was conveyed in both languages interchangeably. In spite of this, all the parents of class 6 children interviewed in this study saw their children as not just bilinguals, but as Anglophone bilinguals. This was captured in the following response from a parent:

> I have four children; one is Francophone, the first one. The other three are Anglophones. Two passed through Cambil; they are now in Anglophone secondary schools in Bamenda. The last one is in her fifth year in CamBil; she too will become an Anglophone. [...] All my children are perfectly bilingual, even the first one is very good in English. [...] To me, it is their success in life that matters and they have shown interest in English education so I have to support them.

This shift from the perception of linguistic identities along territorial lines to purely linguistic competence and medium of instruction is not unconnected to the work of teachers and the school culture. It reveals a potential for an educational system to influence cultural and language ideologies significantly. The socio-affective relationship between teachers, pupils and parents as well as the sharing of pedagogic responsibilities between school and home discussed above are all complementary motivational factors.

Within the period of my involvement in the school, mention was never explicitly made of Anglophones or Francophones in the discourse of the administration. However, teachers made explicit reference to the economic and technological as well as demographic advantages of learning English in the classes. One of the teacher respondents recounted the following:

> I tell my children every time that English is very important in the world because everybody is learning it. It is the most widely spoken language; French is not even the second. Look at the poorest countries in Africa; they are mostly French-speaking, but countries like South Africa and Nigeria, Ghana and Tanzania are more developed than us. If they learn English, they will be able to interact with scientists from developed countries like the U.S., and Britain; even China and Japan which are technologically advanced countries also speak English.

A fallout of such assertions can be found in the discourse of pupils who variously made reference to the fact that they wanted to be able when they grow up to go and study in the United States, the United Kingdom or South Africa. Statements of future ambition like 'I want to be a doctor, so I will go and learn in America'; 'Auntie Barbs said that if I want to be a pilot, I must study hard in English so that I can go to Britain'; 'I am happy to be in class 6 because I am not afraid of English' are illustrations of how teachers influence children's language attitudes.

In terms of pupils' own self-perception, it was revealed that in the final year of primary school, although they had acquired a proficiency in both languages sufficient for them to continue to secondary school in either medium of instruction, identities were created according to the chosen medium of instruction. In class 6, pupils saw themselves as Anglophones, and it was difficult to spot in their friendship group formation, especially during playtime, any discrimination between children from Anglophone homes and Francophone homes. Rather, whenever in my conversation with pupils I made reference to Francophones, they were quick to refer me to their friends in *Cours Moyen 2* (the French-medium class). Statements like, 'If you want to speak French, go there' (pointing to the French-medium classroom), or 'This is an English class, not a French class' point to a new identity formation which is strengthened by the class 6 teacher himself through the encouragement of an in-group dynamics that makes these pupils see themselves as different. Although it was clear that they still had proficiency problems in English, and that they used French extensively at home and in school when communicating with children from other classes, they seemed to have a shared opinion when speaking to me: that they were Anglophones by virtue of the medium of instruction they had chosen. In this study, therefore, pupils' *linguabridity* was very evident, but this was secondary to their constructed identities as Anglophone bilinguals.

Discussion and conclusion

The purpose of this study was to investigate the role that teachers play in influencing the decisions of Francophone pupils and their parents in choosing English-medium education in a context in which two subsystems of education coexist. Language policies have often been led by countries' political visions, with little or no consideration of the material and human resources necessary to make such policies effective. In the case of Cameroon, political changes emanating from a complex colonial experience led to the adoption of English and French as 'neutral' languages which, far from resolving the problem of multiethnicity and multilingualism, created instead stronger ethno-linguistic identities that have threatened the very unity for which the two languages were adopted. The political transformations the country has encountered over its 50 years following independence have seen the neutrality of both languages trampled upon by the emergence of socio-political and socio-cultural discontent amongst Cameroonians. The English language in Cameroon has for a long time been treated as the language of the minority Anglophones and, therefore, given second place to French. Cameroon still remains a predominantly French-speaking country, and its political and economic relationship with France and other French-speaking countries is still overwhelming. It is not certain that this relationship will be changed soon; rather there are indications that the relationship with France is being continuously strengthened at all levels of the country's socio-political set-up. However, trends recently show a rising quest for English-medium education, a situation which has been variously explained by historians, sociologists and linguists.

This present study/this chapter was based on the premise that the examination of the linguistic situation in Cameroon has so far focused on the macro factors (e.g., the international status of English and national policy) that have motivated Francophones to study English as a language or to adopt it as a medium of education for their children, but such an assumption has overlooked the role that teachers can play in consolidating, enhancing or even determining such a motivation. It is difficult to sustain the assumption that the global importance of English and the policy of the government of Cameroon to promote bilingualism in schools are sufficient motivations for parents and children to embrace English-medium education. For this reason, it was important to examine other micro factors that can influence or even sustain language choices. This study focused on those factors that motivate Francophone children to pursue English-medium education in contexts dominated by French and by a more imposing Francophone identity. More particularly, it examined the school/classroom dynamics, investigating especially the role of teachers in influencing such decisions. The results have shown that teachers do, indeed, play an important role in encouraging English-medium education. This can be seen at three levels, namely, through the socio-affective relationship which they create with learners and their parents, their pedagogic practices and the language ideologies and attitudes they convey to learners.

The findings of this study point to the importance of investing in teacher education and teacher quality as an important part of language planning and policy. Drawing from the voices of learners, parents and teachers themselves, this study aligns with previous research elsewhere (e.g., Buckingham, 2003; Maged, 1997) which argues that a teacher's pedagogy is the critical determining factor in the quality of what pupils learn or, as Buckingham (2003: 71) affirms, 'the single most important influence on student achievement is teacher quality'. The results of this study are a reminder for governments and other institutions investing in English-language pedagogy and English-medium education to pay more attention to the development of teacher education as an important factor in designing, planning, implementing and fostering English-medium education.

Engagement priorities

My main focus in this chapter has been on the role of teachers in influencing learners' choice of medium of instruction in a context in which two foreign languages compete. While it is obvious that teachers play an important role in learning, it is not always the case that their perspectives, or even those of other education stakeholders like parents and learners themselves, are taken into consideration in language policy enactment. Maybe this is because, in most cases, a foreign language is introduced only as a subject in a school curriculum that is transmitted through a national language. But, in many countries-in-transition, where national languages have been relegated to family circles and foreign languages given official status, or where national and foreign languages compete as the medium of instruction, there may be a need to reconsider the status and role of teachers alongside that of other education stakeholders like parents and learners, themselves, in defining language policy. The following issues maybe worth exploring:

1. To what extent can language teachers influence language policy, and how may policymakers benefit from involving teachers in the policy-making process?
2. Why would parental involvement in teaching/learning be particularly relevant in primary education?
3. How may we reconcile the institutional need to encourage bilingualism with the personal need to pursue education in a particular language?

Appendix

Table 4.1 Timetable/Emploi de temps Class 5/Cours Moyens 1 (CM1)

Time / Heure	Monday / Lundi	Tuesday / Mardi	Wednesday / Mercredi	Thursday / Jeudi	Friday / Vendredi
07h25–07h40	DEVOTION AND INSPECTION RASSEMBLEMENT				
07h40–08h10	Citizenship–Civics	Hygiene	Citizenship–Moral education	Education à la santé	Citizenship–Human Rights
08h10–08h55	Maths	Lecture	English language/Grammar	Grammaire	English language/Reading
08h55–09h30	English language/Reading	Conjugaison	Maths	Histoire	Maths
09h30–10h15	Geography	Géographie	English language/Composition	Production d'Ecrits	Eng. Lang. Dictation/Spelling
10h15–11h00	History	Les mesures	Geography	Géometrie	Maths
11h00–11h10	SHORT BREAK RECREATION				
11h10–11h40	Education civique et morale	Science/Health education	Education civique et morale	History	Education civique et morale
11h40–12h10	Lecture /Expression orale	Maths	Lecture/Expression orale	Maths	Conjugaison
12h10–12h45	Nombres & numération	English language/Vocabulary	Nombres & numération	Science/Environmental education	Problèmes practiques
12h45–13h10	LONG BREAK PAUSE PAUSE				
13h10–13h40	Sciences/Milieu vivant	English language/Grammar	Orthographe d'Usage	English language/Vocabulary	Sciences Techno
13h40–14h10	Grammaire	Maths	Sciences/Ed. environnementale	Drawing/arts and craft	Activités pratiques
14h10–14h40	Production d'Ecrits	Hand writing	Initiation à l'Informatique	Club activities	Initiation to computer studies
14h40–15h10	Vocabulaire	Home economics	Musique/Chant	Club activities	Sports

Suggested further reading

Coleman, H. (ed.) (2011). *Dreams and Realities: Developing Countries and the English Language*. London: British Council.

A collection of chapters that represents a powerful contribution to the growing debate about the role of English in the world today.

Graddol, D. (2000). *The Future of English?* (Revised Edition). London: The British Council.

This book takes stock of the unassailable position of English in the world and explores the long-term impact of technological, economic and demographic shifts on the spread of English.

Ebong, B. (2004). *The Use of Indigenous Techniques of Communication in Language Learning: The Case of Cameroon*. Gottingen: Cuvillier Verlag.

This book explores, through questionnaires, the motivating effects of the use of indigenous strategies like drama, songs, folktales, riddles and proverbs on students from six French-medium secondary schools in Cameroon.

References

Anchimbe, E. A. (2005). Anglophonism and Francophonism: the stakes of (official) language identity in Cameroon. *Alizes: Revue Angliciste de la Réunion*, 25/26: 7–26.

Anchimbe, E. A. (2007). Linguabridity: redefining linguistic identities among children in urban areas. In E. A. Anchimbe (ed.) *Linguistic Identity in Postcolonial Multilingual Spaces*. Newcastle: Cambridge Scholars Publishing, pp. 66–86.

Ayafor, I. M. (2005). Official bilingualism in Cameroon: instrumental or integrative policy? In J. Cohen, K. T. McAlister, K. Rolstad and J. MacSwan (eds) *Proceedings of the 4th International Symposium on Bilingualism*. Somerville, MA: Cascadilla Press, pp. 123–42.

Buckingham, J. (2003). Class size and teacher quality. *Educational Research for Policy and Practice*, 2: 71–86.

Coleman, H. (2010). *The English Language in Development*. London: British Council.

Dicklitch, S. (2011). The Southern Cameroons and minority rights in Cameroon. *Journal of Contemporary African Studies*, 29(1): 49–62.

Ebong, B. (2004). *The Use of Indigenous Techniques of Communication in Language Learning: The Case of Cameroon*. Gottingen: Cuvillier Verlag.

Esch, E. (2012). English and French pedagogical cultures: convergence and divergence in Cameroonian primary school teachers' discourse. *Comparative Education*, iFirst Article: 1–19.

Focho, G. N. (2010). Language as tool for global education: bridging the gap between the traditional and a global curriculum. *Journal of Research in Innovative Teaching*, 3(1): 135–48.

Focho, G. N. (2011). Student perceptions of English as a developmental tool in Cameroon. In H. Coleman (ed.) *Dreams and Realities: Developing Countries and the English Language*. London: British Council, pp. 137–60.

Gardner, R. C. (2007). *Gardner and Lambert (1959): Fifty Years and Counting*. Available at: http://publish.uwo.ca/~gardner/docs/CAALOttawa2009talkc.pdf [Accessed 20/05/12].

Gardner, R. C and Lambert, W. E. (1972). *Attitudes and Motivation in Second-Language Learning*. Rowley, MA: Newbury House.

Graddol, D. (2000). *The Future of English* (Revised Edition). London: The British Council.

Hasman, M. A. 2004. The role of English in the 21st century. *TESOL Chile*, 1(1): 18–21.

International Monetary Fund (2010). *Cameroon: Poverty Reduction Strategy Paper*. IMF country report No. 10/257. Available at: http://www.imf.org/external/pubs/ft/scr/2010/cr10257.pdf [Accessed 25/05/12].

Jenkins, J. (2006). Current perspectives on teaching world Englishes and English as a lingua franca. *TESOL Quarterly*, 36(3): 265–74.

Konings, P. and Nyamnjoh, F. B. (1997). The Anglophone problem in Cameroon. *The Journal of Modern African Studies*, 35(2): 207–29.

Kuchah, K. (2009). Early bilingualism in Cameroon: where politics and education meet. In J. Enever, J. Moon and U. Raman (eds) *Young Learner English Language Policy and Implementation: International Perspectives*. Reading: Garnet Education, pp. 87–94.

Kuchah, K. (in progress). *Context Appropriate ELT Pedagogy: An Investigation in Cameroonian Primary Schools*. Unpublished doctoral thesis, Centre for Applied Linguistics, University of Warwick.

Kuchah, K. and Pinter, A. (2012). 'Was this an interview?' Breaking the power barrier in adult-child interviews in an African context. *Issues in Educational Research*, 22(3): 283–97.

Law No. 98/004 of 14 April 1998 to Lay Down Guidelines for Education in Cameroon.

Lewis, A. (1992). Group children interviews as a research tool. *British Education Research Journal*, 18(4): 413–21.

Maged, S. (1997). *The Pedagogy of Large Classes: Challenging the 'Large Class Equals Gutter Education' Myth*. Unpublished M.Phil dissertation, University of Cape Town, South Africa.

Mayall, B. (2008). Conversations with children: working with generational issues. In P. Christensen, and A. James (eds) *Research with Children: Perspectives and Practices*. London: Routledge, pp. 109–22.

Mbuh, J. (2000) *Inside Contemporary Cameroon Politics*. Available at: http://docs.indymedia.org/ twiki/pub/MainJusticeMbuh/ICCPC2.doc [Accessed 08/06/12].

Mforteh, S. A. (2006). Cultural innovations in Cameroon's tower of Babel. *TRANS Internet-Zeitschrift für Kulturwissenschaften*, 16. Available at: http://www.inst.at/trans/16Nr/03_2/mforteh16.htm [Accessed 08/06/12].

Ministry of National Education (1999) *A Guide for Primary School Head Teachers*. Yaounde: CEPER S.A.

Ngwana, A. S. (2009). *Cameroon: Genesis and Reality of the Anglophone Problem*. Available at: http://topics192.com/2009/02/cameroongenesis-and-reality-of.html [Accessed 23/05/12].

Pinon, R and Haydon, J. (2010). *The Benefits of the English Language for Individuals and Societies: Quantitative Indicators from Cameroon, Nigeria, Rwanda, Bangladesh and Pakistan: A Custom Report Compiled by Euromonitor International*. London: British Council.

Pinter, A. (2011). *Children Learning Second Languages*. Basingstoke: Palgrave Macmillan.

Ryen, A. (2001). Cross-cultural interviewing. In J. F. Gubrium and J. A. Holstein (eds) *Handbook of Interview Research: Context and Method*. London: Sage Publications, pp. 335–54.

Secretariat General of the Presidency of the Republic (1984). *Revised Constitution of the Republic of Cameroon*. Yaounde: National Printing Press.

Secretariat General of the Presidency of the Republic (1996). *Constitution of the Republic of Cameroon*. Yaounde: National Printing Press.

Shulman, L. (1986). Those who understand: knowledge growth in teaching. *Educational Researcher*, 15(2): 4–14.

Siraj-Blatchford, I., Sylva, K., Muttock, S., Gilden R. and Bell, D. (2002). *Researching Effective Pedagogy in the Early Years*. Department for Education and Skills Research Report Number 356.

Tembe, J. and Norton, B. (2011). English education, local languages and community perspectives in Uganda. In H. Coleman (ed.) *Dreams and Realities: Developing Countries and the English Language*. London: British Council, pp. 114–36.

Tudor, I. (1993). Teacher roles in the learner-centred classroom. *ELT Journal*, 47(1): 22–31.

Ushioda, E. (2008). Motivation and good language learners. In C. Griffiths (ed.) *Lessons from Good Language Learners*. Cambridge: Cambridge University Press, pp. 19–34.

Warschauer, M. (2000). The changing global economy and the future of English teaching. *TESOL Quarterly*, 34(3): 511–35.

Wolf, H. G. (2001). *English in Cameroon*. Berlin: Mouton de Gruyter.

5
The Integration of Content and Language as a Driving Force in the EFL Lesson

Darío Luis Banegas

Introduction

English is a foreign language in Argentina, where Spanish is the official language. Although other languages such as Portuguese, French, Italian and German may also be taught in state secondary education, English is the only subject taught two hours a week over the six years of secondary education regardless of curricular orientations. Not only is it studied at school but also at private language institutes throughout the country, where students of all ages enrol to learn it as a private activity for different purposes. Some students simply like the language; others are interested in English-medium songs and films, and others believe it will be crucial for their professional future. Also, sometimes against their children's will, parents send them to a language institute as a plus in their formal education.

Needless to say, this context creates circumstances in which EFL teachers may have students in secondary education who have already mastered the contents of the official English curriculum. This situation may be similar to other EFL contexts in which students may learn English faster at language institutes than at secondary schools. This chapter examines how, in response to such contextual needs and conditions, teachers and students turn to Content and Language Integrated Learning (CLIL) models as a framework for co-developing motivation, and how they thus assume agency over the teaching and learning processes they jointly create.

First, I offer a brief description of ELT in Argentina so that my accounts of local and contextualised pedagogies may have a global resonance. Surprisingly, we teachers and researchers usually find that we have more contextual similarities than we suspect. Such a description will naturally lead me to introduce the challenges some teachers face and the reasons for exploring a richly localised CLIL approach.

Second, I explain the whys of CLIL in a nutshell and then I examine experiences in Argentina's secondary education from different parts of the country. I analyse how this new approach motivates teachers and students in various ways based on current research carried out by Argentinian teacher-researchers and my own research. From a global perspective, these experiences in Argentina may have echoes in other EFL settings since increasing professional and state educational demands call for more context-driven approaches to promote and encourage the learning of English. Initially, our pedagogies may be anchored in European frameworks, but we live in very different, equally rich settings. Given these conditions, opportunities and demands, teachers and students may need to discuss ways in which they work as a team so as to strengthen their motivations to learn and teach in formal education.

ELT in Argentina

Why do teachers and students possibly need to examine their own motivations and create spaces for collaboration and negotiation? To address this question we need to understand the local context, and so I will briefly describe the state secondary sector where most of my teaching experience comes from, and examine the need for motivations to be negotiated and co-developed and how this could be achieved through a CLIL-based approach.

Secondary education comprises six years and, on average, students study around 13 subjects per academic year. Students usually have English once or twice a week, and most start learning English when they begin secondary school at age 12. Although it only takes two hours of the weekly school timetable, English is the only subject present throughout the whole six years. Because of the scarcity of qualified teachers, some students may have the same teachers for four or even five years. When this is the case with my own students, I often tell them in the first lesson that 'this is the beginning of a long love-hate relationship'.

Teachers are expected to conform to an official curriculum usually designed by a politically appointed group of specialists. It is a top-down style of curriculum implementation. Despite the prescriptive nature of the official curriculum, the guidelines offered act as suggestions for teachers to adapt according to their own contextual needs and qualifications. It is a prescriptive, yet not restrictive, curriculum. Recent curricula offer traditional Communicative Language Teaching (CLT) and Task-Based Learning (TBL) and the more innovative CLIL as three approaches that teachers can implement throughout secondary education. Secondary school students, it follows, may learn English through three different ways – with CLIL being implemented in the last two years, as local specialists agree that it is fruitful when students already know the language as a system. In addition, the Ministry of Education does not impose a particular coursebook, either locally or internationally produced. In theory, each teacher may choose their favourite book. In practice, however, teachers work collaboratively and each school may opt for one or two titles in the market.

Nevertheless, the context also presents another alternative for the learning of English: private language institutes which may be found anywhere in the country. They could be locally run or part of national and international associations. Their courses may be tailored and intensive, and the teacher–student ratio is significantly lower than the state sector ratio. For instance, as a teacher at a language institute I may have six students, but at a regular school I may have around 35 students. This private learning alternative is taken by teenage students who are interested in learning the language faster, and in another environment, or because their parents consider it essential for better career prospects. This may mean that students attend secondary school in the morning and private English lessons in the afternoon or evening. Such an alternative makes the landscape more complex.

When this private learning starts at a young age and continues through adolescence, many students may start year 1 in secondary schools with basic knowledge of English already. As years go by, the gap between the language institute and the state school is wider, causing a number of issues. On the one hand, not all students in a given class attend English private lessons. Teachers then may have a multi-level class with students who are total beginners, others who have had private English for a couple of years and a few others who are studying to take international exams such as First Certificate in English (FCE). On the other hand, those students who already know some English may not be interested in the EFL lessons because they have already mastered the curriculum content. Under these circumstances, teachers are faced with the issue of providing new alternatives which offer these students new learning opportunities.

In an attempt to narrow these gaps among students, classes may be rearranged according to levels of English proficiency at some schools. Teachers find this regrouping more comfortable because they can offer more personalised assistance to their students. However, even though the high-level students are placed together in one class, there is still the issue of what course to develop for them since the curriculum does not contemplate alternative procedures which exceed the mainstream classes and general curricular aims. Although CLIL is officially recommended, it is not stated how it could be systematically applied over a long period of time. However, as I will suggest, exploring contents agreed between teachers and students may be an innovative and motivating approach to learning English.

At this stage most students may be reluctant to continue with grammar practice, bland topics and skills work following international coursebooks since they have received this type of instruction both inside and outside the school for more than four or five years. They usually voice their need to use the language meaningfully by learning contents related to the school curriculum through English in the English lessons.

As a consequence, these contextual features, demands and needs have prompted teachers to view the integration of curricular content and language learning as a solution. Introducing curricular content in the English lesson following CLIL may improve motivation for both students and teachers since the lack of interest of the former more often than not negatively impacts on the motivation of the latter. Moreover, this interest in enhancing motivation does not flow uni-directionally. Teachers may feel that they need to improve their own motivation to teach. Students may also perceive that in the ecology of a classroom, understanding what motivates all the actors involved will contribute to a richer classroom experience. In other words, students may also realise that a motivated teacher will attract students to learning. Motivation could be co-developed through CLIL, since by definition, the incorporation of contents from the school curriculum or generated by students may help us reflect on shared agency and classroom dynamics (see Banegas, 2012; Coyle et al., 2010; Dalton-Puffer, 2007; 2011; Kiely, 2011). I discuss below the reasons behind choosing CLIL as a means for co-developing motivation.

Why CLIL?

According to authors such as Coyle (2006) and Lasagabaster (2011), CLIL will motivate both students and teachers provided it is responsive to the context in which it is developed. Given the relatively low interest in English as a school subject among students with language institute-generated knowledge of English, Argentinian teachers may resort to CLIL to meet the demands of their settings, making students and teachers themselves want to come to lessons. Coyle (2006) adds that motivation in CLIL lessons may be fostered by teacher collaboration and involvement in curriculum development and the non-prescriptive nature of its models. Motivated teachers, she asserts, breed motivated students who, in turn, will motivate their teachers even more.

In principle, CLIL motivates students because they can learn new contents and revise others which are initially rooted in their own interests and curiosity (Brown, 2007: 168–72; Lorenzo et al., 2010; Seikkula-Leino, 2007). The content relations students may achieve produce a positive impact because they are linked to their personal experiences (Llinares & Whittaker, 2009: 78–85). It is the value of the unknown and the importance of manipulating new concepts that may drive students (And why not teachers?). Richards and Rodgers (2001: 204–15) state that students learn another language more successfully when through it they acquire information, such as curricular content. The focus on either content or language within CLIL has given rise to the CLIL continuum. This continuum moves from content-driven models such as bilingual education to language-driven models such as topic-based lessons or content-based lessons in the EFL classroom. I shall now briefly discuss how language and content are treated regardless of models in the CLIL continuum.

In CLIL, language learning may be organised through three interrelated perspectives comprising the Language Triptych (Coyle et al., 2010). In this triptych, one perspective is *language of learning*, that is, the learning of terminology and phrases which are inherent to the content under study. Secondly, *language for learning* focuses on the language students need to carry out classroom tasks such as contrasting data. Last, *language through learning* makes room for unpredictable language learning because it is concerned with new language emerging from the cognitive process students are engaged in. This latter cannot be managed, and it depends on the teacher's ability to make room for students' demands in situ.

What is key in CLIL, according to Coyle et al. (2010: 29–30), is that content needs to be cognitively engaging to students, with tasks which promote problem solving and higher-order thinking processes. CLIL also involves language proficiency for students beginning to engage in tasks which require complex language derived from complex curricular relations (Kong, 2009: 239–48).

Learners are also engaged in more real meaningful interaction when the process is supported by authentic materials. Drawing on a theory of learning built on students' experiences outside and inside schools, authentic CLIL materials may feature texts about contemporary issues and discourse-based activities. For example, contents may come from geography, as it is highly visual, spatial and contextual. Moreover, authentic materials can come from textbooks as well as from the media in the form of documentaries, news reports and short articles. The experience is richer because students may adopt more equal roles since they can suggest topics, explore different knowledge areas and contribute to materials' and activities' selection through which they can develop their autonomy (Wolff, 2003: 211–15; see also Wolff, 2007; 2010).

Overall, students and teachers feel motivated through content and language integrated learning experiences because they offer possibilities to use the language meaningfully by learning new contents through the language. Within language-driven models, motivation may also increase because topics, lesson dynamics and materials are negotiated in such a way that students are willing to learn because they have been active participants in the process. Along these lines, we may agree that this teacher collaboration, participation in educational change, and student involvement will be possible in settings where democratic undertakings are valued and encouraged. Working towards motivation needs to be conceived as a process with others, to which all involved actors contribute and from which they all benefit.

CLIL experiences across Argentina

Although most recent CLIL incorporations appear to be part of new school curricula, the gradual implementation of CLIL models in Argentina essentially responds to a bottom-up process started by practitioners to deal with the classroom issues mentioned above. In addition, some implementations have been the result of teachers meeting at national conferences or in-service workshops in which teacher–researcher findings are shared (Banegas, 2011). Some teachers, then, may start their own experiences and in so doing are replicating or exploring new models within the CLIL continuum. I should emphasise that the integration of content and language is chosen by teachers themselves from their own exploratory practice outcomes, supported by theory and practice in the field rather than being imposed by ministerial policies. The selection of classroom experiences and practitioner research included below may illuminate the joint motivation-driven goals teachers and students have when they decide to explore the incorporation of curricular content into the regular EFL lesson (see also Anglada & Banegas, 2012).

López Barrios (2008: 40–52) offers an enlightening view of content and language in state secondary education in one central Argentine province through a small-scale investigation which includes textbook evaluation and interviews. He found that international coursebooks offer little in terms of challenging and curriculum-related contents because topics are usually trivial or treated naively. When teachers were willing to incorporate content in their lessons despite the coursebooks at hand, they would resort to their students for topics and materials. Although teachers admitted that their lessons would feature translation, reading aloud and vocabulary focus, they still felt that both their students and they, themselves, enjoyed these lessons for they attempted to introduce controversy and reflection in the ELT agenda. I believe that such an experience calls up the need to produce our own materials and courses so that we can choose the topics and sources which are appealing, relevant and meaningful in our local contexts.

In relation to CLIL materials development, Orce and Llobeta (2008: 86–95) together with Schander and Balma (2008: 264–71) describe classroom practices concerned with the use of film trailers and complete films to teach the target culture, whatever that is in the authors' eyes. In their view, the target culture is a powerful content to incorporate as core subject matter in learning English. Film watching, the authors suggest, could be followed by brainstorming cultural aspects which could be then broken down into subtopics learners may choose from to carry out an Internet search and prepare oral group presentations. The authors put forward the belief that it is language that prevails – that is, the incorporation of cultural topics, as it were, fulfils the function of context for skills integration. In their view, they recommend that such a procedure should be explored with secondary school students whose level of English is beyond an elementary stage.

Based in northwest Argentina, Bello and Costa (2011) also used films in their theme-based explorations. Their criteria for content selection were meaningful experiences which could increase their secondary school students' interests, motivation and linguistic improvement. For example, for one lesson these two teachers used an 'I Am Legend' film trailer to activate students' schemata and linguistic knowledge by asking them to solve a puzzle based on the trailer script and images. After this warm-up, they discussed literature, and science fiction as a genre, to express the future. In addition, using the same trailer to refer to biology, they had their students brainstorm ideas around virology and then compare their previous knowledge with a text about what a virologist does.

Last, Castellani et al. (2009: 272–75), from Buenos Aires, report an experience carried out in the first year of an arts-oriented secondary school in which students are taught arts in the EFL lesson, thus combining content and language. The authors highlight the need to develop materials targeted to future art and music specialists from a local point of view. For this type of experience, it is vital that materials and activities should reflect students' interests and needs. To achieve this, it is the teachers involved who need to become active in materials design because the market does not offer suitable materials for learners involved in these types of school projects. Together with this emphasis on context-responsive materials development, the authors acknowledge the fact that this experience takes the CLIL framework as just a guide despite the fact that the aim is to introduce content in the English lesson, consequently placing themselves at the language end of the CLIL continuum. Furthermore, this experience does not seem to be simply a collection of topic-based classes, since all the materials are carefully sequenced and follow a cohesive pattern having one same subject matter, the arts, as core. From my knowledge and position, this is a rich and serious content and language integration experience as it features the following aspects: collaborative teamwork among EFL teachers, materials development in the hands of those teachers and, above all, systematicity in terms of didactic procedures, contents selection and management for materials purposes.

The experiences briefly reported above paint a picture of different CLIL models and adaptations in varied contexts within Argentina. In addition to those practitioner accounts, I will put forward my own experience of exploring language-driven CLIL through action research (Banegas, 2013).

CLIL through action research

Brown and Jones (2001: 44) suggest that every action has a cause and is a possible cause for changes. The explorations discussed above encouraged a group of three teachers and myself as a teacher–researcher to implement language-driven CLIL at a secondary school in southern Argentina. We agreed that action research, given its transformative nature, would be our method-ological framework. By definition, action research seeks to promote cyclical reflection and action in such a way that its outcomes stimulate professional development and generate theories anchored in specific settings. Professional development could be significantly enhanced when teachers work collabora-tively. In our experience, this was realised through regular group meetings, materials development, discussions and classroom observations.

When we designed the three action-research cycles we lived through, we agreed that our main aim was to offer our teenage students a meaningful expe-rience in the learning of English as a school subject. These students learnt English at language schools and, therefore, the school curriculum did not offer anything new in terms of language learning. It was our students' aim also as they demanded the same in their own words and through demotiv-ating behaviours such as poor classroom participation and attention. The plan of achieving such an aim through language-driven CLIL included the development of our own materials as a response to our perceived coursebook-dependent practices and the poor contextualisation and irrelevant topics that coursebooks presented. This step revealed that our motivation was also under investigation and that, in fact, we aimed at not only improving our students' motivation but also our own.

We believed that in order to raise our students' motivation we had to create spaces characterised by democratised and negotiated practices. Teaching prac-tices need to be systematic as regards needs analysis and the outcomes must be then incorporated into the ELT curriculum. This needs analysis should contemplate not only what students bring into the classroom but also what teachers are willing to offer together with their strengths and weaknesses. In so doing, teachers and students will relate to each other from a point of view which acknowledges their internal drives. The concept of democratised and negotiated teaching practices involves increasing students' participation. This meant sharing responsibility for our practices and acknowledging the importance of our students' voices as an irreplaceable resource in a class-room environment. Rather than perceiving their participation as a threat, we perceived this challenge as an invitation to renew the school curriculum with our students' help. We believed that the co-construction of social practices of reference entailed developing, together, a framework which represented all our interests and needs.

In the case of language-driven CLIL, our action-research explorations led us to ask students to vote for topics derived from school subjects. We also asked them to suggest possible sources of input and activities. Since the exchanges we facilitated with the students had revealed that the topics and activities found in coursebooks were unappealing, we decided to include their suggestions in our teacher-developed materials. I shall now elaborate on the effect that topics, sources, and activities exercised on our students and us teachers.

As regards topic selection, we asked our students to have a say, since we had perceived that a topic linked to their interests and curiosity would be the driving force behind all our efforts and pedagogical planning. Even when the suggested topics were not our favourite, we were still determined to accept our students' decisions and plan our CLIL lessons accordingly. The topics the students voted for ranged from the history of rock and roll to Nazis in Argentina, drug decriminalisation and the universe.

Once we had the topics, we moved on to collect sources such as videos from YouTube, texts from Wikipedia, newspaper articles and subject textbooks. These sources included our students' preferences. While they suggested audiovisual sources such as documentaries, film trailers, and interviews, we also incorporated written texts. We realised that, without previous agreement, we had all chosen authentic sources. In our students' eyes, the use of authentic sources provided them with meaningful opportunities to learn English and pay attention in class. Other criteria for materials selection were relevance, comprehensible input, and transferability potential to our context.

In relation to activities, we regularly met once a week to organise and discuss our lessons and materials. Individually we adapted, if necessary, our chosen texts and developed activities around them. As a team we discussed our options and provided and received feedback about our ideas. Although we taught different lessons for different classes, we still felt that collaboration was vital to keeping us motivated and on track. One of the teachers, Sandra, expressed it thus:

> Sandra: *Esto del CLIL me sirve y me ha dejado ver otras posibilidades, animarme a otras cosas.* [This CLIL is useful and has allowed me to see other possibilities, to do other things.]

Similarly, another colleague valued the possibility of developing our own language-driven CLIL materials:

> Aurelia: *Esto de hacer los propios materiales, te alienta, a mí me encanta lo que estamos haciendo (...)* [Making our own materials encourages me; I just love what we're doing.]

In relation to complementing the coursebook with our materials, Sandra put forward how the latter had improved the classroom atmosphere:

> *Sandra: Yo utilizo el libro como de repaso digamos. Pero cada dos, tres clases les tengo que traer algo más. Pero la verdad que está buenísimo. Algunas cosas les interesan, otras no, pero es algo distinto, todos prestan atención y ya es como que lo esperan, ¿me entendés?* [I use the book as a revision, let's say. But every two, three lessons I have to bring them something else. But the truth is that this is awesome. Some things are interesting, some others aren't, but it's something different, everyone pays attention, and it's something they already look forward to, you see?]

When we noticed the benefits of our first lessons, we planned further language-driven CLIL lessons in which the focus was on language practice, vocabulary learning, and, above all, listening and speaking skills practice. In addition, there were activities which responded to the Language Triptych, but work on grammar, for example, was peripheral through awareness-raising activities or not included. We found it difficult to develop grammar activities based on authentic sources. However, when we used texts, discourse features tended to be highlighted.

At the end of each action-research cycle, we asked the students for feedback concerning our lesson management, materials developed and future topics. Taking into account their feedback, we met to reflect about our own emotions and practices. Aurelia explained the effect that her students' feedback had on her:

> *Aurelia: El hecho de poder tener el feedback de ellos te hace repensar la forma en que confeccionás el material. Por lo general el profe de Inglés es el libro.* [The fact of having their feedback makes you rethink the way you develop the materials. In general the teacher of English is the coursebook.]

In general, the students showed that their motivation was linked to our motivation as teachers. They believed that our new attitude and our identity reconfiguration as teachers who were less coursebook-dependent had allowed them to see the learning experience under a new light:

> *Student 1: Cuando viene a hablar de lo que trajo es diferente porque la postura del profesor cambia.* [When (the teacher) comes to talk about what he brought, it's different because the teacher's attitude changes.]
> *Darío: Como que en definitiva es el profesor que hace la clase más interesa.* [Like, in the end it's the teacher who makes the lesson more interesting.]
> *Student 1: Sí, participa más el profesor sino es como 'abrí el libro y hacelo vos'. Es como que participa más el profesor cuando trae sus cosas. Sino es como que*

el chico está participando y el profesor te dice 'yes or no'. [Yes, the teacher participates more, otherwise it's, like, 'open the book and do it'. It's, like, the teacher participates more when he brings his things. Otherwise it's like the kid is only participating and the teacher just says 'yes or no'.]

In addition, the students perceived that they had developed their language skills because the activities – which we developed based on their interests – seemed to be relevant. Even when the activities were similar to those found in coursebooks, the context-responsive nature of the topics put these activities under a new light:

> *Student 2: En la clase habíamos podido hablar más, pensar más y poder decirlo, compartir más opiniones, más ideas. No era solamente la parte de gramática, de hablar, escribir, completar. [That in class we could talk more, think more and be able to say it, share more opinions, more ideas. It wasn't just grammar, speaking, writing, completing]*
> *Student 3: Lo que pasa que el tema, los temas están buenos. Son interesantes, entonces te da ganas de saber.* [The thing is the topic, the topics are cool. They're interesting and so you feel like you want to learn.]
> *Student 4: Para mí que son iguales pero como es un tema que te interesa por ahí prestás más atención.* [To me they're the same but it's, like, because the topic is interesting, you pay more attention.]

At this stage, Sandra and Aurelia had already highlighted how motivating this experience was and our students' perceptions of us seemed to confirm this. More importantly, our students themselves noticed, as in the excerpts above, that their motivation had increased through participation and attention:

> *Darío: ¿Qué otras cosas notaron?* [What else did you notice?]
> *Student 1: Que empezaron a participar todos. Empezaron a hablar gente que no participaba mucho.* [That everyone started to participate. People who would never participate started to speak.]
> *Darío: Eso, ¿a ustedes les parece que aumentó la participación?* [That, do you think that it raised participation?]
> *Student 5: No sé si la participación, pero sí la atención. Cuando estábamos debatiendo de anorexia, todos escuchaban.* [I don't know about participation, but it raised attention. When we were debating about anorexia, everyone was listening.]

We felt that by having addressed contents which were related to a curriculum subject and were derived from our own students' interests and previous knowledge, classroom participation was higher. In addition, they used the language meaningfully and tried to incorporate the language for/of/through learning in the activities we had planned. I may conclude, then, that their motivation increased and so did ours, because we proved that their motivation drove us to improve our practices which, in turn, drove them to participate and to pay attention more in class as we became autonomous and creative teachers. Thus, the exploration of language-driven CLIL through action research revealed that classroom motivation is a dynamic construct which emerges from student and teacher motivation in synergy.

Motivation negotiation in language-driven CLIL

Based on the experience outlined above, CLIL may be a valuable option to co-develop and foster motivation among teachers and students provided that the content is negotiated with the students. However, negotiation also includes sources of input and activities. When teachers and students discover their interests, needs and demands, the learning process irradiates new possibilities through which their roles and identities are reconfigured, always in relation to one another. Teachers and students become active agents by co-developing materials and offering suggestions which will feed into the classroom dynamics and materials development.

Language learning through content, whether it is deeply embedded in the L1 curriculum or in the social context, is what makes language-driven CLIL relevant and meaningful. All pedagogical approaches and every single coursebook feature topics and themes which may relate to general culture, popular knowledge or trivia. Topic-based lessons and texts about sports, healthy eating, or Australia are common in ELT. If CLIL only incorporates these topics superficially, I may argue that there is nothing new about CLIL. What is not frequently found is a text or a selection of topics related to scientific knowledge and school subjects treated in such a way that they are cognitively engaging without inadvertently underestimating students. On the other hand, even the most ordinary topics could become crucial and enlightening when authentic sources and activities are used to stimulate the students at a cognitive level.

Drawing on a metaphor from physics (language and content integrated for real), I view motivation negotiation in the language-driven CLIL classroom as a matrix in which different forces interact. Naturally, it is the teacher who sets CLIL as the approach that will help learners achieve the shared aims. It is also the teacher who acts as a force that facilitates the moving of students through CLIL. However, because all motivation may be eventually intrinsic, such moving may be hindered if the motivations are significantly different. If the teacher-led CLIL consists of topics and sources which only represent the teacher's motivation, and such topics and sources are generally rejected by the students because they have other motivating topics in mind, the friction will obstruct the learning and teaching processes.

In physics, identical surfaces facilitate movement with minimal friction. In CLIL, or any approach in fact, similar or aligned motivations facilitate learning. Even when teachers and students acknowledge the fact that their motivations as regards topics may be dissimilar, there should be still room for negotiation which needs to emerge from mutual understanding and reflection. From my experience, it may turn out that a topic that students see under a poor light becomes relevant once they understand it or are able to contribute to it with their own knowledge, experiences and sources. It could also work the other way as I may become engaged after listening to their accounts. More often than not, students' preferred topics are linked to what they do not know rather than to what they already understand. Although it may be asserted that the first steps for successful learning materials and approaches are text collection and text selection (de Graaff et al., 2007: 607–08; Tomlinson, 2003: 110–16), I think that we need to consider topic selection as the cornerstone of our endeavours. Topic selection must be the alpha of CLIL models, especially when we claim that we aim at integrating language and curricular content in our lessons. If in a language-driven CLIL model the language will be learnt through contents but these are somewhat imposed, little language learning may be achieved because students will not feel inclined to participate or pay attention. Because intrinsic motivation may reside in students' interests in certain topics and tasks, these have to be relevant in their eyes so that they feel moved to collaborate (Ryan & Deci, 2000: 56–7). Their positive attitude to learning may instil enthusiasm among teachers who will then respond more positively to students, thus establishing an interactive relationship between teacher and student motivation (Dörnyei & Ushioda, 2011: 190–91).

Conclusion

I opened this chapter by providing an overview of ELT in Argentina and how language institutes pose state secondary schools (where the official curriculum is taught) with a challenging question to address: What shall we do with the language institute students in the secondary school EFL lesson? Such an issue has triggered the exploration of language-driven CLIL models across Argentina. My own personal and team experiences through action research provide an account of what motivates teachers and students to embrace CLIL and, more specifically, what benefits teachers may gain when developing their own materials through different possible frameworks. In CLIL pedagogies it is vital that contents, sources and activities emerge from the intersection between the school curriculum and students' interests and cognitive development.

Above all, learning is about discovering. Foreign language learning becomes an engaging activity when knowledge of the world is approached through it.

English becomes a powerful tool for asking and answering questions, setting positions about historical issues and putting across cause-effect relationships between two entities. In Greek mythology, several gods and heroes were punished by being given a task that is mechanically repeated for eternity. We as teachers do not want to use the same coursebook all our professional lives or impose our agendas so as not to leave our comfort zone. Our students do not want to learn over and over again that verbs add an –s in the third person singular in present simple affirmative. Teachers and students may be willing to explore different ways of accessing knowledge, since inquisitiveness, the irreplaceable root of our life (Bordelois, 2010: 110), is what drives us to suggest topics, to develop materials and to offer sources and experiences.

Engagement priorities

CLIL pedagogies which shape and are shaped by collaborative development between teachers and students entail a number of areas which are worth exploring. Student–teacher collaboration for effective CLIL seems to be based on students' proficiency, the extent to which topics and materials can be negotiated and the relevance attached to content complexity in an EFL lesson. Given these apparently necessary conditions for good CLIL practices, it may be enriching to delve into the following concerns:

1. To what extent can students choose topics and materials for the EFL lesson?
2. Could language-driven CLIL through authentic sources improve students' grammar and all skills equally?
3. What relevance should content learning have in assessment when, after all, the subject is EFL?
4. Does CLIL only benefit proficient students?
5. Can CLIL be carried out by teachers who are not proficient L2 users?
6. Do students truly engage with cognitively demanding content and activities in the CLIL lesson?

Suggested further reading

Dale, L. and Taner, R. (2012). *CLIL Activities: A Resource for Subject and Language Teachers*. Cambridge: Cambridge University Press.

This handbook features more than 50 CLIL activities to focus content, language and cognitive skills, and assessment. The authors emphasise the motivational force of subject-related topics strictly found in the school curriculum.

McCall, I. (2012). Score in French: motivating boys with football in Key Stage 3. *Language Learning Journal*, 39(1): 5–18.

The author reports the development and implementation of a curriculum around football to foster motivation and fight underachievement among boys in a French class.

After one school year of projects and teacher-developed materials around football, boys (and also girls) found French learning more engaging.

Mearns, T. L. (2012). Using CLIL to enhance pupils' experience of learning and raise attainment in German and health education: a teacher research project. *Language Learning Journal,* 40(2): 175–92.

This action-research-based report signals that CLIL is mainly motivating among high-achievers. Results indicate that while students' enjoyment of the German class-room increased, their confidence in their own progress was affected by the type of tasks introduced.

References

Anglada, L. B. and Banegas, D. L. (eds) (2012). *Views on Motivation and Autonomy: Selected Papers from the XXXVII FAAPI Conference.* San Martín de los Andes: APIZALS.

Banegas, D. L. (2011). Content and language integrated learning in Argentina, 2008–2011. *Latin American Journal of Content and Language Integrated Learning,* 4(2): 32–48.

Banegas, D. L. (2012). Integrating content and language in English language teaching in secondary education: models, benefits, and challenges. *Studies in Second Language Learning and Teaching,* 2(1): 111–36.

Banegas, D. L. (2013). *Teachers Develop Content and Language Integrated Learning Materials through Collaborative Action Research in Argentina.* Unpublished doctoral thesis, Centre for Applied Linguistics, University of Warwick.

Bello, P. and Costa, L. (2011). CLIL in action. *IATEFL Voices,* 220: 6–7.

Bordelois, I. (2010). *Del Silencio Como Porvenir* [Of Silence as Future]. Buenos Aires: Libros del Zorzal.

Brown, H. D. (2007). *Principles of Language Learning and Teaching* (Fifth Edition). White Plains, NY: Pearson Longman.

Brown, T. and Jones, L. (2001). *Action Research and Postmodernism. Congruence and Critique.* Buckingham/Philadelphia: Open University Press.

Castellani, E., Dabove, C. and Colucci, L. (2009). Teaching EFL or teaching art? In D. Fernández (ed.) *XXXIV FAAPI Conference Proceedings: Teachers in Action. Making the Latest Trends Work in the Classroom.* Bahía Blanca: FAAPI, pp. 272–75.

Coyle, D. (2006). *Content and Language Integrated Learning: Motivating Learners and Teachers.* Available at http://blocs.xtec.cat/clilpractiques1/files/2008/11/slrcoyle.pdf [Accessed 15/4/11].

Coyle, D., Hood, P. and Marsh, D. (2010). *CLIL: Content and Language Integrated Learning.* Cambridge: Cambridge University Press.

Dalton-Puffer, C. (2007). *Discourse in Content and Language Integrated Learning (CLIL) Classrooms.* Philadelphia: John Benjamins.

Dalton-Puffer, C. (2011). Content and language integrated learning: from practice to principle? *Annual Review of Applied Linguistics,* 31(1): 182–204.

deGraaff, R., Koopman, G., Anikina, Y. and Westhoff, G. (2007). An observation tool for effective L2 pedagogy in content and language integrated learning (CLIL). *International Journal of Bilingualism and Bilingual Education,* 10(5): 603–24.

Dörnyei, Z. and Ushioda, E. (2011). *Teaching and Researching Motivation* (Second Edition). Harlow: Pearson.

Kiely, R. (2011). Understanding CLIL as an innovation. *Studies in Second Language Learning and Teaching,* 1(1): 153–71.

Kong, S. (2009). Content-based instruction: what can we learn from content-trained teachers' and language-trained teachers' pedagogies? *The Canadian Modern Language Review/La Revue canadienne des langues vivantes*, 66(2): 233–67.

Lasagabaster, D. (2011). English achievement and student motivation in CLIL and EFL settings. *Innovation in Language Learning and Teaching*, 5(1): 3–18.

Llinares, A. and Whittaker, R. (2009). Teaching and learning history in secondary CLIL classrooms: from speaking to writing. In E. Dafouz and M. Guerrini (eds) *CLIL across Educational Levels*. London: Richmond, pp. 73–88.

LópezBarrios, M. (2008). Content – the stuff ELT is made of. In D. Fernández (ed.) *Using the Language to Learn and Learning to Use the Language: What's Next in Latin America. XXXIII FAAPI Conference Proceedings*. Santiago del Estero: FAAPI, pp. 40–51.

Lorenzo, F., Casal S. and Moore, P. (2010). The effects of content and language integrated learning in European education: key findings from the Andalusian bilingual sections evaluation project. *Applied Linguistics*, 31(3): 418–42.

Orce, E. and Llobeta, E. (2008). Unveiling the mystery: crime film trailers and their use in the English language class. In D. Fernández (ed.) *Using the Language to Learn and Learning to Use the Language: What's Next in Latin America. XXXIII FAAPI Conference Proceedings*. Santiago del Estero: FAAPI, pp. 86–95.

Richards, J. and Rodgers, T. S. (2001). *Approaches and Methods in Language Teaching* (Second Edition). Cambridge: Cambridge University Press.

Ryan, R. M. and Deci, E. L. (2000). Intrinsic and extrinsic motivations: classic definitions and new directions. *Contemporary Educational Psychology*, 25(1): 54–67.

Schander, C. and Balma, B. (2008). CLIL+ educational technology: a lesson framework. In D. Fernández (ed.) *Using the Language to Learn and Learning to Use the Language: What's Next in Latin America. XXXIII FAAPI Conference Proceedings*. Santiago del Estero: FAAPI, pp. 264–71.

Seikkula-Leino, J. (2007). CLIL learning: achievement levels and affective factors. *Language and Education*, 21(4): 328–41.

Tomlinson, B. (2003). Developing principled frameworks for materials development. In B. Tomlinson (ed.) *Developing Materials for Language Teaching*. London and New York: Continuum, pp. 1–14.

Wolff, D. (2003). Content and language integrated learning: a framework for the development of learner autonomy. In D. Little, J. Ridley and E. Ushioda (eds) *Learner Autonomy in the Foreign Language Classroom: Teacher, Learner, Curriculum and Assessment*. Dublin: Authentik, pp. 211–22.

Wolff, D. (2007). CLIL: bridging the gap between school and working life. In D. Marsh and D. Wolff (eds) *Diverse Contexts – Converging Goals: CLIL in Europe*. Frankfurt: Peter Lang, pp. 120–30.

Wolff, D. (2010). Developing curricula for CLIL: issues and problems. In B. O'Rourke and L. Carson (eds) *Language Learner Autonomy. Policy, Curriculum, Classroom. A Festschrift in Honour of David Little*. Bern: Peter Lang, pp. 103–20.

6

Motivational Challenges for Gulf Arab Students Studying Medicine in English

Diane Malcolm

Introduction

The Arab Gulf region, comprising the countries of the Gulf Cooperation Council (GCC) – Saudi Arabia, Kuwait, the UAE, Qatar, Oman and Bahrain – is among the regions of the world where tertiary institutions have proliferated in the past few decades, as their governments have attempted to provide higher education opportunities for burgeoning numbers of young, increasingly educated and globalised nationals. Private colleges and universities offering a wide choice of majors to GCC high school graduates have also spread. In most of these new institutions, the principal language of instruction in technical and scientific fields is English (Zughoul, 2003), yet the level of English required to be an effective college student in these settings is often far beyond what most public-school graduates from GCC schools have achieved. As a result, most colleges in the region include compulsory English language and academic skills training in a foundation or preparatory programme as a pre-requisite to acceptance to the degree courses. Medicine is among the most prestigious and desirable of the professions in the GCC, so acceptance into a medical college is an aspiration for many of its brightest students and a source of pride for their families and communities. In GCC countries, students typically enter medical college directly from high school, study for six years then intern for a year before becoming fully qualified MDs. Arabian Gulf University (AGU) in Bahrain, where I have taught for over 20 years, is one of the longest-established medical universities in the region and the first in the GCC to follow a problem-based learning (PBL) approach. It is also unique in being the only regional medical college that is supported by all the GCC countries, providing scholarships for qualified nationals according to a quota system for each country. Up until very recently, AGU did not provide its students with basic English skills training in a foundation year, but English courses with a focus on English for medical purposes have always been a credited part of the Year One programme, which also includes basic science, lecture-based courses, and is seen as a 'filter year' in which pass marks in all courses are required to proceed to Year Two, the medical phase. Although, unlike those who study in ESL settings, these Arab students live and study in a familiar environment, they face a number of challenges to their motivation and self-esteem as they adapt to their new role and, perhaps most importantly in the initial phase, to the demands of studying academic content for the first time through the medium of English. This chapter describes some of these challenges as students themselves perceive them, guided by the 'person-in-context' relational model (Ushioda, 2009) that highlights personal, affective variables rather than cognitive ones, in order to facilitate teachers' understanding of the many background factors that affect the individual's attitudes, responses and ultimate success or failure as a medical student studying in English in the Arab Gulf region. It is hoped their experience may also have relevance for English teachers of tertiary level students studying for specific professional aims in other, non-English settings, as an example of a phenomenon that is becoming increasingly prevalent in today's globalised educational setting.

English learning background of Arab public-school graduates

The English language proficiency levels of Arab learners of English entering Arab universities to pursue degree courses in regional institutions can vary widely depending on their previous schooling, but the majority of applicants have attended public schools. Rabab'ah (2005) describes a typical experience in Jordan, where public–school students experience English as a school subject taught largely in Arabic, with little or no communicative use of the language, and very little opportunity for out-of-school contact with English speakers. The problems of school English courses as reported by Clarke (2006), Qashoa (2006) and O'Sullivan (2004) for the UAE setting include classes that are teacher-dominated, where translation and memorisation are widely used techniques; readings act as a vehicle for vocabulary, structure, and pronunciation practice rather than content; and the classroom focus is on exam preparation rather than communication. Suleiman (1993) reported the Arab learners of his study (Libyan, Saudi, Jordanian and Palestinian) found their English classes in their home countries were boring, repetitive, not challenging, emphasised grammar over conversation, and their teachers had poor pronunciation and used Arabic more than half the time. As a result of such instruction, students who enter universities are often at a low proficiency level, despite having had several years of high school English courses (Dwaik & Shehadeh, 2010; Rabab'ah, 2005).

Motivation of Arab students of English

Studies investigating Arab tertiary level students' motivation to learn English generally categorise their motivation as 'instrumental' (Diab, 2006; Suleiman, 1993; Vogt & Oliver, 1998) as they report students have a clear purpose in mind relating to the need to learn English: a requirement for their college major, a necessary step for their future careers and professional development, or fulfilment of family expectations (Suleiman, 1993: 44). Another term used is 'required' motivation (Dwaik & Shehadeh, 2010), in which passing an English course is detached from any real life purpose, but is a compulsory part of the educational syllabus. Because of the perceived status of English as the language of international communication, even Arabs with hostile attitudes to English speakers view its acquisition as a necessity for progress. For example, Zughoul (2003: 106) states:

> Despite the hegemonic and imperialistic nature of English, it is still badly needed in the Arab world for the purposes of communicating with the world, education, acquisition of technology and development at large.

English may also be viewed as the dominant, or prestige, language of the educated GCC national, at the expense of Arabic, a situation that is seen as unavoidable but threatening by some academics and by the students themselves (Clarke, 2006). Gulf Arab students who wish to study medicine in a regional college have little option but to study in English, regardless of their attitudes to the language. It is accepted that, even in Saudi Arabia, where it is not used as a language of wider communication as much as in the other GCC states, English is taken for granted as the 'medium of instruction especially in medicine and engineering' (Al-Haq & Smadi, 1996).

Instrumental or integrative motivation

While the term 'instrumental motivation' had earlier acquired a somewhat negative connotation as being associated with superficial, pragmatic language learning – compared to what was considered a more enabling 'integrative' motivation' which assumed a desire to understand and assimilate to both the target language and culture – nowadays the term integrative motivation in its original formulation has lost its applicability to the motivating factors affecting English learners in the globalised setting (Dörnyei & Ushioda, 2011: 87). Instead, new motivational paradigms, such as the L2 motivational self-system (Dörnyei, 2005; 2009), person-in-context relational view (Ushioda, 2009; 2011), possible selves (e.g., Oyserman & Marcus, 1990), and complex dynamic systems (Dörnyei & Ushioda, 2011: 88) have been proposed to account for the fluctuating nature of motivation, as well as the individual and situational elements that form a backdrop to the process of language learning over time.

Apart from the immediate need to master English for their medical studies, many students of medicine are motivated by their long-term goals and their vision of an ideal future self, or 'instrumentality-promotion' self-regulatory motivation (Higgins, 1998; 2000), a type of instrumental motivation that fires the imagination and spurs the students to persist in their efforts. For most first-year students, however, the immediate and pressing need to pass the year is at the forefront of their efforts, and achieving this goal the primary focus of their studies. Thus, their 'ought-to' self is related to Higgins's concept of 'instrumentality-prevention' motivation, in which the driving force for first-year students is not to fail the first-year courses, disappoint their parents and, consequently, have to leave the university.

The present study

Study background

For the past several years, I have interviewed over 30 AGU medical students, individually or in small focus groups, in order to discover the problems they face in dealing with their medical studies in English. These interviews, mostly conducted with first- and second-year students, inevitably touched on affective issues relating to students' perceptions of how their studies were proceeding; problems they had faced and overcome; initial responses to the demands of studying medicine in English; sources of help and encouragement; and the role of the teacher in facilitating their English improvement. For this chapter, focus group interviews specifically aimed at investigating student motivation were conducted with two groups of students. The first group comprised three students now in the medical phase (Years 2 and 3), including one who had taken a preparatory year at a university in Saudi Arabia before transferring to AGU, another who dropped out of first year in order to study English intensively in New Zealand before coming back to complete Year One at AGU, and a third who was given the chance of taking a specially arranged semester of foundation English in lieu of completing Year One, which he was in danger of failing. The second focus group was made up of students currently enrolled in Year One, who were among the first batch of students to be accepted after completing a full year of foundation-level English at AGU. Most of these students had been, or are currently, in my Year One English classes, and had given their permission for the interviews to be recorded. All the students are male and from Saudi Arabia. The focus group interviews averaged around one hour in length and were conducted in English in my office; then the recordings were transcribed and the transcripts reviewed for comments related to motivational factors. Relevant comments were also included from previously conducted interviews with male and female nationals of Bahrain, Kuwait, UAE, and Saudi Arabia. Their remarks were then grouped according to the following recurring themes: background factors including family and societal expectations, previous education and training, adjusting to a new environment and different learning demands, and coping with affective threats to their self-esteem and study focus. In particular, I wanted to focus on how these factors function both to stimulate and inhibit motivation, as related to the 'ideal' versus the 'ought-to' self of the L2 motivational self-system (Dörnyei, 2009) or the 'instrumentality-promotion'/'instrumentality-prevention' model proposed by Higgins (as summarised in Dörnyei & Ushioda, 2011: 88). Finally, I wanted to examine these students' perceptions of the importance of English proficiency in their studies and future profession and the role of the teacher in supporting their language learning efforts. Students are not identified by name but by the year of study at the time of the interview (Year 1, 2 and 3). The questions posed to the students are listed as an Appendix.

Students' perspectives on motivation

Background factors affecting student motivation: personal factors, family expectations, social setting, and attitudes

Applicants for the AGU medical school undergo a screening interview as part of the entrance requirements. Typically, when asked why they wish to become a doctor, they will mention that it has been their dream since childhood. This has become such a cliché that some interviewers cannot conceal their amusement at hearing the same story recycled. One interviewee remarked:

> I remember when I do the interview, they laughed at me. I told him when I was a child, I see a doctor (as) something big, important or like this, and then from that time it was my ambitious, I want to be like this guy (Y1)

Nevertheless, the dream of becoming a doctor is widely seen as the most important source of motivation, but often the dream has been strongly influenced by family expectations and personal events:

> You say motivation, I think a person has a dream, the dream will be his motivation. And if he has some reasons, I had my grandmother, she dead [died], and she told me, 'Ahmed, I want to see you doctor.' And I think I have to be doctor, and not just be doctor...she death [died] from wrong mistake [of the] doctor's. And then I want to be surgical, cardio-surgical doctor, because I don't want to see more people death from doctor mistake or I see people and I can't help him. Beside my dream, it is more responsible my grandmother told me I want to see you doctor. Sometimes I feel I don't want to complete [continue] but when I remember what she told me, I think I want to do it. (Y1)

While family hopes can act as a motivator to keep on going through tough times, the fear of failure and returning home in disgrace also has a powerful influence on motivation:

> [In first year] I [was] very, very afraid to fail. I will disappoint my family, and myself, and my relatives. All of them see me in good position, then I [am] back in [my home]. Bad picture. (Y3).

Expectations from the community and friends also play a part, and put additional pressure on students to pass:

> Even my neighbors (say), 'Welcome doctor, welcome doctor, welcome.' I say to them, 'Don't say doctor, I still in year one.' We didn't deserve this word, until we finish at least four years. (Y3)
>
> When I fail or something, I think my close family they would support me, but others from my family members, they think that he's a bad guy. They don't think, okay, maybe they have sons and they study basic subjects and they be [do] good because it's easy. But when someone study medicine and fail, it's [a] big problem. They think, okay, he's a loser. Everything in life, he can't do anything. (Y1)

Another student, whose father had died, had to convince his mother to let him study in Bahrain, rather than in his home country. As the eldest son, this Saudi student was expected to take on an active role as head of the household, according to tradition:

> When I choose to study medicine in Bahrain, [my mother] said: 'No. You will be away.' And you know in my age it's the first age to be like, like the father of the family and she will miss this thing. But when my uncles, her brothers told her, it's very big chance and most students want to be in your son's situation she agreed. And now she thanks God. (Y1)

AGU medical students from other Gulf countries must move to Bahrain which, while still an Arabic-speaking Islamic country, is an open society compared to some of its neighbours, notably Saudi Arabia, and has gained a reputation for being a 'party place'. Students must combat these negative stereotypes:

> Saudi people when they come to Bahrain and they come back to Saudi Arabia, they have bad picture about...what happening in Bahrain. [They think it's] just for fun. We told our relatives there is good universities in Bahrain and good people and this is one benefit of travelling. You know the cultures of another country, you meet people from another countries, you know all their cultures. (Y2)

And also they think this university it's easy, it's Bahrain. In Bahrain it's easy, you can take certificate without hard study. (Y3) Yeah, [they think] you can buy certificate. This is the idea in the people in Saudi Arabia. But actually it's harder. (Y3)

Adjusting to the new educational setting and threats to self-esteem

Low proficiency in English is at the root of many of the problems students have in their first-year experience of studying in the AGU medical college. The failing grades they obtain largely as a result of their poor English are at odds with their self-image as excellent students, based on their high school leaving results. One student who did poorly in the first set of exams was asked why he didn't give up at that point, and he expressed it like this:

I was afraid of, you know, come early to my father and he...sent me here, so I think, 'I will try, month, two months and then I will see.' [So the main thing that kept you here, was, you didn't want to disappoint your father?] Not just that, even disappoint myself, because I feel in my high school, you know, I am good student, I can do whatever I want. (Y2)

For me, I was the honest [most honored] student in my high school...I get 97 in my high school, but when I came here I felt like the worst student in this university. For the second week, I lose maybe two three kilo from my weight. I can't eat, just I'm thinking. Yeah, and there was Eid [Eid Al Fitr, a major Islamic holiday] after the two weeks...it's was for me the worst Eid in my life. (Y3)

Even students with better English skills face difficulties handling the amount of reading and information-processing demanded by the first-year science courses:

I remember the first week when we had the biology and physiology I was very depressed and I was very disappointed, because I said, 'Oh my God it's too much.' I stayed for one page maybe one hour approximately. And I told myself, 'My God what can I do?' (Y1)

Dealing with large amounts of technical reading matter in English is not the only problem, however. Having to motivate oneself to read and study the required subjects that are uninteresting is another issue:

The problem was that we took subjects, like epidemiology, that they were very, very dry for us. So, because of that I was thinking from my side, why have I chosen medicine. I think business or something like that is better than medicine. But after a while I changed my opinion and I say to myself, 'sure I have some difficulties here and whenever I go there, I will have the same difficulty because they have their own language and I have here in my medical college, my own language. So I have to deal with it and I have to be very happy because I have chosen medicine from the beginning.' (Y2)

The students who joined Year One after taking an English foundation year also found that adjusting to the study atmosphere of Year One had an effect on their motivation. Full of confidence after their success in improving their English, they had hopes of rising to the top as their studies progressed:

In the beginning I had enormous motivation and I think about the honor board but [now] my ambition to take 80; that's my level and I will work hard to achieve this. (Y1)

When asked what brought about these lowered expectations, this student had two explanations.

Because physics I got so bad grade because we don't have good basic education in Saudi Arabia, the marks, yes, and some students also. When you sit in the lecture hall you see just three or four just talking all the time. They don't let you have a chance to ask. The teacher want[s] to teach something, and when he start, they say everything and he go to the other slide. Okay, let him give us the information. Because he thought we understand everything. Yeah, he thought that all of us, we are the same. (Y1)

Many of the students admitted to Year One have graduated from international schools, so they are both fluent in English and accustomed to the kinds of interaction expected from college-level instructors. The experience of attending lectures with these fluent students is intimidating to those without that background and serves to demotivate them, temporarily at least. As one student put it:

In foundation year, we are the same, sort of, we are the same [level]. And I think it's more motivate than this year. And there are a few students they are, I think they are up the ah normal level who graduated from international school or something in Saudi Arabia, they already get physics and chemistry. So they come here they know the most information and it's easy for them but they laugh about you when you said anything. Okay you are better because you have more experience and you have another kind of education but it's not fair, you make me [have] less ambition when you laugh. (Y1)

However, this feeling is short-lived as these students realise that the English and interactional skills of these international school graduates are not always a guarantee that they will achieve the highest marks.

> I told the student, English is not the key for pass, in this university. If you don't study, you will never/pass. My friend, his level when he came was very, very bad. But he pass Year One, and Year Two and now he's in Year Three. This [being weak in English] is not an excuse. (Y3)

The attitude of some of the professors is also a factor in demotivating students. A physics professor who, students complained, taught at a level far beyond their understanding, had a powerful effect on their motivation, although his intention was probably the opposite:

> [The physics professor] teach us for the high level, but if he come in the first lecture and he told you 60 percent for the students [last year] they failed in my exam and 60 percent will fail, no problem, it is normal. How you will feel in the first exam and he told you this? He want[s] you [to] suddenly be a high level, [but] we just finished high school. (Y1)

In order to understand his lectures, students record and then spend hours transcribing them. While students complain about the amount of pressure they are under to do well in Year One, at the same time they accept that this is expected of medical students, and has a purpose:

> Here [they should teach] the basic, [in] the premedical, it have to be the basic, but they make it the most pressure and you don't have time for anything. Maybe... they think to make us in pressure because they want to see who will want to be a doctor... The physics professor... said that your work in medicine, or in college, in medical college, it's to suffer (laughs). And it's right. (Y1)

Many of the adjustments these students have to make are common to all students in transition from high school to college studies, not just those studying for academic purposes in their home countries. What makes it harder for these Arab medical students, of course, is the fact they must also study in English. Understanding how English proficiency is involved in their motivation to learn is the one factor that is of most relevance to their English instructors, especially as related to the kinds of language support that can most facilitate student progress.

The importance of English and the role of the instructor

General English ability is closely aligned with students' success at AGU, and students' poor English level is a subject that frequently recurs in incidental conversations with medical college professors, most of whose own first language is not English. Nevertheless, it is assumed that English is the first language of learning medicine, though it may not always be the only language used to convey content. As one student remarked:

> In this time the English is now the mother of the language in all the world. And when you can speak English fluently you can live in anywhere – in China, Russia, in America, in Arabian Gulf. And all the science, the good science, like medical, engineering, computer science, almost (all) the language of this science is by English.

Public-school graduates, particularly those who did not have the chance of a foundation year to improve their English skills, consider their first-year experience to be mostly concerned with improving their English, especially as related to their medical studies:

> The most benefit for us, English in Year One. The most benefit [beneficial] subject/*yanni*/[I mean] in Year One, the English, for us. Okay, biology, Year Two you can repeat it and you can understand it. It's okay, but English you have to study hard in Year One. (Y3)

In particular, students praise the study of medical terminology:

> You know the name of organ, name the process, name the tools or instruments, what we used it in the surgical process or take biopsy or investigations. It's very, very good, very helpful. (Y3)

Those students who completed a foundation year before being accepted to Year One also recognised how much they owed to the programme:

> We can understand everything. If we sit in the lecture, we can understand the lecture. But if we just graduate from high school and we came here, we will be, like: He talk about [what]? I don't know, in the language I don't know (Y1)

This student had already taken a year in another college in Saudi Arabia, but had not been accepted into medical school there because of his low grades, which he attributed to his low proficiency in English. From this experience, and because of his determination to do medicine even if it meant losing another year, he said:

> So I came here, to improve my English and also to be in a good college like AGU. If they put me in first year when I had [the admission] exam I will

choose to go to the foundation year. Because I know that, if it's one year of studying English it will be very helpful. That's what happened. (Y1)

One of the criteria for admission to AGU is high school final scores. Students with science and English averages below 95 per cent are not normally admitted. However, grade inflation is prevalent in public schools, and a mark in the 90s in the final exam in one GCC state does not necessarily equate to that in another country. To illustrate the extent of unpreparedness, one student recounted his experience when taking the admissions exam which I administer:

I [was] shocked when you stand up at that exam. You speak, you spoke English, you said, '[Stop working] after 5 minutes.' Even I couldn't write my name in English. I felt I am so stupid. (Y2)

It may be evident to most English teachers that a student with so little experience of English as a 'real' language rather than as a high school subject has little chance of passing a first year of medical school crammed full of difficult lectures, readings, and exams that depend so heavily on comprehension of the language. This is not such an uncommon situation in the Arab world, however. Rabab'ah (2005: 182) states that in Arab universities students are accepted into English departments 'without taking into consideration their proficiency level or whether or not they will be able to manage in a program of English studies'. Our university is supported by the governments of five different GCC countries, and a predetermined number of seats are assigned to each. Although in theory students must meet the university criteria for acceptance, in practice it is very difficult to reject candidates selected by their country for a scholarship to study medicine, or to insist that they meet an internationally recognised English standard before entry. Thus, before the foundation programme was established, Year One English classes were likely to contain students of widely divergent proficiency levels. In such a situation, student motivation is put to the test, while teacher support is a key factor.

Student views of the English teacher

Faced with students whose English skills are so far below what is expected by their medical college professors that failure is virtually inevitable, their instructor may feel disheartened and dismissive of their needs. Nevertheless, the effort to help those cast into these difficult waters is not unappreciated. Over the years, I have dealt with many students who were initially almost unable to say a word in English in my class and certainly understood very little. Yet the strength of their drive to succeed and strong self-image, bolstered by family expectations and their previous positive experiences as high achievers can result in their overcoming the odds, through hard work, advice, and help from more fluent or upper-year friends and relatives. Teacher encouragement and support are also seen as an important source of motivation. As one of my former students put it:

> I think if you didn't push me to learn, I wouldn't be here. [The role of the teacher is] not just to teach us, [but] to know, you know, [find out] what's our problem, what do we need from you [not] just to give us information [Or to just] give the subject and go through the door. The relation between the teacher and student is bigger than this. (Y3)

These students also have quite clear ideas about what is needed to improve their English. Apart from learning medical terminology, these often relate to improving their speaking skills:

> I think the group discussion is a good way to learn. The best way. (Y2)
>
> No, I think the best way to learn, it's by presentation. (Y2)
>
> Presentation for speaking just, and to break the shy[ness]. (Y2)
>
> Yes, first you have to break the wall between you and English, then group discussion, to improve your skills. (Y3)

Fluent speaking is often equated by these students with proficiency in English and, as described above, they are often intimidated in lectures and in English class by the fluency of international school graduates. Students who had been in the intensive English foundation programme the previous year also regretted the drop in fluency they experience in Year One, when more time is spent in poring over textbooks and listening to difficult, information-dense lectures than in interactive, communicative English enhancement activities:

> Now, in Year One, I think our English, not the general part but speaking part, it's decreased, because sometimes when I want to talk or when I went to talk with [my foundation] teacher, I find that it's different than the last year... because I lost some skills. (Y1)

These students went on to discuss how their teacher's actions affected their motivation:

> I think the teacher sometime give you some motivation... when I attend in [Teacher X's] class [in the foundation year] I think I get some information, but unfortunately I was with [Teacher Y] I'm sorry but what I want said it, I remember she never get up from her chair. All the time she was sit[ting] and start talking about his house and summer [holidays]. Okay but you didn't... teach us how we have to talk and how we learn the grammar. (Y1)

This student felt he had gained so little from the foundation classes that he enrolled for private English tuition, at considerable expense, to coach him to the required International English Language Testing System (IELTS) level for admission to AGU Year One.

Other characteristics of teachers that these students criticise or praise illustrate how importantly they view the teacher's role. In their view, a poor teacher is inactive, gives little information, has poor pronunciation or is a bad speaker, expects students to learn the language on their own without guidance and has little patience for student error or confusion. A good teacher is active in the class, gives good, detailed explanations, is willing to repeat, and creates an encouraging, unthreatening environment. Most importantly, the teacher must push the student to learn, as one upper-year student advised:

> Push them, because any student, he's just come from Saudi Arabia, 'okay, open country, can do anything.' And now he is alone, he can do anything. But if the university [will] push them, give them more homework... more tests, and more book[s], I think they will get better. (Y3)

Summary of motivational factors

Studying in the GCC setting

The experience of these Arabic-speaking medical students studying through the medium of English in, or near, their home countries, illustrates the many challenges to their self-esteem and motivation they must face and overcome in order to reach their goals. While students in the GCC setting have easier access to family and friends than those studying in L1 English settings, they may also be under greater pressure to succeed thanks to the constant reminders of the high expectations placed on them, such as being called 'doctor' when they return to their home villages. Furthermore, students' pride in being accepted into a medical school is undermined by negative attitudes to the university and its setting in their home countries, devaluing the degree they are working toward, due to the society's lack of acknowledgement or understanding of the hard work involved in achieving it. One student stated that he was offered free tuition at a private university in his home country but refused because these schools 'don't teach as good as other universities[. T]hey cheat, and there is bad things happen[ing] there'. Unfortunately, the bad reputation of these money-making institutions may have tarnished the image of more legitimate and established universities.

Changing image as a student

On a personal level, students must reconcile differences in their self-image, from confident, top-of-the-class student in high school, to anxious, near-failing student in Year One medical school. The negative vision of returning home as a dropout ('a loser'), and the problems this will create for their family, acts as 'instrumental-preventive' motivation. At this point the 'dream' of the ideal self – the future doctor – may be the only spur that keeps the student on track. As one student put it, 'If you thought about if you be a doctor how you will feel if you save one life... this is what give you motivation, so stop thinking about leave or something like that'. The necessity to work hard and 'suffer', reinforced by their professors, is seen as a rite of passage for a medical student, and even a source of pride. Anticipation of top marks in medical school becomes tempered by the pressure of exams, lectures, and readings, and students lower their expectations, hoping just to pass rather than being on the honour board.

Future selves as motivators

The vision of themselves as successful future doctors is for these medical students very much intertwined with competence in English and, thus, learning English has an 'instrumental-promotion' focus, related to the 'ideal' L2 self. Students are also sustained in their motivation by examples from their families and the social setting of doctors who have studied abroad in English L1 countries and, as such, are held in higher respect when they return. One student put it like this: 'When you go out and you return with good grade(s), all the people will respect you, and the mind will change about you'.

Institutional policy

Students accepted into the university in spite of their low levels of proficiency in English face an almost insurmountable challenge. While realistically these students should be redirected to an English foundation programme, in reality, as noted above, often government or university policies mandate direct entry. In fact, at AGU this has been the policy until quite recently, meaning that the English courses which are a required part of Year One had to accommodate students of a wide proficiency range in the same class.

Finding ways to improve English proficiency

With the exception of students who have graduated from English-medium international schools, all first-year students face an adjustment phase in which they must find ways to deal with the English problem. One second-year student described his initial reaction like this: 'When I come here and I see everything in English, I start hating this language'. He also admitted feeling depressed and lonely at first, and in need of family support: 'I every day call my mother on the telephone and she [said], "You can do it, you can make it easier"'. With time, as his understanding grew, and as he succeeded in passing his courses, his view of English changed. He was heartened by comments of his relatives and friends: 'They said that the English is... the easiest language and the Arabs... can learn fast any language, any other language'. As evidence for this, he stated that his uncle had mastered German in six months in order to continue his studies in Germany. By the time this student reached second year, the English problem was largely overcome, and he took pride in being asked by one of the fluent students for his lecture notes:

> I feel like I improved in English because last night H. come to me. He said, 'M. I want your pathology notes.' I felt like proud, of myself because last year I asked him to explain the meaning. I asked him about meanings and now he wants notes, not meaning. (Y2)

Other students decide their best course of action is to drop out temporarily and upgrade their language skills elsewhere before being readmitted to the university, such as the student whose brother advised him to go to New Zealand to avoid failing the year. For those who elect to stay, the required English courses and the relationships built up in these classes with the teachers and fellow students help to counter students' feelings of confusion, demotivation, and low self-esteem. Unlike lecture courses, English classes are small, and constitute a non-threatening, supportive and accessible learning setting. Importantly to students, they are also credit courses, and good marks in English can help to improve students' overall averages as they struggle to pass the first year. Two guiding principles have helped shape the content of AGU English courses over the years: accommodating students' interest in English for medical purposes and creating opportunities for English improvement for students of a wide range of proficiency levels. To meet the first aim, course materials focus on the language of basic sciences, and include a programmed study of medical terminology as well as a number of assignments that require researching medical texts, dictionaries, and online resources for in-class oral and written presentations. Less proficient students get additional support from the self-access centre, staffed by a fluent speaker of Arabic and English who also directs discussion sessions for fluency practice. Students are also encouraged to develop their autonomy and English skills by organising and carrying out each semester a self-directed project on an aspect of English they would like to improve. These required out of class activities are included in the course evaluation, to encourage students to expand their English learning efforts while appealing to their desire to get marks for their work.

Conclusion

In many ways, the challenges faced by the Gulf Arab students I encounter every day in my English for medical purposes classes are common to students entering tertiary level education in other settings. Many have experienced the highs of being a top student in high school, followed by plummeting self-esteem and feeling unprepared, stupid, and voiceless in the new language and new setting. In the difficult period of adjustment, the long-term dream of becoming a medical professional helps to sustain these students' motivation while the day–to-day encouragement and advice of friends, relatives, experienced others, and teachers buffer short-term blows to the ego. What is different for these students, of course, is the need to upgrade their English language competence rapidly, while handling all the personal and study challenges of college-level studies. Administrative policy at AGU may stipulate English competence as a requirement for admission but, as is the case in other regional institutions, it is also subject to political and fiscal realities that bend these requirements. In this situation, teachers also face motivational challenges in providing the means to 'push' students who are often underprepared students to maintain their study focus while upgrading their English language proficiency as rapidly as possible.

Engagement priorities

The common practice of importing into the Gulf Arab countries Western models for tertiary education has had many benefits in providing better opportunities for its citizens as well as enhancing national prestige and setting the groundwork for future progress and modernisation. At the same time, mismatches between the regional culture and tradition, different primary and secondary school practices and standards, and those expected in Western academic institutions with similar aims often give rise to conflicting social and personal expectations with consequent effects on motivation for both students and instructors. Although enormous expense and effort are often involved in setting up these programmes, to date little investigation has been done of recurring problems and controversies that affect them, as well as of the effects on individual participants. These issues include the following:

1. While it is generally accepted that English is the language of medicine, and competence in the language a great benefit to students in the field, the emphasis on its acquisition seems to cast the students' native language of Arabic into a subordinate role. To what extent does this undermine students' self-concept and self-esteem, and what are the immediate and long-term effects on their motivation?
2. One of the contentious issues at AGU has been the establishing of a foundation year. Some feel scholarship students should be admitted directly to first year and compete on the same footing, regardless of their English background. They argue students will forget their high school science and waste their time and the government's money if they do not take the year seriously. Are there differences in motivation according to whether students enter a

degree programme directly from high school, in spite of low English proficiency, or after a year's foundation in the language? How can teachers in a foundation programme motivate their students to stay focused on passing the language requirements when they must wait another year to start their medical studies?

3. As noted in this chapter, in this academic setting students of very different levels of language proficiency are placed in the same academic courses. What are the mechanisms that allow students with low proficiency in English to maintain their motivation when competing with more fluent students and when facing failure?

4. Based on their previous experiences in the school setting, many Arab students consider the teacher the giver of marks, and the process of awarding marks as open to negotiation. On the other hand, their instructors view marks as something to be earned, and improvement, not inflated grades, the measure of success. What teaching practices can help motivate students to take on greater responsibility for their own learning, become less teacher-dependent and develop their own ways to assess their language gains?

5. Learners in this study noted the effect of their teachers, both in English and science subjects, on their motivation. What part is played by teacher attitudes toward, and involvement with, their students in enhancing or detracting from their motivation to succeed in their academic studies and future profession?

Appendix: Questions posed during focus group interviews about motivation

1. What do you think of when I say motivation? What pushes you to do something, such as becoming a good English speaker? Is there anything in your background that motivated you to study medicine?

2. How important did you think it was to learn English before coming to this university?

3. Did you notice a difference when you started to study in Year One (for foundation students)? In what way was it different? How did you feel then?

4. Was there ever a time when you felt you wanted to leave and thought you couldn't do medicine? How did you keep yourself from leaving at that point?

5. Do you think your family or friends had an influence on you or helped to motivate you? How?

6. What was the biggest challenge you thought you would face when you came here? What have been some of the challenges you had to face since you came?

Suggested further reading

Ushioda, E. (2011). Motivating learners to speak as themselves. In G. Murray, X. Gao, and T. Lamb (eds) *Identity, Motivation and Autonomy in Language learning.* Bristol: Multilingual Matters, pp. 11–24.

This article draws attention to learners as fully rounded individuals with distinct personalities and contextualised identities, rather than as mere 'language learners', de-personalised and language-deficient ciphers. The importance of autonomy-promoting activities that draw out learners' unique, 'transportable' identities is highlighted.

Ryan, R. and Deci, E. L. (2000). Intrinsic and extrinsic motivations: classic definitions and new directions. *Contemporary Educational Psychology,* 25: 54–67.

This article offers a comprehensive description of the two major conceptualisations of motivation, while expanding the definition of extrinsic motivation to include different degrees of external control and self-regulation. Motivational concepts are linked to the human need for autonomy, competence, and relatedness.

Zughoul, M. R. (2003). Globalization and EFL/ESL pedagogy in the Arab world. *Journal of Language and Learning,* 1(2): 106–46.

The author presents a polemic on the spread of English in the Arab region and its potential impact on English teaching practices.

References

Al-Haq, F. and Smadi, O. (1996). The status of English in the kingdom of Saudi Arabia (KSA) 1940–1990. In J. Fishman, A. Conrad and A. Rubel-Lopez (eds) *Post-Imperial English: Status Change in Former British and American Colonies.* Berlin: Mouton de Gruyter, pp. 457–84.

Clarke, M. (2006). Beyond antagonism? The discursive construction of 'new' teachers in the United Arab Emirates. *Teaching Education,* 17(3): 225–37.

Diab, R. L. (2006). University students' beliefs about learning English and French in Lebanon. *System,* 34(1): 84–96.

Dörnyei, Z. (2005). *The Psychology of the Language Learner: Individual Differences in Second Language Acquisition.* Mahwah, NJ: Lawrence Erlbaum.

Dörnyei, Z. (2009). The L2 motivational self system. In Z. Dörnyei and E. Ushioda (eds) *Motivation, Language Identity and the L2 Self.* Bristol: Multilingual Matters, pp. 9–42.

Dörnyei, Z. and Ushioda, E. (2011). *Teaching and Researching Motivation* (Second Edition). Harlow: Pearson.

Dwaik, R. and Shehadeh, A. (2010). Motivation types among EFL college students: insights from the Palestinian context. *An-Najah University Journal of Research,* 24(1): 333–60.

Higgins, E. T. (1998). Promotion and prevention: regulatory focus as a motivational principle. *Advances in Experimental Social Psychology,* 30: 1–46.

Higgins, E. T. (2000). Making a good decision: value from fit. *American Psychologist,* 55: 1217–230.

O'Sullivan, A. (2004). Reading and Arab college students – issues in the United Arab Emirates Colleges of Technology. *Proceedings of the First International Online Conference on Second and Foreign Language Teaching and Research.* Available at: http://www.readingmatrix.com/onlineconference/proceedings2004.html [Accessed 24/02/12], pp. 1–14.

Oyserman, D. and Marcus, H. R. (1990). Possible selves and delinquency. *Journal of Personality and Social Psychology*, 59(1): 112–25.

Qashoa, S. H. (2006). *Motivation Among Learners of English in Secondary Schools in the Eastern Coast of the UAE*. Unpublished master's thesis, British University in Dubai.

Rabab'ah, G. (2005). Communication problems facing Arab learners of English. *Journal of Language and Learning*, 3(1): 180–97.

Suleiman, M. (1993). *A Study of Arab Students' Motivations and Attitudes for Learning English as a Foreign Language*. Unpublished doctoral dissertation, Arizona State University.

Ushioda, E. (2009). A person-in-context relational view of emergent motivation, self and identity. In Z. Dörnyei and E. Ushioda (eds) *Motivation, Language Identity and the L2 Self*. Bristol: Multilingual Matter, pp. 215–28.

Ushioda, E. (2011). Motivating learners to speak as themselves. In G. Murray, X. Gao and T. Lamb (eds) *Identity, Motivation and Autonomy in Language Learning*. Bristol: Multilingual Matters, pp. 11–24.

Vogt, C. and Oliver, D. (1998). *Kuwait University Students' Attitudes Toward English and An English-Based Curriculum*. Kuwait: Kuwait University Faculty of Medicine. (ERIC Document Reproduction Service No. ED422 714)

Zughoul, M. R. (2003). Globalization and EFL/ESL pedagogy in the Arab world. *Journal of Language and Learning*, 1(2): 106–46.

7
Motivation and the Transition to University

Lindy Woodrow

This chapter focuses on the motivational profiles of English for academic purposes language learners in Australia. It has emerged from a research project that examined a wide range of issues concerning the academic performance of 'foundation college' students in Australia (Woodrow et al., 2011). The chapter focuses on motivation and how this changes over time for a cohort of international students during their foundation programme and through their first year of undergraduate university study. Information was collected using questionnaires and interviews on three occasions: at the beginning of their foundation course, after one semester of their undergraduate course and at the end of their first year.

English for academic purposes learners are interesting to consider from a motivational point of view because they are engaged in both academic learning and English language learning. English has become the lingua franca of academic communication and so plays a vital role in students' lives. For these students, the academic content they are studying is delivered in English, they are learning English and they are living in an English-speaking country. For this reason, theorising in motivation from both an academic perspective and a language learning perspective may provide a clearer picture of their motivational profiles. This chapter considers the motivation of these students in terms of their goal orientations and whether this changes over time. In the first instance, issues concerning international students are discussed. This is followed by a description of the research project, which tracked the motivation of the students over 18 months. This period included the transition from the foundation college to university setting, from a language learning/content-based instruction setting to a solely academic setting. Finally, implications for addressing the needs of international students are discussed.

Universities worldwide are seeing a much greater diversity in the student population than previously. Universities want to represent the full spectrum of society, while young people are choosing to have an international experience as part of their education. The focus of this chapter concerns issues relating to international students studying at Western English-medium universities. These universities have an ever-increasing demand for places from international students. This moves the learning of English as a second language into a significant position worldwide. The chapter addresses issues concerning English for academic purposes in Australia; however, such issues are applicable to a range of academic settings that provide tertiary education in English to speakers of other languages.

Australia is a popular destination for students from neighbouring Asian countries who wish to receive a Western university education. The majority of international students come from China. A Western education is highly valued in these countries for a number of reasons. In the first instance, it is easier to enter an Australian university than the top-tier universities in countries such as China. The competition for places in Chinese universities is fierce. Second, Australian universities like to recruit international students because they bring in much-needed capital through fees. A further reason is concerned with migration. Many students come to Australia with the intention of acquiring a permanent residents' visa, which has many benefits. Some intend to settle in Australia permanently. Yang (2007) found that the three top reasons for Chinese students choosing Australia as a study destination are: the perceived higher quality of education, future migration opportunity and lower cost of living and tuition fees than other Western countries.

There are a number of university entry pathways for international undergraduate students. Potential students need to meet academic and language entry requirements. The academic university entry requirements must be benchmarked with Australian school qualifications. These include international certificates such as an international baccalaureate. However, benchmarked standards are not available for many school qualifications in the Asian Pacific region. A foundation programme can overcome this difficulty, since students can enter the college with their local school qualifications and, providing they achieve the necessary grades in the foundation programme exit tests, they are assured of a place on their chosen university course. English proficiency university entry requirements can be satisfied in many ways. Typically, students need to achieve 6.5 on the International English Language Testing Service test (IELTS). However, Coley (1999), for example, found no fewer than 61 different types of English proficiency measures as being acceptable. One pathway is through a foundation programme. The language entry requirements for a foundation programme are lower than the university requirements as the students receive English instruction. Again the students need to achieve an acceptable grade in the foundation programme's exit test.

The term 'foundation programme' needs further clarification to situate the research described in this chapter. This study investigated students from a university-affiliated foundation college. This college has approximately 800 students enrolled at any one time. It provides programmes for international undergraduate students intending to study at universities in Australia. Most of the enrolled students intend to study at the affiliated university. The college offers three programmes: 34 weeks, 40 weeks and 59 weeks. Eligibility for the programmes depends upon the student's academic and English proficiency entry scores. The programme is full-time with around five hours of instruction per day. Students receive English for academic purposes (EAP) instruction in the areas of humanities, science or the arts, depending on their chosen field. They also receive instruction in a range of subjects broadly related to their intended undergraduate fields of study. However, the curriculum is not directly informed by the intended academic subjects the students will study. The teachers in the foundation programme are recruited to teach English or specific subjects. While there is some link with the academic departments in the university the teachers are not university academics. The majority of students (40 per cent) enrol on business and economics degrees, and the largest national group is from China.

The foundation type of programme is becoming more common as a preferred method of pre-sessional training English language training preceding academic courses for international undergraduate students both within Australia and offshore. There is evidence that international students who study on this type of programme are more likely to succeed academically than other international students (Wilson et al., 2008). Much attention in the research literature has focussed on the primacy of English language proficiency (Kerstjens & Nery, 2000; Woodrow, 2006). It is argued that while adequate English proficiency is essential for academic success at university, other factors play a part (Storch & Hill, 2008). This study addresses the issue of motivation in light of university adaptation of a cohort of foundation programme students as they progress from their pre-sessional course to the end of their first year of undergraduate studies. These students are studying in an ESL environment and come from neighbouring countries. When considering language learning motivation, the majority of research focuses on issues which may not be relevant to this group of language learners. The obvious goal of this foundation college group is to successfully gain a degree taught in English at a particular Australian university. This suggests that issues concerning identification with the target language group in societal terms, an area central to much research in L2 motivation, may not be salient. Previous research in language learning motivation has focussed on goal orientations informed by cultural and linguistic factors. In the case of pre-sessional EAP, these may not be sufficient. Two types of motivational goals may be reflected in such learners' profiles: that of language learning and that of academic learning. Language learning motivation and mainstream academic motivation have followed different research tracks and are rarely considered together. This study adopts the conceptualisation of goals based on self-determination theory. This conceptualisation has been applied in both language and academic studies. It also uses goal-orientation theory used in school education.

The majority of studies into English language learning motivation have been conducted in either bilingual language environments such as Canada or foreign language environments such as Europe and Asia, and much of this research focuses on the social goals of language learners. Little research has focussed on the large group of English language learners who elect to study in English at universities in English-speaking countries. These learners have both language and academic goals. Arguably, for this group of language learners, motivation is very specific and cannot be accounted for by the previously mentioned type of studies. These learners also have academic goals.

To investigate the motivation of foundation students, five types of motivational goals were considered. These reflect theorising in language learning and education. One important issue in motivational goals is the extent to which they are internally or externally driven. In Deci and Ryan's (1985) self-determination theory, these are conceptualised as intrinsic and extrinsic goals. An intrinsic goal orientation reflects engagement with a task based on interest or pleasure gained from the task. An extrinsic goal orientation reflects engagement with a task based on a desire to achieve a particular outcome. This conceptualisation of goals has been applied in language learning by Noels and colleagues (Noels et al., 2003).

While studies in academic motivation have also used intrinsic and extrinsic goals, goal-orientation theory studies focus on slightly different learning goals. Originally proposed by Ames (1992), the conceptualisation of goals focuses on mastery goals and performance goals. Mastery goals (also known as task and learning goals) are internal orientations very similar to intrinsic goals. These goals reflect an interest in learning and pleasure derived from academic tasks. Performance goals (also known as ego or ability goals) reflect orientations to outperform others and to display knowledge. These orientations are self-referent and are classified as being *approach* or *avoid*. A performance *approach* goal reflects a desire to be the best in the class and to gain respect from teachers, whereas a performance *avoid* goal reflects a goal to avoid looking stupid or incompetent (Midgley, 2002). Current research into goal orientations indicates that individuals can hold multiple goals (Pintrich, 2000) rather than holding a mastery goal or a performance goal.

The study

Until recently the predominant approach to research in language learning has been quantitative and cross-sectional. Typically a questionnaire is filled out on one occasion. This instrument captures a static description of an individual's motivation. However, such methods fail to capture changes in motivation over time and situation. The transition from school to university is a time of great change for students, so a longitudinal research design seemed more applicable for this study. The participants in this study face changes in their lives, both in terms of transition from one level of education to another, and also in terms of cultural adaptation moving from one culture to another. The participants in this study come from different educational backgrounds that emphasise different skills and values. For example, in an Australian educational setting, the emphasis is on developing critical ability; whereas, in many Asian educational settings, the emphasis is on the transmission and reproduction of knowledge (Ballard & Clanchy, 1997). Therefore, transition to university presents new international undergraduates with many challenges. To attempt to capture these changes as students move from a foundation college programme to university, a longitudinal study was conducted. Data were collected on three occasions through questionnaires and semi-structured interviews. The first round of data was collected while the participants were still at the foundation college; the second round was collected at the end of the first semester. This was approximately six months into their undergraduate study. The third round was collected at the end of their second semester, which was approximately 12 months into their undergraduate study.

The study reflected a range of variables considered important in academic adaptation: self-efficacy, perceived difficulty, values, motivation, self-regulation, academic performance and English performance. This chapter is concerned with motivation in relation to adaptation to university. The questionnaire to measure motivation orientation used a five-point Likert scale (1 = not at all true of me; 5 = totally true of me) and included questions about goal orientations from an academic and language learning perspective:

1 I want to learn new things (intrinsic/mastery).
2 I want my parents to be proud of me (extrinsic).
3 I want my teachers to think I am successful (performance approach).
4 I want to avoid failing (performance avoid).
5 I want to contribute to my country's development (extrinsic).
6 I want to get a good job (extrinsic).
7 I want to be the best student in the class (performance approach).
8 I feel good when I am using English (intrinsic).
9 I feel good when I do well in my studies (intrinsic/mastery).
10 I feel good when I master something very difficult (intrinsic/mastery).
11 I feel guilty if I do not do well (performance avoid).
   (alpha reliability: phase 1 = 0.83; phase 2 =0.88; phase 3 = 0.84)

In phase one at the foundation college the questionnaire was given to students during regular class time. There were 341 participants (M = 158; F = 179; missing = 4). In phase two and three, questionnaires were sent electronically to the students. Understandably, the response rate was much lower because the students had dispersed upon completing their foundation courses. In phase two 99 (M = 36; F = 63) of the original cohort responded, and in phase three 91 (M = 37; F = 54) of the original cohort responded. The nationalities of the participants were divided into four main categories. In the Chinese category students from China, Hong Kong, Macau, Taiwan and Singapore were included. In the Asian category students from Korea, Thailand, Cambodia, Malaysia, Myanmar, the Philippines and Japan were included. Middle Eastern participants included students from Iran and Saudi Arabia, while the European category included students with British nationality and Turkish students. Table 7.1 shows nationalities of the participants.

After each questionnaire a number of students took part in interviews to investigate more deeply issues of motivation. In phase one, 14 participants were interviewed; in phase two, 27 participants were interviewed and in phase three 23 participants were interviewed.

The data from the questionnaire was analysed using SPSS computer software. In the first instance descriptive statistics were computed for each data-collection round. Table 7.2 presents the descriptive statistics for this data. The results indicate that there were differences in the means over the three rounds of data collection with the scores generally going down.

To examine the changes in motivation more closely, the variables were compared over the three phases. In the first instance data collected during the phase-one foundation programme were compared to that collected in phase two during the first semester at university. There were 99 matched participant pairs. The questionnaire data was analysed for significant differences ($p < 0.05$) using paired sample t-tests. To indicate the strength of the relationship between the variables, effect sizes were calculated using eta squared. These are interpreted as 0.01 (small effect), 0.06 (medium effect) and 0.13 (large effect). The analysis indicated significant differences between phase one and phase two in terms of reported motivation orientations The results showed motivation orientations were lower at university than at the foundation programme. Two

Table 7.1   Nationality of participants

Nationality	Phase 1	Phase 2	Phase 3
Chinese	275	79	63
Asian	42	14	19
Middle East	15	3	6
European	4	2	2

Table 7.2 Descriptive statistics for questionnaire items

Item	Phase 1		Phase 2		Phase 3	
	M	SD	M	SD	M	SD
1 Learn new things	4.38	0.80	4.14	0.83	3.80	0.96
2 Parents proud	4.54	0.75	4.38	0.83	4.09	1.00
3 Teachers think successful	4.06	0.98	3.89	1.02	3.69	1.08
4 Avoid failing	4.43	0.91	4.38	0.81	4.09	0.94
5 Contribute country	3.81	1.02	3.67	1.08	3.61	1.04
6 Get a good job	4.70	1.20	4.50	0.80	4.28	0.86
7 Best student	3.70	1.20	3.47	1.19	3.28	1.14
8 Feel good using English	3.70	0.93	3.64	1.08	3.56	1.06
9 I feel good do well	4.53	0.77	4.34	0.80	4.22	0.861
10 I feel good master difficult	4.32	0.92	4.48	0.86	4.15	0.86
11 Feel guilty not do well	3.88	1.08	3.76	1.03	3.94	0.96

of the significant differences were with the intrinsic variable about learning new things (t = 2.67, $p < 0.05$) showing a medium effect (eta squared = 0.06); and the extrinsic variable referring to getting a good job (t = 2.149, $p < 0.05$) showing a medium effect (eta squared = 0.05). There were also some variables that indicated a moderate effect, however, the significance level did not quite reach $p < 0.05$. These were extrinsic orientation of making parents feel proud (eta = 0.04) and the intrinsic orientation of feeling good when performing well (eta = 0.04).

A further t-test analysis was run comparing the data from phase two during semester one of university and phase three at the end of semester two at university (54 matched participant pairs). The results showed motivation orientations were lower at the end of the first year at university than during the first semester. The repeated measures t-tests indicated that three of the motivation variables showed significant differences between phase two and phase three. These were the intrinsic orientation to learn new things (t = 3.11, $p = < 0.05$) showing a large effect (eta squared = 0.15); the extrinsic orienta-tion of making parents proud (t = 2.08, $p < 0.05$) showing a medium effect (eta squared = 0.07); and the extrinsic motivation of getting a good job (t = 2.15, $p < 0.05$) showing a medium effect (eta squared = 0.08). The variable referring to the intrinsic orientation of feeling good when mastering something diffi-cult approached significance (t = 1.88, $p < 0.05$) showing a medium effect (eta squared = 0.06).

The analysis clearly indicated that motivation dipped over the span of the research. This unmistakably outlines the need for further support for such students at both the pre-sessional and in-sessional level.

The questionnaire was followed up with interviews to provide more in-depth insights into the motivation orientations and the adaptation of the participants

Table 7.3 Coding analysis of interview data

Motivation	Intrinsic	Extrinsic	Perform approach	Perform avoid
Phase 1				
Strong	6	11	13	1
Weak	8	3	1	13
Total	14	14	14	14
Phase 2				
Strong	21	18	17	7
Weak	6	9	10	20
Total	27	27	27	27
Phase 3				
Strong	15	12	19	3
Weak	8	11	4	20
Total	23	23	23	23

to academic life. Semi-structured interviews were held on three occasions during the 18-month period. The participants talked about their experiences and aspirations during their studies. They talked about how they adapted to university, the problems they encountered and how they felt during the period in question. The interviews were audio-recorded and transcribed. The transcriptions were coded in the first instance according to the variables in the study. In this chapter the focus is on motivation. Table 7.3 presents the coding analysis of participant responses.

In phase one (foundation college) the data showed an overall strong motivation among students with a weighting towards extrinsic and performance approach goals. In phase two (semester one) the respondents showed high levels of intrinsic motivation indicating a developing interest in their academic studies. In phase three (semester two) the participants reported high levels of performance approach goals. This perhaps reflected a concern with academic assessments. The following section considers each phase in more detail.

During the phase-one interviews the participants talked about their hopes and aspirations at university. In general, the students were all optimistic, confident and looking forward to their studies. The motivators they reported were extrinsic, mostly linked to pleasing parents and the ultimate goal of getting a good job:

> I want to do better than my parents' generation, have a nice job and get a money and also I think that success is important because my life is only once so maybe I can live better when I succeed. (Yong)

The reference to parents was constant throughout the three data-collection sessions. Some of the participants felt pressure to perform well because their parents had invested a great deal of money to enable them to be educated in Australia. This was particularly true of the Chinese participants, who often came from one-child families. Their parents were very proud of their achievements and the students were motivated by this:

> My parents spent a lot of money to let me study here and so I have to make them proud. (Jane)
> I'm the only child so I have to do good to make them proud of me...and they have sacrifices a lot of happiness of being with me, sacrificed a lot of please and things. (Wang)
> In my country they expected me to come with a certificate, with a good mark, so that's what keeps me try harder because I feel it's not only for me it's for my parents as well. (Hamid)

Some of the participants referred to a feeling of a perceived temporary easing of academic pressure at the foundation college. They indicated that getting into university had demanded a lot of effort, and they expected the university course to be very demanding, but at the foundation college they could relax somewhat:

> Because I have been very hard-working in the past year and very high pressure, now I want to relax a bit. (Lin)
> Yeah, actually after I come to Australia I feel more comfortable to start...ah. My home country there is too much push, push you. (Chen)

In the phase-two interviews the students seemed to be more strongly intrinsically motivated in comparison to phase one. This contrasts with the findings from the questionnaire and could be accounted for by self-selection. Perhaps the students who volunteered to take part in the interviews were more motivated generally.

> I am quite enthusiastic when learning new things. I'm quite happy to get to know more that's all new. (Harry)

Wei reported an intrinsic drive despite the perceived negative consequences. He clearly believed that his way would result in lower grades:

> Some students just copy from other students material but I just did it on my own and even though I didn't get a really high mark, but it's not low as well. (Wei)

In phase two the participants seemed to have had lost their optimism and were struggling to adapt to their new academic situation. They reported that while the foundation course had prepared them well they were surprised by the impersonal nature of university courses and the size of the classes. Many had expected to make friends with local students but this did not happen. They found the discussions in tutorial session particularly challenging:

> It was not as easy as I thought. I was frustrated at the beginning. I hardly understood the lectures. I am doing an Arts degree. The four units I enrolled last semester are Anthropology, Sociology, Psychology and Economics. What I found difficult is the English. It is hard to catch the words after listening. Another difficulty are the concepts, especially in Sociology and Anthropology. I was quite afraid in the tutorials, because students are all from different countries, and speak fluent English. However, my English is not very good. I communicated with them but not good at it. The interaction was limited to greetings only, so I was not able to make friends with them...at the University, we had classes once a week, and I only met classmates for one hour. Unless I approached them very actively, it was hard to make friends with them. (Ng)

From an extrinsic perspective the participants seemed concerned with their grades. The foundation college grades did not seem to be in alignment with the university grades, so some of the participants felt disillusioned because they received low grades on their assignments:

> I just keep gradually lower marks from what I have been expecting. Maybe after one month during the exam I get quite high and I have an interest or enthusiasm to keep studying but if I just like, what I thought, I get very low mark and then I'm quite not happy. It just quite boring. (Xin)

Some referred to grades in light of the expectations of their parents:

> Every weekend I tell them (parents) about my study, but to be frank for the low marks I never tell then. I never tell my parents I just tell them about the high marks. (Thuy)

In phase three the participants reported that the work was getting harder as their courses progressed. Some participants had lapsed into a state of unmotivated procrastination:

> I'm not studying hard enough. Not hard enough this semester. I'm trying. I failed at many things and I'm falling behind the level they teach...I return

home I just play the guitar and then some stuff...but after two or three week you have do nothing and then you realise that you need to do something and then you start doing the revision then you found that there's a loss of things. (Shirley)

If I don't catch up with the work then I'll just fall behind and I'll be in big trouble when it comes to the exam. So that's kind of what motivates me as an international. (Harry)

Other motivators showed up in the data with students thinking ahead to winning scholarships or student exchanges:

I've applied for the exchange to America. I need to work hard in this year's subjects to get a good result in order to go to America. (Sophie)

Significant others emerged as a source of motivation, or even demotivation, for some:

I met many students who are really passionate for their studying...I'm the kind of person who around me are very passionate then I'm going to be passionate as well. (Nan)

She (his girlfriend) does help a lot. If I don't work hard then she will feel disappointed in me. Something like that. (He)

In terms of a lack of motivation:

I don't feel passionate...I have one friend from the same country she is the same as me she is not really motivated she got into pharmacy because her parents wanted her to do something like medical and stuff...for most of the students in pharmacy, it's like that. (Tran)

Clearly from the data the participants held multiple goals, and over the 18-month period their goals and enthusiasm changed. However, all but one of the participants passed all their courses and all adapted to their academic lives. There were no failures and no dropouts from this group.

Theoretical and research implications of the study

Despite the large number of international students at Western universities and the status of English as lingua franca of academic communication, there is relatively little published research into this group of English learners/users. The majority of Western universities have an increasing number of international students. In Australia, international university students come from neighbouring Asian countries, with the majority from China. Once these students have achieved entry into university, many stop formal English learning. Their language learning activity may be restricted to looking up unknown vocabulary. However, they have not achieved native-speaker competence in English. As such, this group does not sit entirely within the language learning motivational theoretical framework. By considering theorising from educational psychology it may be possible to capture issues of learning faced by this large and important group.

There are many obstacles for new undergraduate students when they start university. However, in the case of international students this is greatly intensified because they are not confident in English. Gu et al. (2010) refer to learning shock which reflects the emotional strain and the social, cognitive and affective problems international students face. The evidence in this study focussed on two shifts in learning environment: that from studying in the student's home country to foundation college, then the shift from the foundation college to the undergraduate course at university. The major academic shifts may be accounted for by Ballard and Clanchy's (1997) analysis of international students studying in Australia. They classified the teaching and learning situation in Asian countries as being 'reproductive', with excellence being represented by a recall of information as measured by formal examinations. Students are not expected to question knowledge or the teacher. In Western educational systems the emphasis is on developing critical skills, and asking questions is a very important part of this. While the foundation college courses focussed on academic reading and writing, there was evidence that the students had problems with oral communication in tutorial settings in which academic discussion is the main focus.

One significant result of this study is the support for motivation as a dynamic construct. The study indicates fluctuations in motivation over the 18-month period and shifts in the academic and social concerns of the participants. The study shows that motivation is the drive behind academic engagement, and this study confirms the view that motivation is dynamic in nature (Dörnyei and Ushioda, 2011). There is a need for further research in this area to consider in more depth the situated nature of motivation as influenced by contextual factors. In this study, social influence emerged as a motivator, with reference to parents and significant others. Parental influence on academic outcomes at a university level is under-researched. This may be because Western students are less likely to perceive parental pressure as a factor in their lives. However, the majority of the respondents in this study came from Confucian heritage cultures. One of the central tenets of Confucianism is filial piety whereby children have an obligation to their parents. In the case of the current cohort this was made more salient because the students were mostly funded by their parents and so felt a strong obligation to succeed. It should be noted, though, that the perception of parental pressure or influence can be perceived as positive or negative (Woodrow, 2011). Since parents play such an important role in international students' lives, it is an area that would benefit from further investigation.

This study measured five types of goal orientations. Intrinsic and extrinsic goals have received some attention in the research literature, but the application of mastery and performance goals is not widespread in language learning. This study showed that such a conceptualisation is of value when examining the motivation of international university students.

Practical implications of the study

The discussion of the practical implications emerging from this study focuses on providing and maintaining a motivating experience for international students at English-speaking universities. From a general academic perspective, students are more likely to be motivated if they are presented with manageable but challenging tasks and when they have control over the learning tasks (Schunk et al., 2008). In the pre-sessional classroom this lends support to the notion of scaffolding techniques whereby an individual learner is supported by teachers and peers to achieve a challenging task. Support is gradually removed until the student can complete the task alone. A sense of control may be achieved by individual and group project work which develops a sense of pride on the part of the student.

In the case of pre-sessional EAP students, perceived relevance is a motivating force. The foundation students in this study were most comfortable in their university classes when they had received some background instruction in the subject area, and were least comfortable when they enrolled in a new academic unit with content outside their existing knowledge. This suggests that the foundation programme should have a closer alignment with the university programmes. In order to achieve this, a closer relationship between the subject academics at university and pre-sessional students via the pre-sessional institution would be beneficial. This could take the form of attending lectures or of specific content-related reading and writing tasks.

In this project the participants lost optimism and motivation when they made the transition from the foundation college to university. This they attributed to unfamiliarity with the expectations of the undergraduate academic experience. In the first instance they found the delivery of the courses unfamiliar. They were required to take part in large impersonal lectures and then to participate in tutorials. To help pre-sessional students it should be possible to provide authentic academic experiences which could reflect the lecture and the tutorial methods of course delivery. In the second instance the grades in the pre-sessional course were not closely aligned with the university grading system. The university grades were much tougher. While it is acknowledged that it may not always be possible or desirable to change a marking scheme within a language school, it should be possible to have some tasks that accurately reflect university level grades.

The fluctuation of motivation and the reports of the experiences of this group of students suggest that there is a need for continued support of international students. Pre-sessional courses tend to focus on the goal of achieving English proficiency entry requirements of the university. Often, there may be relatively little focus on the students' future needs at university. The current study suggests that ongoing support at least throughout the first year of undergraduate studies would be beneficial. This support could take the form of traditional in-sessional language and academic support provided by the university or the setting up of a formalised peer mentoring system whereby new students are partnered with experienced students who guide them through the first-year experience. The results of this study point to the importance of social support and significant others. A peer mentoring programme could contribute toward a satisfying academic experience in this regard. In addition to this, attention should be paid to the grouping of students in academic classes to develop social relationships. The use of out-of-class tasks can also facilitate relationships.

Engagement priorities

The implications of this study centre on the dual focus of motivation for language learning and motivation for academic study. Both pre-sessional institutions and universities have the responsibility to develop and *maintain* student motivation. To do this English teachers need to establish a closer link between language learning activities and content learning activities and tasks that are on university academic courses. How such a synergy may be actualised is the focus of the engagement points below:

1. How can perspectives in academic motivation inform EAP practices?
2. How can pre-sessional EAP courses and universities collaborate to provide more motivating academic training?
3. What are the benefits of peer mentoring for international students?
4. How do you think such a programme might be organised and monitored?
5. What are the major issues in group work that can influence motivation and learning? What are the advantages and disadvantages of mixing local and international students?

Suggested further reading

Schunk, D. H., Pintrich, P. R. and Meece, J. L. (2008). *Motivation in Education: Theory, Research and Applications* (Third Edition). Upper Saddle River, NJ: Pearson.

This book provides an excellent overview of motivation in educational settings. It is particularly good in its consideration of the classroom implications of various motivational constructs. Chapter 5 contains an overview of mastery and performance goal orientations.

Woodrow, L. J. (2012). Three perspectives on goal orientations. In S. Mercer, S. Ryan and M. Williams (eds) *Psychology for Language Learning: Insights from Research, Theory and Practice*. Basingstoke: Palgrave Macmillan.

This chapter provides an overview of three conceptualisations of goal orientations: integrative and instrumental; intrinsic and extrinsic; and mastery and performance goals in English language learning.

Ballard, B. and Clanchy, J. (1997). *Teaching International Students: A Brief Guide for Lecturers and Supervisors*. Deakin, ACT: IDP Education Australia.

This short book is informed by research conducted in Australia. It considers the problems of adaptation faced by international students and offers some suggestions for how lecturers can help.

References

Ames, C. (1992). Classrooms: Goals and structures and student motivation. *Journal of Educational Psychology*, 84(3): 261–71.

Ballard, B. and Clanchy, J. (1997). *Teaching International Students: A Brief Guide for Lecturers and Supervisors*. Deakin: Education Australia.

Coley, M. (1999). The English entry requirements of Australian universities for students of non English speaking background. *Higher Education Research and Development*, 18(1): 7–17.

Deci, E. L. and Ryan, R. M. (1985). *Intrinsic Motivation and Self-determination in Human Behavior*. New York: Plenum.

Dörnyei, Z. and Ushioda, E. (2011). *Teaching and Researching Motivation* (Second Edition). Harlow: Pearson.

Gu, Q., Schweisfurth, M. and Day, C. (2010). Learning and growing in a foreign context: intercultural experiences of international students. *Compare*, 40(1): 7–23.

Kerstjens, M. and Nery, C. (2000). Predictive validity in the IELTS test: a study of the relationship between IELTS and students' subsequent academic performance. *IELTS Research Reports*, 3: 85–108.

Midgley, C. M. (ed.) (2002). *Goals, Goal Structures and Patterns of Adaptive Learning*. Mahwah, NJ: Lawrence Erlbaum.

Noels, K., Pelletier, L. C., Clement, R. and Vallerand, R. (2003). Why are you learning a second language? motivational orientations and self-determination theory. *Language Learning*, 53(S1): 33–64.

Pintrich, P. R. (2000). Multiple goals, multiple pathways: the role of goal orientation in learning and achievement. *Journal of Educational Psychology*, 92(3): 544–55.

Schunk, D. H., Pintrich, P. R. and Meece, J. L. (2008) *Motivation in Education: Theory, Research and Applications* (Third Edition). Upper Saddle River, NJ: Pearson.

Storch, N. and Hill, K. (2008). What happens to international students' English after one semester at university? *Australian Review of Applied Linguistics*, 31(1): 1–17.

Wilson, R., Hughes, J. and Anditomo, N. (2008). *USPF Tracer Study Final Report*. Sydney: University of Sydney.

Woodrow, L. (2006). Academic success of international postgraduate education students and the role of English proficiency. *University of Sydney Papers on TESOL*, 1: 51–70.

Woodrow, L. (2011). College English writing affect: self-efficacy and anxiety. *System*, 39(4): 510–22.

Woodrow, L., Hirsh, D. and Phakiti, A. (2011). *Academic Performance of ESL Graduates from USFP*. Sydney: University of Sydney.

Yang, M. (2007). What attracts mainland Chinese students to Australian higher education. *Studies in Learning, Evaluation, Innovation and Development*, 4(2): 1–12.

8
Digital Games and ELT: Bridging the Authenticity Gap

Alastair Henry

Introduction

In this chapter I will suggest that in cultural contexts such as Sweden, where English is an integral part of young people's everyday lives and is encountered and used in a range of out-of-school domains, a particular challenge facing teachers is not so much generating motivation to succeed in long-term competency goals, but rather engaging students in day-to-day classroom activities. Based on the idea that self-authenticity can have a motivating force (Gecas, 1991; Vannini, 2006; Vannini & Burgess, 2009) and drawing on James Paul Gee's recent work on affinity spaces (Gee, 2005; Hayes & Gee, 2010), I will argue that teachers of English need to create learning opportunities whereby students can experience the types of creative and self-relevant interaction commonplace in digital gaming. This does not mean that teachers should look to leisure-time domains with an eye to the wholesale import of youth culture content into the classroom but, rather, that greater scope should be given to aesthetic and personal expression in activity design. In arguing that there is a growing authenticity gap between the English that students learn in school and the English they use outside, I will begin the chapter by looking at the sorts of things young people in Sweden do in their free time.

English inside and outside of school

From having been essentially just a school subject only a couple of decades ago, English is now an integral part of the everyday lives of young people in Sweden, particularly those who are frequent Internet users and digital game players (Sundqvist & Sylvén, 2012). This shift in students' encounters with English has serious implications for teaching, not least in terms of motivation. In an alarming evaluation of the state of secondary school English teaching in Sweden, the Swedish Schools Inspectorate (2011) identify two entirely different cultures in which English is encountered – one in school and one out of school – with very few crossovers between the two. Echoing the view of Simensen (2010: 482), who contends that the currently 'most pressing question from an educational point of view is the discrepancy between the language pupils are exposed to in the media and society in general, and the language they meet in the educational system', the Schools Inspectorate concludes that building bridges between these two cultures is of the utmost importance.

The discrepancy between in- and out-of-school encounters with English has real effects on classroom motivation and is something teachers are increasingly confronting in their professional practice. In observations of nearly 300 lessons, as well as analyses of extensive interview and questionnaire data, the Swedish Schools Inspectorate (2011) found that, for some students, English lessons have little to offer in developing language competence and, instead, provide a welcome opportunity during the school day to relax and switch off. The nature of this disengagement is neatly summed up by one practising teacher's recent reflection on the motivational challenges she now encounters in her daily work:

> As a teacher, I often feel stunned by the miracle of learning; 12-year-old pupils arrive to lesson one in a French course with almost no prior knowledge of the language at all and then, after a few months, they are able to understand texts and to communicate with others to some extent. Sometimes I wonder how it happened. Since most pupils come across very little French outside of school, I conclude that the pupils learn the greatest part of the French they know at school and at home, doing homework.
>
> Teaching English is different since the pupils have studied the language for several years when I meet them, at the age of 13–16, and since they are surrounded by English outside of school, watching TV, listening to music or playing computer games, for instance. The miracle of learning that I experience when teaching English is of a different kind; sometimes I am amazed by the fluency and range of vocabulary some pupils demonstrate when they leave school at the age of 16. The two hours of English provided by school every week could hardly explain the level of some pupils' proficiency; it seems likely that they have also benefitted from contacts with the language outside of school. This group of pupils sometimes seems slightly bored at school; it is not always easy to create challenging English lessons on different levels at the same time. (Olsson, 2011: 1)

That students learn lots of English outside the classroom is by no means a new phenomenon. Ten years ago, in a national evaluation of Swedish secondary school education (National Agency for Education, 2004), more than 50 per cent of students reported that they learned as much if not more English outside of the classroom. At the same time, along with maths and Swedish, English was rated as one of the most important subjects in school. Students reported a pleasant classroom environment and, along with music, physical education, home economics and crafts, English was rated as one of the most enjoyable subjects. While the picture painted by the national evaluation is undoubtedly a positive one, there are perhaps early indications even here that students are beginning to take a rather relaxed approach to learning English in school. Its ranking in terms of interest and enjoyment alongside other less demanding and academically more peripheral subjects may be an indicator, as identified by Olsson (2011) and the Schools Inspectorate (2011), that students' growing confidence in their ability to learn English in their free time means that, most of the time, it is fine just to coast along in class.

So where might this rather laid-back approach to classroom work stem from? What sorts of things are students doing in their free time that lead them to believe they can learn more English outside school and can afford to sit back and take it easy in class?

It is quite apparent that in the last 10 years the types of things young people do in English have changed radically. Even though English-language interactive games such as *Sim City*, *Doom* and *Warcraft* have been around since the beginning of the 1990s, it was not until the mid-2000s with the increase of affordable PC ownership and high-speed Internet connections, and advances in graphic design in games such as *The Sims* (2000), *World of Warcraft* (2004) and *Counter-Strike* (1999), that gaming lost its 'nerdish' tag and became a mainstream activity for young people of both sexes. As we will see, digital gaming (both role-playing and casual gaming) is today the most common leisure-time activity among young people in Sweden.

Digital gaming

Quite a lot is known about the leisure-time activities of young people in Sweden. Since 2005 the National Media Council (*Mediarådet*) has regularly produced data on the population's media use. As the most recent report clearly shows, the biggest change in young people's leisure-time activities over the past five years has been the shift away from watching TV and DVDs, playing console-based offline digital games and hanging out with friends in real time, to online PC-based digital game playing and social networking via PCs and mobile phones. While social networking – via, for example, *Facebook* and MSN – takes place almost exclusively in Swedish, online and offline computer and console-based gaming is done entirely in English. Before looking at the types of digital games young people most commonly play, I will first look more closely at some of the trends in young people's media use and free-time activities in recent years (Swedish Media Council, 2005; 2006; 2010).

- In 2005 38 per cent of 9–16 year-olds had a computer in their bedroom. In 2010 this figure had increased to 61 per cent. This can be compared to TVs in bedrooms, which in both 2005 and 2010 was 55 per cent.
- Face-to-face after-school contact with friends has declined dramatically over the period. In 2006 74 per cent of 9–16 year-olds reported that this was a common activity. In 2008 this had decreased to 64 per cent, and in 2010 to just 58 per cent.
- Across the period, after-school Internet use has increased. In 2006 49 per cent reported Internet use as a common activity. In 2010 the corresponding figure had risen to 59 per cent.
- Watching TV and reading books have both decreased substantially in recent years. While in 2006 56 per cent of 9–16 year-olds reported watching TV as a common after-school activity, only 47 per cent did so in 2010. For reading books and magazines the number of students reporting it as a common after-school activity fell from 30 per cent in 2006 to just 19 per cent in 2010.
- In 2010 24 per cent of boys were frequent users (more than 3 hours per day) of computer/TV games; 24 per cent of girls were frequent users of mobile phones.
- The most common Internet activities reported in 2010 were watching film clips (72 per cent) and playing online games (64 per cent).
- Gender differences in all areas of media use have diminished over the period.

It is evident, then, that rapid changes have been taking place in young people's recreational habits and patterns of socialising. While the total amount of time spent in English-language environments might not have changed quantitatively (children and young people have been watching United States-produced TV programmes with Swedish subtitles and listening to English language music for years),[1] the sorts of things that they do in these environments has changed a lot. Today, digital gaming not only provides the greatest exposure to English, but also the most intense experiences. Digital gaming is not just a pleasant way to pass the time, like watching TV and DVDs. It offers more than this. Players interact intensively both with other players and the game itself. As critical linguist and professor of pedagogy James Paul Gee explains, when playing well-designed digital games 'players feel a real sense of agency, ownership, and control. It's *their* game' (Gee, 2008: 318).

The four most popular digital games played by young people aged 12–16 in Sweden, all of which are English-language mediated, are *Counter-Strike* (*CS*), which 18 per cent of young people report playing regularly; *World of Warcraft* (*WoW*), 13 per cent; *Call of Duty 2 – Modern Warfare* (*CoD*), 10 per cent; and *The Sims 3*, 7 per cent (Swedish Media Council 2010). In addition, 9 per cent of young people report playing generic so-called 'casual' online games. Each of the big four games has its own particular characteristics.

> *Counter-Strike* is an online FPS (First Person Shooter) game played either with opponents via the Internet or, commonly in Sweden, in specially designed local area networks at so-called 'LAN meets'. Players are assigned to two teams – one comprised of terrorists and the other of special forces – who fight against each other in a range of different environments.
>
> *Call of Duty* is another online FPS where the action takes place in either contemporary or WWII battlefield settings. Players control individual soldiers who, either alone or together with other players, carry out military operations.
>
> *World of Warcraft* is a Massively Multiplayer Online Role-Playing Game (MMORG) where thousands of players can be linked to a single server. Players belong to a guild and together combine specialist individual knowledge and skills to fight either against monsters in special dungeons or groups of other players.
>
> *The Sims* is a strategic relationship game in which players control the daily activities and social lives of one or more virtual characters. Unlike the other games there are no missions to be undertaken or points to be gained. Originally developed for PCs, *The Sims* games can now be played on game consoles or mobile phones.

Although a full analysis of these four games is beyond the scope of this chapter, it is important (particularly for non-game-players) to appreciate the intensity of the interaction that takes place when playing. All four games encourage, and often demand, cooperation, communication and user-generated input. Because players need to build up sophisticated repertoires of knowledge and skills, and because in games like *WoW* single players cannot advance in the game without the help of others, communication and cooperation are essential. In contemporary digital games interaction takes place not just with other players, but with the game itself, something that, using terms such as 'authorship', many researchers (e.g., Corliss, 2010; Gee, 2008) have emphasised. Analogous to the Web 2.0 concept of 'prosumerism' (online activity that involves both 'use' and 'production', see e.g., Goddard & Geesin, 2011; Thorne & Black, 2008), authorship refers to the unique input of individual players, and is a process that is highly creative and reflexive. Players inhabit and interact in worlds they themselves help to create. Like many other researchers, Corliss emphasises the creative experience of digital gaming:

> Through our interactions, we become part of the game, accumulating a degree of authorship always mediated by the constant evaluation of (reward or penalty for) our actions within the game world; these interactions are intensified by a distinct physicality through which we come to embody our digital play and our game learning. (Corliss, 2010: 7)

In a series of influential works in which he analyses the types of learning that take place when playing digital games, Gee (2003; 2008; 2009) explains how games develop deep feelings of agency. Amongst other things, good games, he argues, mean that players:

- co-design the game through their unique actions and decisions;
- are encouraged to take risks, to explore and to try out new ideas;
- have the opportunity to customise the game to suit their own playing and learning styles;
- become producers and not just consumers;
- learn to view the virtual world through the eyes and values of a distinctive identity that is constructed 'from the ground up' (Gee, 2008: 318).

Classroom English

As we have seen, a new type of student seems to have turned up in the English classroom in recent years. Surprisingly proficient in many aspects of English, particularly vocabulary (Sundqvist & Sylvén, 2012), but also in processing written information and sometimes also in oral production and interaction, these students do not seem to feel the need to overexert themselves in class (Swedish Schools Inspectorate, 2011). What sort of classroom environment, though, do these students meet? Has there been much change in teaching approach over the same period? The answer, as we might expect, is probably very little. Even though teachers in Sweden have extremely wide discretion in terms of the choice of content, working approaches and assessment methods, they are nevertheless heavily reliant on textbooks (Swedish Schools Inspectorate, 2011), with three out of four English teachers using commercially produced textbooks in essentially every lesson (National Agency for Education, 2006). Indeed, compared to teachers of other subjects, English teachers use textbooks to a greater extent and generally tend to use a single book around which they base their teaching (National Agency for Education, 2006). While, like other subjects, individual project-type work has become common in recent years, in the 2011 curriculum a return to more teacher-led classroom instruction was clearly signalled. It is therefore no exaggeration to say that, compared to the radical transformations that have recently been taking place in young people's free-time activities, it has been pretty much business as usual in the English classroom. Practices that a decade or so ago captured students' attention – when English outside the classroom was encountered mostly via music, film and youth- as opposed to adult-oriented TV programmes (such as the currently popular *Family Guy, Desperate Housewives* and *2½ Men*) – may not work as well now. A decade ago many of the most highly proficient students probably owed their abilities to hard work in the classroom. Now, this may not necessarily be the case. For students who spend hours in digitally mediated English-language environments outside of school and, moreover, are aware that this is where they gain much of their skills, the English of today's classrooms may by comparison seem less meaningful. Less 'real'. A credibility problem seems to be emerging. There would appear to be an authenticity gap between the two different worlds.

How, then, should we as educators understand and address the emergent phenomenon of a gap between English in school that is still primarily taught as a foreign language (i.e., where textbooks dominate and the focus is on the acquisition of vocabulary, production, reception and, of course, grammar), and the English that outside of school forms the self-evident medium for some of the most personally meaningful activities in which young people currently engage? What does this mean for us as teachers, and what consequences does this have for the way we design lessons? In the remainder of the chapter I will address these questions, arguing that in many classrooms students will rarely have the opportunity to engage in the types of self-congruent activities and forms of learning that are characteristic of the digitally mediated environments they inhabit outside of school. I will begin, however, by briefly looking at authenticity in the sense that it is traditionally understood in language education.

Addressing the authenticity gap

That language classrooms poorly replicate patterns of interaction in real life has long been recognised. Framed in terms of authenticity, academic debate on the problem of the artificiality of classroom language use has largely centred on language production, tasks, assessment and, most commonly, the content of learning materials. Although very little research has been carried out, Gilmore (2007) points to a widespread belief among researchers and teachers alike that authentic learning materials have a positive effect on students' motivation. Justifications offered include the idea that authentic materials are inherently more interesting because they are 'real' and have a 'real' message to convey, that authentic materials can be selected to meet students' specific needs and that motivation is enhanced when students realise they can actually cope with 'real' texts. In studies that have been undertaken, results have, however, been inconclusive, leading Gilmore (2007) to conclude that there is very little empirical evidence in support of the claim that authentic learning materials have a positive effect on motivation.

Even if we were to accept the idea that authentic texts – and, for that matter, authentic tasks and authentic forms of assessment – have positive effects on motivation, it is questionable, as a single strategy, whether a greater emphasis on authentic materials is likely to make any inroads into students' perceptions of a credibility gap between leisure time and classroom English. As a means of addressing this developing problem, the time may have come to start thinking beyond the motivational effects attributed to the authenticity of artefacts (texts, learning materials and tests), and instead consider how perceptions of authenticity in engaging with the language might impact on motivation. By broadening the focus in this way it may become possible to better understand why it is that students who spend hours engrossed in English-mediated activities outside of the classroom – and who are convinced that such practices form important sites for their learning – seem happy to disengage from classroom activities.

Authenticity as motivation

As a result of Dörnyei's (2005; 2009) recent work on the motivational function of future self-guides, the driving force behind the effort needed to learn a foreign language is today understood in terms of the learner's identification of her-/himself as a future user/speaker of the target language. Pioneering in the true sense of the word, Dörnyei's research has offered new ways of thinking about language learning behaviours and opened up new vistas of enquiry. In particular, by reconceptualising motivation as a consequence of self-related processes, Dörnyei has made it possible for L2 researchers to draw on a wealth of theoretical and empirical research from mainstream psychology, thus making it possible, as MacIntyre et al. (2009: 50) put it, 'to map out new conceptual linkages by taking the self as the starting point'. One area that could be usefully explored using a self-based approach is the issue of authenticity – not in its artefact/textual sense, but in the sense of engaging with the language. Let me explain what I mean.

From an 'artefact' perspective, authenticity can be regarded as an evaluative description of the extent to which we perceive something to be real or genuine. Something authentic is what it purports to be: the real deal. Just as authenticity can be used as an evaluation of an object, that is, an authentic text, an authentic Ming Dynasty vase or an authentic Donna Karan shirt, so too can it be used in the evaluation of the self or, more precisely, the evaluation of the self at a particular moment in time and engaged in a particular type of activity. In both situations we are making an appraisal. When we consider the authenticity of an artefact, the judgment we make would appear to be fairly clear-cut – it either is or is not a Donna Karan shirt. This we do on the basis of not only the evidence at hand – that is, the cut, the material, the stitching and, importantly, the label and the tags – but also in relation to an implied referent, that is, a similar shirt that would be hanging on a rail in the Donna Karan shop on Madison Avenue. When considering possible courses of action or when evaluating our engagement in ongoing actions, we make similar assessments. We base our appraisal on emergent evidence – that is, what we are doing, why we are doing it and for what purpose – which we then compare with an implied referent. In such situations, the referent we use to judge the authenticity of our actions is the collection of core conceptions that we hold about ourselves and which define who we are. Thus, when we evaluate current courses of action, what we are doing is asking 'is this me?' (Gecas, 1991; Vannini, 2006). This, as Vannini and Burgess (2009: 104) explain, involves a contextual appraisal of our authenticity:

> [T]he indicator of realness or authenticity is the degree of congruence between one's actions and one's core self-conceptions – consisting of fundamental values, beliefs, and identities to which one is committed and in terms of which one defines oneself. When actions are congruent with core self-conceptions, one's self is affirmed and one experiences authenticity; when one's actions do not reflect or affirm one's core self, one feels inauthentic. This is not to deny that people do not rationalize self-incongruent behaviors or find ways of accounting for such conduct. Rather, our claim is intended to suggest that when actions are defined to be congruent with one's values one will feel affirmed and thus authentic.

From a psychological perspective, then, authenticity is the experience of being true to one's self in doing something that fits with who we feel we are, and which coheres with our own particular view of the world. In this sense experiences of authenticity are linked to other emotions and sensations, such as pleasure, satisfaction, contentedness and self-esteem. And, just as with other affective dimensions of motivation, we will be encouraged to do something if we believe that the activity is authentic and involves things that cohere or are congruent with our sense of self – see also Noels' (2009) recent discussion of authenticity from an Self-Determination Theory (SDT) perspective.

The polar opposite of authenticity is inauthenticity, which people struggle to avoid because it involves negative feelings of self-contempt and meaninglessness (Gecas, 1991). However, because inauthenticity implies engagement in senseless, meaningless activities, it is a self-state rarely encountered. Much more commonly, as Vannini and Burgess (2009) explain, people experience a sense of what they call *frustrated authenticity*. This arises when the individual feels unable to act in congruence with her/his self-values and, as a consequence, feels frustrated, agitated, dissatisfied and unfulfilled. Not surprisingly, such feelings have a negative impact on the willpower and determination to pursue the activity in question.

To be sure, many language students will have, among their set of core ideas and self-concepts, conceptions of themselves as someone who, for example, is responsible, goal-oriented and conscientious. And these types of self-conception will, of course, generate motivated classroom behaviours. But this is not the type of self-congruent behaviour that, according to Vannini and Burgess (2009), generates feelings of authenticity. This is because authenticity encompasses an additional element; an aesthetic dimension. Referring to the work of Fine (1996), who suggests that feelings of being authentic in carrying out working tasks are closely related to the aesthetic evaluation of the things that are produced, Vannini and Burgess argue that that authenticity is experienced not just in any type of self-congruent behaviour but, specifically, by engagement in activities from which aesthetic pleasure is derived.

If we now return to considering the way in which young people in Sweden encounter English outside and inside school, the concept of authenticity – and in particular Vannini and Burgess' identification of the importance of the aesthetic evaluation of the products of creative processes – seems to form a useful lens through which to consider differential engagement in English-medium activities.

In the creative activities involved in playing the most popular digital games in Sweden (*WoW, CS, CoD* and *The Sims*), pleasure and satisfaction are derived not simply from the sense of achievement (for example, in taking out bad guys and destroying evil monsters), but also in the aesthetics of the game in creating/customising appealing avatars and developing sophisticated strategies. It is in this way that players can achieve a sense of congruence between core values (who I am) and current activities (what I am doing). The self is affirmed, the individual feels authentic and is motivated to continue with current and similar activities.

But, of course, playing online or offline digital games is not the only arena in which English functions as a creative medium in young people's lives. In the activities of the English classroom, steered by a curricular focus on communicative competence, students are required to be creative in their use of language when writing essays and book summaries, giving oral presentations, or participating in group discussions. However, these types of creative process differ in the emotional resonance they have for the participants, and herein, I suggest, lies one of the causes of the authenticity gap. Quite simply, productive language use in the classroom is unlikely to match the more deeply meaningful and self-relevant experiences that young people gain in online environments. In particular, two important factors are often lacking; the value placed on individual creativity and on the desire for satisfaction with outcomes and end results.

Here, it is important to point out that the research carried out by Vannini and Burgess (2009) was not with young computer gamers but with an entirely different group of participants: middle-aged university academics. Although, at first glance, playing multiplayer online role-playing games such as *World of Warcraft* and *Counter-Strike* and doing scientific research might seem worlds apart, they have much in common. Both involve immersion in highly complex contexts. Both demand sophisticated problem-solving skills. Both require dedication and perseverance over long periods of time. Both presuppose an ability to collaborate with others. Both reward innovation and creativity and, most importantly, both activities are highly aesthetic practices that provide participants with 'peak' experiences of self–world fusion.

Turning to look more closely at Vannini and Burgess' (2009) findings, two specific motivational factors seem to emerge: the value of creativity and the desire to achieve end-product satisfaction. When invited to consider the motivational factors in their work, the researchers interviewed talked about, for example, 'the excitement of doing something new and creative' and 'the creative process and the beauty in the realised form as its ultimate expression'. They also highlighted the 'satisfying success of solving a difficult problem after months or years of work' and the pleasure gained in 'arriving at results and figuring things out' (Vannini & Burgess, 2009: 110–11). Explaining how specific motivational experiences gained in one context can impact on motivation in others, Vannini and Burgess make the following important observation:

> To suggest that the aesthetic pleasure associated with creation, innovation, and discovery is a motivator is not the same as arguing that these are needs or forces that drive all individuals, always and in all occasions. Rather, we are simply suggesting that the meaningfulness of aesthetically appreciating one's work is significant enough and valuable enough to *orient one toward seeking similar experiences*. (111) [my emphasis].

This, as I see it, seems to encapsulate not only the essence of the relationship between authenticity and motivated behaviour, but also the sense that there might be a gap between different types of activity. Just as the university teachers did not view all of their work in the same way – research and administrative tasks did not provide anything like the same levels of aesthetic appreciation – so might it be the case that students' experiences of their use of English differ between the domains of digital gaming and school. Thus, it is not the case that materials used, nor for that matter communicative activities in classroom English, lack authenticity. Nor is authenticity lacking because interlocutors are imaginary or topics of discussion lacking in salience. Rather, the authenticity gap may result more from an *orientation to seek similar experiences* to those gained in digital gaming and in a search for similar types of self-congruent aesthetic experience.

Vannini and Burgess' idea that people involved in aesthetically creative activities orient toward seeking similar experiences in others is an intriguing one and resonates well with another discontinuity, namely Gee's (Gee, 2005; Hayes & Gee, 2010) identification of a gap between the sorts of learning processes implicated in digital game playing and the learning processes that take place in school. Approaching the authenticity gap from a different angle, I will now take a closer look at Gee's ideas and, in particular, his concept of the affinity space.

Affinity spaces and authenticity

In his recent research, Gee (2005) has developed the notion of the affinity space as an alternative to Lave and Wenger's well-known concept of 'communities of practice' (Lave, 1996; Lave & Wenger, 1991; Wenger, 1998). As opposed to a focus on the *membership* of a community, Gee instead chooses to focus on the *spaces* in which people interact. In his critique, Gee's point is that people relate to, and form an affiliation with, the activity taking place within a particular space and not, in Lave and Wenger's terms, with the other members of a community (Gee, 2005).

So what is an affinity space? What does it look like? Although a comprehensive discussion of the characteristics of affinity spaces lies beyond the scope of this chapter (interested readers are referred to Gee, 2005), of the 11 features Gee identifies, it is important in the context of the current discussion to highlight the generative use of knowledge and the sharing of resources. Characteristic of an affinity space is the ability for people to generate knowledge for particular purposes, which can be used either by themselves or by others (Hayes & Gee, 2010). Knowledge is, therefore, not an exclusive accomplishment, commodity or preserve. Rather, it is something generated in interaction with others and shared, both directly and indirectly, with other individuals.

Although in developing the idea of affinity spaces Gee draws on his analyses of real-time strategy computer games such as *Age of Mythology* (Gee, 2005; Hayes & Gee, 2010) and the anime card game *Yu-Gi-Oh* (Gee, 2005), his project extends beyond gaming and online environments. In his work, Gee is always interested in the juxtaposition of informal and formal learning and the characteristics of the environments in which they take place. In particular his aim is to focus on differences in knowledge-generation processes in schools and contemporary popular culture (Hayes & Gee, 2010). Thus, in his work the affinity space functions as a counterpoint against which classroom practices can be critically examined.

One of the most important differences between learning practices in school and the types of learning that take place in affinity spaces concerns opportunities for personal expression and creativity. As Gee explains, school environments tend not to encourage students to be innovative, imaginative and creative, nor do they reward the types of personal expression and 'thinking out of the box' commonly valued in affinity spaces:

> Young people today are confronted with and enter more and more affinity spaces. They see a different and arguably powerful vision of learning, affiliation, and identity when they do so. Learning becomes both a personal and unique trajectory through a complex space of opportunities (i.e., a person's own unique movement through various affinity spaces over time) and a social journey as one shares aspects of that trajectory with others (who may be very different from oneself and inhabit otherwise quite different spaces) for a shorter or longer time before moving on. What these young people see in school may pale by comparison. It may seem to lack the imagination that infuses the non-school aspects of their lives. (Gee, 2005: 231)

Thinking back to the previous discussion on authenticity, Gee's point about the differing role of imagination in schools and affinity spaces would seem to resonate rather well with Vannini and Burgess' notion of a frustrated authenticity. In the same way that the highly regulated learning environments of school can limit opportunities for aesthetic creativity, opportunities for students to be imaginative and pursue 'a personal and unique trajectory' are similarly restricted. But there is another and, motivationally speaking, even more important similarity. Gee explains that rather than being oblivious to, or uninterested in, the differing experiences and differences in learning processes characteristic of most classrooms and most affinity spaces, young people are fully attuned to such types of discontinuity. In particular, he makes the point that because 'many young people today have lots of experience with affinity spaces [they] thus have the opportunity to compare and contrast their experiences with these to their experiences in classrooms' (Gee, 2005: 222).

To my mind it is the sense in which students are likely to cross-reference experiences in leisure time and classroom domains highlighted by both Gee and Vaninni and Burgess that, as teachers, we either fail to consider or we conveniently overlook. It is also the reason why both self-authenticity and affinity space theory seem to have particular relevance for English teaching. For students who regularly play digital games, English is much more than just a communicative medium. Everything – from studying online manuals to communication with other players – takes place in English. English is a non-dissociable part of the experience. Thus, when they make comparisons between the communicative activities in the English classroom and the intense and meaningful experiences gained in interacting with other players and game architectures, it may not be surprising that feelings of frustrated authenticity – in the sense of lacking the scope to use the language in the same meaningful and self-relevant ways that it is used in gaming environments – may arise. Full engagement in an activity that lacks the vitality of things done in English in virtual worlds may, thus, become difficult to sustain.

Implications?

Before looking at some of the implications that digital gaming might have on classroom motivation, let me first clarify a couple of points. In developing these ideas, I have focused on a particular type of game: online, real-time, multiplayer role-playing games. Although, as we have seen, large numbers of young people in Sweden play such games – and some of them play them a lot – this is not a universal leisure-time activity. While other forms of English-mediated popular culture certainly involve aesthetic dimensions akin to those envisaged by Vannini and Burgess and have some of the characteristics of Gee's notion of affinity spaces, I am not making any explicit claims in respect of these activities; my focus here is on digital gaming.

It is also important to make clear that, in drawing parallels with self-authenticity and affinity space theory, I am not suggesting that the phenomena these theories describe or the processes they anticipate are the same. Rather, my argument is that both provide useful lenses through which, as teachers of English, we can try to better understand the experiences that many of our students have outside the classroom and the ways in which these experiences lead them to make comparisons with what they learn in school.

So, if these theories can help us understand what young people might see as an authenticity gap between English in school and English outside, what are the implications for classroom teaching? And are there any pointers as to what we can do to increase classroom motivation? I think that there are. However, before outlining some ideas, I want to sound a cautionary note. While I have argued that students are likely to make comparisons between the things they do in English in their leisure time and what they do in school, and that, as Hayes and Gee (2010) have argued, current popular culture constitutes a form of competition for schools and education, the direct import of popular culture into the classroom may bring problems of its own.

As we have seen in the earlier discussion on authenticity, there is a fairly widespread belief among language educators that students respond better to 'real' texts, and many teachers and textbook writers – quite rightly – take young people's interests as a self-evident starting point in instructional design. There is, however, a risk attached in saturating classrooms with the forms of popular culture students are accustomed to in their leisure time. First – as, for example, technology-enhanced learning researcher Mike Sharples has pointed out – students do not, generally speaking, want school to intrude too far into their personal lives. Thus, attempts by teachers to colonise young people's social worlds by, for example, bringing the technologies of social networking into the classroom, may be met with resistance. Consequently, as Sharples explains, there is a need to be clear about 'where the bounds of school lie and where it is not legitimate for formal education to intrude on childhood' (Sharples, 2006: 22).

A similar point is made by the German youth sociologist, Thomas Ziehe (2000). Ziehe's argument is that it is important for young people to maintain identity boundaries between who they are in school, and who they are outside. It is not the place of school, he argues, to encroach on the other life spaces students occupy outside of school. Moreover, Ziehe argues that school has an important role to play in enabling young people to develop differentiated identities which, he believes, are necessary when orientating through the complexity of modern life:

> To be a student is just one dimension of a young lifeform. School cannot possibly embrace the whole range of possible admissions to experience and knowledge any more. And school has a valid priority only when it concerns the young person as *student*, which is just *part of the perspective*. I believe that the distinction between school/young people will and should remain. But still school should *work to build bridges*. (Ziehe, 2000: 60) [emphasis in the original].

In addressing binaries such as school/free time and formal/informal learning, educational theorists have viewed the intersections between them as particularly fruitful areas for developing knowledge and skills. Not surprisingly, structuring metaphors such as 'bridge building' abound in the literature. For example, as a means of forging links between the formal/analytical activities of school and the informal/experiential activities of leisure time, theorists talk in terms of drawing on differing 'funds of knowledge' (Moll et al., 1992), creating 'third spaces' (Bhabha, 1994; Gutiérrez, 2008) and, in an L2 context, developing 'bridging activities' (Thorne & Reinhardt, 2008).

From the range of different theories and approaches based on the idea of making connections between different learning/knowledge domains, I have chosen to consider a number of propositions made by Elizabeth Moje and her colleagues (Moje, 2006; Moje & Hinchman, 2004). One of the reasons for doing this is that Moje, a literacy researcher, takes specific account of motivation in her handling of third-space pedagogies. Another is that, in extrapolating ideas from third-space and literacy development theory to the particular settings of English-language classrooms, Moje's propositions for what she and Hinchman call 'responsive teaching' (Moje & Hinchman, 2004) seem particularly interesting.

Responsive teaching involves the recognition that students' experiences are a necessary part of the processes of knowledge acquisition. However, rather than a 'now and then' filtering of young people's experiences into the classroom, in responsive teaching cross-referencing is systematic:

> This perspective on culturally responsive pedagogy argues that it is not enough to bring cultural experiences into classrooms as a way of helping students to connect more effectively to new ideas or as a way of engaging and motivating students, despite the fact that these are important aspects of culturally responsive pedagogy. Instead, this perspective wants to make a permanent space in the classrooms and schools for knowledges and Discourses that have been traditionally marginalized. (Moje & Hinchman, 2004: 326)

In advocating a 'responsive teaching' approach that can build bridges and create spaces in between school knowledge and ways of knowing that are not normally valued in school, Moje and Hinchman argue that teachers often view the young people they work with in rather reductive terms on the basis, for example, of their ethnic and/or socio-economic backgrounds. Responsive teaching, they explain, means moving beyond basic positional categories and, instead, branching out and attempting to incorporate the different social practices that each young person individually engages in into the teacher's overall understanding of the student. This means being aware of the broad spectrum of knowledges and different ways of knowing that are characteristic of young peoples' home environments, their social and ethnic communities and, most importantly, the popular cultural practices they engage in. Thus, in responsive teaching, not only is there a recognition of different types of knowledge and different types of practice, but also of different identities. Responsive teaching, therefore, means merging 'the needs and interests of youth as persons with the needs and interests of youth as learners of new concepts, practices and skills' (Moje & Hinchman, 2004: 322). Using responsive teaching as a blueprint, and by combining the need for intersubjective relationships identified by Moje and Hinchamn (2004), the motivational importance of self-congruent aesthetic creativity explained by Vannini and Burgess (2009) and the learning potential of affinity spaces described by Gee (2005; 2008), Hayes and Gee (2010), I will now make some suggestions for the development of a pedagogy that, in drawing on students' out-of-school experiences, can enhance classroom motivation.

The first step: a better understanding of young people's cultural experiences

One of the problems facing teachers is developing a better understanding of youth cultural practices. While we usually have a good idea about the *types* of things our students do in their free time – digital gaming, playing team sports, interacting with friends on social networking sites – often we know very little about *what* this involves. Unless we ourselves or people in our immediate social environment have similar free-time interests, we are left to media reports, second-hand information and our own speculation as to what our students actually are up to. As language teachers it is important that we inform ourselves about the things that our students are doing in their free time that involve the use of English. If, as an initial step, we are able to gain greater insights into the activities and language use associated, for example, with playing MMORGs, we will be better attuned to opportunities to bridge between school and free-time English.

There is however another reason why the lack of a nuanced and in-depth knowledge about the types of things our students do can be problematic. As Moje and Hinchman (2004) explain, lack of insider knowledge can mean that we devalue youth cultural experiences, particularly those different from our own. In the case of English there is a particular risk that the type of communicative competence we aim at in teaching can function in a way that puts the informal and highly adapted forms of language used, for example, in digital gaming, on an unequal footing. However, by explicitly recognising the value of non-standard language forms and adopting an inclusive approach to different types of language use, we avoid the risk of appearing to stand exclusively for one particular form of English – school or 'proper' English – which, moreover, is a form pupils rarely encounter outside the classroom. Indeed, if as teachers we expect students to be able to navigate between different types of English that are appropriate in different domains, should not we also be able to do so?

Linking youth culture experiences to target concepts

While there is, of course, a limit to the knowledge we can reasonably be expected to possess about our individual students' free-time activities, an understanding of common, yet for many of us culturally distant, practices is essential in making specific links between target concepts and English-medium activities outside school. As Moje and Hinchman (2004) explain, pulling as many cultural experiences into the classroom as possible may not be particularly effective (cf., Sharples, 2006; Ziehe, 2000 above). Even though students might become temporarily very engaged in a particular activity, it is often difficult for them to make connections between out-of-school experiences and the learning objects that are in focus. For deep content learning to take place, the experiences drawn upon need to be *relevant* to the target concepts (Moje & Hinchman, 2004: 342).

So, what might this idea mean for the classroom teaching of English? I will try and give some examples. In introducing new vocabulary, the rich virtual worlds of digital games could be used to provide contexts in which new words can be situated and described in terms of references to characters, landscapes, activities, processes and so on. Similarly, in written production, different types of composition – for example argumentative, descriptive, contrastive and narrative texts – can be effectively scrutinised and practised using examples from the complex worlds of digital gaming. For instance, important concepts in written communication, such as different forms of text coherence, could be exemplified by looking at good and bad examples found in online strategy manuals.

Placing a greater focus on creativity and personal expression

As we have seen, digital gaming rewards resourcefulness, intuition and imagination. When playing good digital games there is always a demanding yet ultimately achievable challenge. And, in more sophisticated games such as *World of Warcraft* and *The Sims*, great value is placed on authorship and aesthetic creation. The sense of being engaged in a self-congruent activity – playing 'my game', doing something that 'is me' – creates the sort of motivated behaviour rarely encountered in schools (Gee, 2005). While it would be naïve to imagine that classroom teaching, no matter how innovative, meaningful or 'authentic' it might be, could replicate such levels of engagement over sustained periods, a greater focus on creative activities involving personal expression, such as creative writing and role-playing may be important. This is a point Ushioda (2011: 206) also emphasises, arguing that the more teachers are able to create opportunities for students 'to engage and express their own preferred meanings, interests and voices', the more likely effort will be invested in learning.

Similarly, innovation and creative thinking need to be properly recognised and more fully rewarded. As Gee (2003) explains, risk-taking and experimentation are fundamental in digital gaming. Thus, it may be important that in designing classroom activities we explicitly encourage students to test boundaries and to use the language in creative ways. Greater scope for creativity in individually chosen or individually moulded activities such as personalised blog and Wiki compositions may also enhance feelings of self-congruence and authenticity.

Developing networks with affinity space features

In his critique of contemporary classroom practice, Gee (2005) makes the point that, compared to affinity spaces, classrooms reward individual rather than collective achievement, favour individual rather than distributed knowledge, and rarely provide students with opportunities for networking with each other. Given that students' primary use of English is in network environments, this is an area that teachers can and should develop as an important part of their methodology. Setting up student discussion or working groups on the Internet or on the school's intranet, with the teacher as a participant, could be a particularly fruitful initiative. This type of initiative would resonate well with the so-called 'Dogme' approach to communication in which authentic learner-driven conversational interaction between teachers and students is regarded as crucial in developing language skills (Ushioda, 2011). In such environments groups of students could work with either teacher-generated or self-generated problem-solving tasks or cases. Having many affinity space characteristics – such as collaborative working – which students recognise from free-time online activities, students' voices and identities can emerge in student–student and student–teacher interactions in ways that can feel authentic, meaningful and self-congruent.

Conclusion

In this chapter I have argued that in countries like Sweden classroom motivation may be negatively affected by students' perceptions that, compared to personally more meaningful leisure-time activities such as digital gaming, working with English in school can create a sense of frustrated authenticity. Because students are likely to compare in- and out-of-school learning experiences, teachers of English would profit from a better understanding of young people's leisure-time activities. This would enable links to be made between target concepts and culturally situated experiences. Further, because as individuals we orient towards activities that provide us with feelings of self-congruence and authenticity, I have suggested that, when designing instruction, teachers need to provide students with greater opportunities for creativity and meaningful self-expression.

Engagement priorities

Although the in-school-English/out-of-school-English dissonance highlighted in this chapter may not be a universal phenomenon (although see also Taylor, Chapter 3, and Ushioda, Chapter 13, in this volume), the issues raised concerning the extent to which classroom educators should draw on students' experiences of language use outside the classroom are nevertheless likely to be relevant for teachers of most age groups in most contexts. For teachers of English, the ability to critically engage with students' free-time English-language activities, and to know how and when to incorporate aspects of out-of-class English in everyday instruction, are skills that are likely to become of increasing importance. The following are just some of the many issues teachers need to address:

1. To what extent, if at all, might there be a gap between in- and out-of-school English in the part of the world where you live and work? How do you see future trends? How do you see the future development of in-school/out-of-school discrepancies in exposure to, and use of, English?
2. Might there be other ways of addressing the gap between school and free-time English than those suggested here?
3. Is it always necessary to try to bridge between the different domains of English use/exposure when teaching? What about the case of students who are academically motivated? What about students who have little contact with English in their free time?
4. In what sense might the gap suggested here be a gendered phenomenon? Might, for example, 'frustrated authenticity' be more of a problem for boys?
5. As discussed in the chapter, commentators such as Ziehe (2000) argue that there should be clear dividing lines between school and free time, and that it is not the place of education to colonise leisure-time domains (see also Stockwell, Chapter 9, in this volume). Do you agree? By extension, is there not a case for arguing that there should be a clear distinction between the English that is learnt in school and that acquired outside?

Note

1. In 2010 the most popular TV programme for children and young people aged 9–16 was *The Simpsons. Family Guy* and *2½ Men* were popular among boys, while *Desperate Housewives* was the most popular programme for girls aged 12–16. *Hanna Montana* was the most popular programme for girls aged 9–12. All of these programmes, with the exception of *Hanna Montana*, which is dubbed, are English language with Swedish subtitles.

Suggested further reading

Gee, J. P. and Hayes, E. (2010). *Women as Gamers: The Sims and 21st Century Learning.* New York: Palgrave/Macmillan.

In this recent publication, James Paul Gee and Elizabeth Hayes continue their work on the ways in which digital games stimulate deep learning, here based on a series of case studies of women who play *The Sims.*

Readers interested in Gee's work on learning are recommended to visit his website – *jamespaulgee.com* – where many of his extremely accessible and thought-provoking publications are freely available to download. In addition to the publications listed in the references section below, his article 'Getting over the slump: Innovation strategies to promote children's learning', although aimed at L1 teachers, also makes very worthwhile reading for teachers of English as a second language.

References

Bhabha, H. K. (1994). *The Location of Culture*. London: Routledge.

Corliss, J. (2010). The social science of digital games. *Games and Culture*, 6(3): 3–16.

Dörnyei, Z. (2005). *The Psychology of the Language Learner*. Mahwah, NJ: Lawrence Erlbaum.

Dörnyei, Z. (2009). *The Psychology of Second Language Acquisition*. Oxford: Oxford University Press.

Fine, G. (1996). *Kitchens: The Cultures of Restaurant Work*. Berkley: University of California Press.

Gecas, V. (1991). The self-concept as a basis for a theory of motivation. In J. Howard and P. Callero (eds) *The Self-Society Dynamic: Cognition, Emotion and Action*. Cambridge: Cambridge University Press, pp. 171–88.

Gee, J. P. (2003). *What Digital Games Have to Teach us about Learning and Literacy*. New York: Palgrave Macmillan.

Gee, J. P. (2005). Affinity spaces: from 'Age of Mythology' to today's schools. In D. Barton and K. Tusting (eds) *Beyond Communities of Practice: Language, Power and Social Context*. New York: Cambridge University Press, pp. 214–32.

Gee, J. P. (2008). Game-like learning: an example of situated learning and implications for opportunity to learn. In P. A. Moss, D. C. Pullin, J. P. Gee, E. H. Haertel, and L. J. Young (eds) *Assessment, Equity, and Opportunity to Learn*. New York: Cambridge University Press, pp. 200–21

Gee, J. P. (2009). Literacy, digital games, and popular culture. In D. Olson and N. Torrance (eds) *The Cambridge Handbook of Literacy*. New York: Cambridge University Press, pp. 313–25.

Gilmore, A. (2007). Authentic materials and authenticity in foreign language learning. *Language Teaching*, 40: 97–118.

Goddard, A. and Geesin, B. (2011). *Language and Technology*. Milton Park: Routledge.

Gutiérrez, K. (2008). Developing a sociocultural literacy in the third space. *Reading Research Quarterly*, 43(2): 148–64.

Hayes, E. R. and Gee, J. P. (2010). Popular culture as a public pedagogy: design, resources and affinity spaces. In A. Sandlin, B. Schultz, and J. Burdick (eds) *Handbook of Public Pedagogy*. New York: Routledge, pp. 185–93.

Lave, J. (1996). Teaching, as learning, in practice. *Mind, Culture and Activity*, 3(3): 149–64.

Lave, J. and Wenger, E. (1991). *Situated Learning: Legitimate Peripheral Participation*. Cambridge: Cambridge University Press.

MacIntyre, P. D., Mackinnon, S. P. and Clément, R. (2009). The baby, the bathwater, and the future of language learning motivation research. In Z. Dörnyei and E. Ushioda (eds) *Motivation, Language Identity and the L2 Self*. Bristol: Multilingual Matters, pp. 43–65.

Moje, E. (2006). Motivating texts, motivating contexts, motivating adolescents: an examination of the role of motivation in adolescent literacy practices and development. *Perspectives* 32(3): 10–14.

Moje, E. and Hinchman, K. (2004). Culturally responsive practices for youth literacy learning. In T. L. Jetton and J. A. Dole (eds) *Adolescent Literacy Research and Practice*. New York: Guilford, pp. 321–50.

Moll, L. C., Amanti, C, Neff, D. and Gonzalez, N. (1992). Funds of knowledge for teaching: using a qualitative approach to connect homes and classrooms. *Theory into Practice*, 31(2): 132–41.

National Agency for Education. (2004). *Nationell Utvärdering av Grundskolan 2003* (National evaluation of compulsory school in 2003). Stockholm: Skolverket.

National Agency for Education. (2006). *Läromedlens Roll i Undervisning* (The role of learning materials in teaching). Stockholm: Skolverket.

Noels, K. (2009). The internalisation of language learning into the self and social identity. In Z. Dörnyei and E. Ushioda (eds) *Motivation, Language Identity and the L2 Self*. Bristol: Multilingual Matters, pp. 295–313.

Olsson, E. (2011). *'Everything I Read on the Internet is in English': On the Impact of Extramural English on Swedish 16-Year-Old Pupils Writing Proficiency*. Licenciate thesis, Faculty of Humanities, University of Gothenburg.

Sharples, M. (2006). How can we address the conflicts between personal informal learning and traditional classroom education? In M. Sharples (ed.) *Big Issues in Mobile Learning*. Nottingham: Nottingham University, pp. 21–4.

Simensen, A. M. (2010). English in Scandinavia: a success story. In D. Wyse, R. Andrews and J. Hoffman (eds) *The Routledge International Handbook of English, Language and Literacy Teaching*. Milton Park: Routledge, pp. 472–83.

Sundqvist, P and Sylvén, L. S. (2012). World of VocCraft: computer games and Swedish learners' L2 vocabulary. In H. Reinders (ed.) *Digital Games in Language Learning and Teaching*. Basingstoke: Palgrave Macmillan, pp. 189–208.

Swedish Media Council (2005). *Ungar Och Mediar 2005: Fakta Om Barns Och Ungas Användning Och Upplevelser av Medier* (Young people and the media 2005: facts on children and young people's media use and experiences). Stockholm: Regeringskansliet.

Swedish Media Council (2006). *Ungar Och Mediar 2006: Fakta Om Barns Och Ungas Användning Och Upplevelser av Medier* (Young people and the media 2006: facts on children and young people's media use and experiences). Stockholm: Regeringskansliet.

Swedish Media Council (2010). *Ungar Och Mediar 2010: Fakta Om Barns Och Ungas Användning Och Upplevelser av Medier* (Young people and the media 2010: facts on children and young people's media use and experiences). Stockholm: Regeringskansliet.

Swedish Schools Inspectorate. (2011). *Engelska i Grundskolans Årskurser 6–9 Kvalitetsgranskning* (A quality assessment of English in secondary school grades 6–9). Report 2011:7. Stockholm: The Swedish Schools Inspectorate.

Thorne, S. L. and Black, R. (2008). Language and literacy development in computer-mediated contexts and communities. *Annual Review of Applied Linguistics*, 27: 133–60.

Thorne, S. L. and Reinhardt, J. (2008). 'Bridging activities', new media literacies, and advanced foreign language proficiency. *CALICO Journal*, 25(3): 558–72.

Ushioda, E. (2011). Language learning motivation, self and identity: current theoretical perspectives. *Computer Assisted Language Learning*, 24(3): 199–210.

Vannini, P. (2006). Dead Poets' Society: teaching, publish-or-perish, and professors' experiences of authenticity. *Symbolic Interaction*, 4: 1–20.

Vannini, P. and Burgess, S. (2009). Authenticity as motivation and aesthetic experience. In P. Vannini and J. P. Williams (eds) *Authenticity in Culture, Self and Society*. Farnham: Ashgate Publishing Ltd, pp. 103–20.

Wenger, E. (1998). *Communities of Practice: Learning, Meaning and Identity*. Cambridge: Cambridge University Press.

Ziehe, T. (2000). School and youth: differential relation. Reflections on some blank areas in the current reform discussions. *Young*, 8: 54–63.

9
Technology and Motivation in English-Language Teaching and Learning

Glenn Stockwell

Introduction

Advances in technology have made it easier for teachers and learners of English to access a wide range of resources in terms of authentic input and communication with native and non-native speakers of English around the world. From the early days of computer-assisted language learning (CALL), there has been discussion of how technologies can play a role in motivating learners in learning a language (e.g., Warschauer, 1996), and as technologies have become more sophisticated, the growing range of uses of technology in and out of the classroom increases the potential for enhanced motivation. My own teaching context is a large private university located in central Tokyo, where one might expect that technological advances are far more than those of many other countries around the world, including Europe and the United States. In my experience in discussions with colleagues and attending international conferences, there are more commonalities than differences in problems that are encountered regarding implementing technology for learning purposes and, for this reason, I have kept this discussion at a more general level, as the implications are likely to be of relevance to teachers regardless of where they are based.

As Dörnyei (1999: 525) very rightly argues, 'motivation is one of the most elusive concepts in applied linguistics and indeed in educational psychology in general'. There has been a great deal of discussion about motivation in language learning over the past half a century or more, but the last few years have seen a renewed interest in motivation in the field, and a number of books have appeared recently (e.g., Dörnyei & Ushioda, 2009; 2011; Murray et al., 2011), laying testimony to its importance. Increased motivation has often been given as the justification for the introduction and use of technology in language learning environments, but what is the nature of the relationship between motivation and technology? And what are the characteristics of the motivation for using technology for learning a second language? To address these questions, it is important to examine research into CALL and how it explicitly and implicitly refers to motivation, not only in the learning process, but also in the selection and use of technologies. Obviously, research into CALL is exceptionally broad, but there is a body of research which looks at why teachers use CALL, and how technology can assist learners to build and maintain their motivation in learning English.

Thus, this chapter looks at how technology can be used in the English-language classroom, and how these uses can link to motivation. It begins with looking at general issues associated with technology and motivation, including a brief discussion of the so-called inherent motivational benefits of using technology. It then considers the issue of motivation for using technology from both the teacher's and learner's perspective, followed by an overview of communication technologies that have come into the mainstream in English-language teaching and learning, and how these can impact motivation. These include writing for a real audience through blogs and social networking tools (e.g., Lee, 2009) and the potential benefits of anonymity that may be seen in different types of communication tools such as virtual worlds (e.g., Deutschmann et al., 2009). The chapter continues with an examination of mobile technologies for language learning, and explores the concept of private and studying spaces (cf., Stockwell, 2010). The chapter concludes by considering the local and global issues associated with using technology for English-language learning, and how motivation may be affected by the technologies that are available in both more- and less-technologically advanced regions.

Technology and motivation

Inherent motivational effects of technology

The issue of the inherent motivating effects of technology in education is hardly new, and teachers have long held the view that introducing new technologies into language learning environments has the potential to boost learner motivation. Apart from the novelty effect of engaging with a new technology (e.g., Fox, 1988), such claims were founded on the idea that computer-assisted instruction allowed for more individualised instruction and provided opportunities for learner control and rapid, non-judgemental feedback (see Warschauer, 1996 for a discussion). While much of the early research came from general education environments that did not focus specifically on second language learning, the predominantly drill-based vocabulary and grammar activities meant at the time that it maintained its relevance to computer-based language learning activities as well. Developments in networking technologies, however, enabled language education to take on a somewhat different nature, and environments emerged in which students were not constrained to work alone or in small groups on standalone machines, but could be linked to teachers or other students, increasing the potential opportunities for communication. Initially, this was limited to synchronous exchanges within a single classroom (e.g., Kelm, 1992), but was followed shortly by studies investigating new tools as they appeared, such as email (e.g., Warschauer, 1995), Internet Relay Chat (IRC) over the World Wide Web (e.g., Hudson & Bruckman, 2002), and text-based virtual worlds known as MOOs (Multi-user domain Object Oriented) (e.g., Shield, 2003). Aside from the obvious benefits of interacting with a wider range of interlocutors both in and out of the classroom, networked communication tools were linked to motivational increases through interacting with a real audience (Hoffman, 1994), and reduced anxiety through more anonymous exchanges (Beauvois, 1995). In addition, learners indicated that they could feel part of a community and overcome isolation, and that they could learn about different people and cultures (Warschauer, 1996), all of which were deemed as enhancing motivation. The technologies listed above formed the foundations for the majority of the technologies that are in use today, although current research into communication technologies for language learning has taken on a slightly different slant that goes beyond the simple view of equating task engagement with motivation, as is discussed later in this chapter.

Although the reasons above are not unrelated to the intrinsic nature of the motivation to use the various technologies described, to a large degree they do refer to the tasks and activities which are performed through these technologies rather than to the technologies themselves. In returning to the issue of the *inherent* motivational effects of technologies, it is important to consider the reasons behind the view that technologies motivate students to learn a language. As stated above, earlier research referred to a novelty effect of learning through technology (also see Murray, 1998), whereby the initial enthusiasm for using a new technology was compared to a child with a new toy. The learners were at first attracted to the so-called 'bells and whistles' of learning through a means that was unfamiliar to them, but what about the long-term effects of this attraction? In addressing this question, it is helpful to consider the context in which this early research took place. In the early 1990s, desktop computers (which made up the overwhelming majority of studies at the time) were still, for the most part, prohibitive to members of language classes and, as a result, many learners only had access to them in educational settings. This was often during class time and frequently under supervision, and the amount of time that learners were able to spend at the computer tended to be quite short. In many cases there were insufficient computers to enable one student to sit at a computer, and learners were required to be put in pairs or small groups or, alternatively, simply engage in other non-computer activities while waiting their turn. While, of course, the functionality of computers at the time was far less than it is today, even with this comparatively limited amount of access to computers, learners quickly became aware of what they could and could not do, and motivation waned according to the degree to which their expectations were (or were not) met.

If we compare this situation to our current day and age, we can see that there is a completely different demographic of both teachers and learners. In these early days of learning through technology, the teacher tended to be absolute in regard to control over the technology (i.e., predominantly only in the class-room and only doing what the teachers said) and to the skills and knowledge possessed regarding the technologies used. Needless to say, learners today are far more discerning about the technologies they use and the ways in which they use them. While Prensky's (2001) 'digital natives' concept has received some criticism in terms of its generalisability (see Bennett et al., 2008), studies have shown that young adult learners are, for the most part, highly technically savvy, at least as far as mainstream technologies such as computers, mobile phones and email are concerned (Kennedy et al., 2008). Indeed, specific studies have shown ownership of technologies to be very high in some countries, such as 98.5 per cent of United States university students owning a computer (Winke & Goertler, 2008), and 100 per cent of Japanese university students owning a mobile phone (Stockwell, 2008). These figures imply that the vast majority of learners will view technologies as something that is natural to possess and use on a daily basis and, as a result, they are unlikely to be impressed with a new technology unless it meets or exceeds their expectations based on their experiences with using the technologies around them. What can be concluded from this is that if technologies in themselves have an inherent motivating effect, this effect is likely to be relatively short-lived, and certainly not long enough for any kind of meaningful language learning to take place.

Regarding sustained use of technologies, studies have given mixed results, but they have generally shown that it is easier to ensure that learners continue to engage actively in activities under supervised conditions than when outside of class. In an examination of learners in Spain and English engaged in tandem email exchanges, Appel and Mullen (2002) found that individual students working with a tandem site outside of the classroom environment sent steadily fewer messages as time progressed compared to those working with the site during class. Many students stopped sending messages altogether, and only 'very highly motivated students' (p. 200) continued with the exchanges until the end of the project. Despite the fact that the same technology was used by the learners, the students who used it outside of class were far less likely to maintain their motivation to continue with the exchanges than were those who undertook the activities in class. This in itself becomes a stark reminder that it is not the technology that motivates learners to study, but the manner and the context in which the technology is used.

It should also be noted that while the teachers had an expectation that learners would continue with the exchanges in much the same way in both the in-class and out-of-class environments, the reality was that learners did not do so unless there was immediate and constant pressure on them. In this situation, one would imagine that the teachers would have decided to ask learners to engage in the exchanges because of the anticipated benefits for their language learning, and that learners would be aware of this fact. Why, then, did learners fail to use the system outside of class? It is possible to envisage that there ended up being a discrepancy between what teachers' expectations for learners were and how the learners perceived the activities that they were asked to do. If this is the case, we can see that problems arise with adopting a technology for learning a language when there are gaps between the teacher's view of what and how technologies should be used and views held by the learners. The following section considers this issue in more depth.

Motivation for using technology

What is it that drives teachers and students to engage in technology use for language learning? As alluded to in the above section, while the ultimate goal of success in acquiring a second language is likely shared by both teachers and learners, there is indeed a range of other factors that must come into play. There are at least three main considerations which need to be kept in mind regarding the use of technology for language teaching:

1. the motivation for teachers to initiate and maintain use of a technology;
2. the motivation for learners to use (and keep using) a technology;
3. whether and how a technology supports or facilitates learners' motivation to learn the language.

Each of these factors is dependent upon the background and experience of individual teachers and learners, as well as the specific characteristics of the learning environment – all of which merge together to form the language learning context. The context in which language learning occurs greatly affects the players within it, and this in turn will have a significant effect on how both learners and teachers select and identify with technologies. The complex range of factors that make up the context occur at individual, institutional and societal levels, each of which interplays with the others to construct the individual circumstances in which teachers and learners find themselves (Stockwell, 2012). The motivation for teachers and learners to use technologies is then a product of this complicated context.

Teacher perspectives

There are several reasons that might be considered as contributing to why teachers would choose to adopt technology in their language teaching environments. In very broad terms, teachers may choose to use technology due to pressure from external sources or, alternatively, they may be self-motivated to use it in an attempt to add something to their language learning environment (see Levy & Stockwell, 2006 for a discussion). Whether the motivation is externally initiated or internally initiated will have a large effect on what technologies are used, how they are used, how they are viewed and even the longevity of their use. Externally initiated pressure invariably comes from the institution in which they are teaching, often as a result of the introduction of technologies – such as a CALL lab, a Course Management System (CMS), or laptop computers – more often than not at quite some expense, and management of the institution is keen to see the outcomes as a result of this outlay. Alternatively, and this is particularly the case in ESL and EFL settings, numerous job descriptions put a requirement on having technology skills, and teachers feel that they must use technologies in order to keep themselves competitive (Kessler, 2006). In these situations, it is quite easy to imagine that the teacher might be an unwilling user of technology in the classroom, a relative novice with technology who has had pressure to use it applied to him or her. Success in implementation of technologies for education tends to be quite varied, and while there is a range of contributing factors, it tends to be very difficult for teachers to introduce technologies, particularly if they attempt to do so without support (Stockwell, 2009). Their motivation to continue using the technology is often a direct result of how long the pressure is kept on them and, in many cases, the degree to which they experiment with technologies remains limited. Ertmer (2005), for example, found that practising teachers who were required to use technologies in their teaching environments were limited to low-level tasks such as word-processing and Internet research, and that their use of technology was directly related to their underlying beliefs about the usefulness of technologies. That is to say, in order to start to use technology and to use it in the long term, teachers must have both the support to do so, as well as see for themselves how technology can play a role within their own specific settings.

In contrast, teachers who are internally motivated tend to have different characteristics from those who are externally motivated, but they also tend to fit into two main categories: those teachers who have a desire to change the environment and feel that technology can help them to achieve this, and teachers who have an interest in technologies (or a specific technology) and wish to use them in their teaching environments. Some teachers will approach the task of introducing technology with preconceptions of what a specific technology can do to motivate their students, such as using hypermedia structures to improve language learning structures (Hémard, 2006), introducing information and communication technologies (ICTs) to promote interaction (Gallardo del Puerto and Gamboa, 2009) or build rapport between teachers and students (Jiang & Ramsay, 2005) or using a CMS to enhance autonomy (Sanprasert, 2010). In each of these examples, teachers have clearly indicated that they believe that the technology of choice will play a positive role in improving the motivation of their learners, and as such it is possible to conclude, then, that the motivation for using the technology is still largely focused on the learners themselves. While also highly motivated to use technologies, teachers who are interested in a specific technology are often curious to see whether or not the technology works in their given environment. This may be some type of system that they have developed themselves (e.g., Baturay et al., 2010), or it may be a new or emerging technology such as Second Life (e.g., Peterson, 2010). In either case, the motivation to use the technology starts with a curiosity, and continued use of the technology is often dependent upon the lifespan of the project (as might be the case with self-developed technologies), or until the technology fades out of popularity.

Dörnyei and Ushioda (2011) identify four main elements with regard to teacher motivation: it has a central intrinsic component, is linked with contextual factors, is subject to change over time, and is subject to negative influences. Linking this to technology use, the potential relevance is immediately obvious. For example, when teachers see success in their environment in terms of positive learner attitudes or achievement of desired learning outcomes as a result of technology, this may serve to motivate them to continue in their use of the technology. Contextual factors have been touched on above but, specifically, teachers may find difficulties in maintaining motivation if they feel overworked or not appreciated for the work that they do. Thus, if teachers perceive that it is too difficult to become competent users of technology, or if there is a lack of training or support, motivation to use technology would be greatly diminished (see Pelgrum, 2001). Most teachers, like many professionals, feel a need to advance in their career over time. If technology can provide a means to promotion or other professional development, the motivation to use it would naturally be stronger. Finally, teacher motivation is likely to be negatively affected by a range of other factors, such as the stressful nature of teaching jobs, an inhibition of teacher autonomy (i.e., lack of freedom to express individuality in their teaching), insufficient training, repetitiveness and inadequate career structures (Dörnyei & Ushioda, 2011). To sum up, then, when teachers make the decision to introduce technology, they do so based on a range of factors that will go beyond the immediate classroom situation. Teachers themselves are individuals who face daily pressures from the institution as well as having their own personal goals, and it is a consolidation of these factors which will dictate how motivated teachers are to use technologies in their language learning environments.

Learner perspectives

As described above, discussions regarding technology use and learner motivation primarily revolve around two main aspects: the motivation for learners to use a technology for language learning, and the relationship between technology use and motivation in language learning. These two factors (and indeed teacher motivation) are by no means mutually exclusive, and it is possible to see that there is in fact a bilateral relationship between them. Motivation to use a technology could very well lead learners to develop motivation to learn a language (although unlikely automatically) and, conversely, sustained motivation to learn a language could result in a desire to use technology. Learners who are interested in Facebook, for example, may see that this tool allows them to interact with speakers of other languages all over the world. While they did not previously have an interest in learning a specific language, they may find that through interacting with others, they want to relate with speakers of a language and converse with them in that language. In this case, while language learning was not the primary objective, it has developed over time as a result of using a certain technology. In contrast, learners who already possess high levels of motivation to learn a language may find that they are looking for alternative ways to increase their opportunities for interaction in the target language, and they join online communities such as Second Life, where they are able to converse with native speakers of the language. In each of these cases, although there were different starting points, ultimately both learners have ended up using technology as a means of improving their target language.

Given that learners may have their own motivations to use technologies, as in the examples above, how is learners' motivation to use technologies sustained? Learners may use technology for language learning in two ways: language learning may take the form of a course that is dictated by a teacher either inside or outside of the classroom, or it may involve spontaneous use by learners acting on their own volition. When learners are in class, it is easier to be monitored by teachers to ensure that they remain on task and complete what is required of them as expected (see Appel & Mullen, 2002), but what happens when teachers are not immediately present is somewhat less clear. In a study of learners of English enrolled in e-learning courses in South Korea, Jung (2011) found that the single most-important factor was interaction – most importantly with other students in the course, but closely followed by interaction with teachers. Learners valued opportunities for both asynchronous and synchronous online interaction, indicating a need for the freedom to contact others when they were available, but at the same time to reply to immediate needs as they arose. Learners also cited support as being a key factor, but this is an aspect that has often been found lacking in many e-learning situations. Learners who choose to use technology for their own independent language learning tend to apply a different set of criteria when choosing technologies.

According to Lai and Gu (2011), in a study of university students from Hong Kong studying a range of foreign languages, learners were more likely to use social networking sites (SNS), such as Facebook, if they set clear goals in their language learning, felt familiar with the technologies and possessed sufficient language skills. Many learners were wary about interacting with others online, opting to give private information only to people that they trusted, but they were then more likely to maintain interactions once they had developed relationships with their online interlocutors. Thus, while clear learner goals certainly contributed to learners making the decision to engage in online interactions, it was the development of interpersonal relationships that was a determining factor in their sustained use.

What of the potential of technologies to sustain motivation to learn a language? Warschauer (1996) argued that students who used computers for writing essays online felt that they were able to learn better and more independently, with more control over their learning and more opportunities to practise English, which ultimately led them to write better, more creative essays. What was it about writing online that led learners to this perception? One of the key points was the fact that they were able to interact with real people, which made the language feel real rather than as something that was simply undertaken in class. When learners are able to see a clear relationship between what happens in their language classes and interactions with speakers of the language they are learning, it follows that they can feel a sense of achievement which can lead to heightened motivation (see Atkinson & Raynor, 1974). Related to this is the notion that technology which is designed to cater to a variety of learners' styles, interests and skill levels can lead to sustained motivation (Strambi & Bouvet, 2003). Language learning systems that track learners' progress and provide feedback about what they have achieved can make it easier to see how they have progressed. Whereas progress in many environments may be relatively unseen, systems equipped with record-keeping facilities that enable learners to see what they have learned and what they still need to study can boost student motivation to sustain their efforts in studying the language.

The literature has also revealed cases in which the use of technology can have an adverse effect, resulting in a reduction in motivation. For example, Chen and Cheng (2008) examined EFL learners enrolled in a writing class in Taiwan who were required to use automatic writing evaluation software to assist them with essay writing during class time. They found that when the learners were expected to use the system without teacher intervention, they became frustrated, finally forming negative opinions of the writing system. In another example, Castellano et al. (2011) required their learners to undertake Internet searches in class, but ultimately concluded that when the learners were required to sift through large amounts of authentic target-language information on the

Internet, they were overwhelmed with the volume of information and were not able to perform the task as expected. Both of these examples illustrate the potential pitfalls of using technology in the classroom and give us insights into what is necessary to avoid inadvertently damaging learners' motivation to study using technology. In the first case, learners lacked the skills to be able to deal on their own with problems as they arose, and required assistance from the teacher, but did not receive it. In the second case, the level of language proficiency required to undertake the task was insufficient for the task they were assigned. What this tells us is that, above all else, the teacher needs to be aware of learners' current ability regarding both technology and language proficiency, and must take care to select tasks which are suited to them. Furthermore, it also tells us that before placing expectations on learners to work unsupervised, sufficient time needs to be dedicated to training them to ensure that they can deal with difficulties as they arise.

Technologies in language teaching and learning

The last decade has seen an explosion of new technologies becoming available to the general public – technologies which add to the already quite-impressive list of tools with which we engage on a daily basis. As described earlier in the chapter, teachers – including language teachers – have been relatively quick in adapting into their educational settings new technologies as they appear. This has had an enormous effect on the language learning environments in which teachers are involved and, of course, this is very true of English language teaching settings as well. This section deals with some of the more mainstream technologies in the CALL literature. The first two, communication technologies and social technologies, specifically look at tools that encourage interaction between learners and their teachers, other students and the wider community, while the last, mobile technologies, considers how learners can capitalise on the tools that they carry with them to enhance their language learning opportunities. It should be pointed out that in recent years, both communication and social technologies are also used through mobile technologies, in particular, smart phones and tablet computers, but the discussion below maintains a more generic view which is applicable to both mobile and non-mobile settings.

Communication technologies

As pointed out in the beginning of the chapter, communication technologies have occupied a central role amongst the range of technologies which are used for language teaching. Some of these have been around for quite some time, such as email and online chat, although research has taken on slightly different characteristics in recent years. While early research into communication tools like email was primarily concerned with language skills, such as vocabulary and grammar, that could be acquired through interactions with native speakers (e.g., Stockwell & Harrington, 2003), more recent research has moved towards examining how a wider range of learner attributes can be developed. In one such example, Fisher et al. (2007) investigated how learners of French and English used an electronic bulletin board system (BBS) in order to interact with native speakers of the other language. They found that the learners not only continued with the interactions without intervention from the teacher, but they also mimicked the formatting of greetings, asked linguistic questions and formulated expressions in the target language to encourage as many responses as possible to questions that they had posed on the BBS.

Increased bandwidth has also seen an increase in other communication tools the use of which has been implemented in language teaching environments as well. Where video-conferencing tools were often plagued by technical difficulties and problems with slow connections, modern video tools are relatively foolproof in terms of installation, and they provide very clear images and sound to users. Using one such system, Adobe-Connect, Jauregi et al. (2012) found that beginner and intermediate learners of Dutch were motivated by being able to see and orally interact with native-speaking partners. While learners at both levels indicated concern regarding being able to succeed in their interactions, they indicated a sense of achievement when communication was successful. In this study, however, it is important to note that learners were interacting with experienced interlocutors who applied specific strategies to encourage the learners in their interactions. Given the comparatively low levels of proficiency of the learners compared with that of other studies, the stance adopted by the researchers was no doubt extremely important in ensuring success in the project.

Social technologies

Social technologies have probably been among the most noticeable developments over the past several years, moving from simpler technologies such as blogs and Wikis, through to more sophisticated ones such as Facebook (see Stockwell & Tanaka-Ellis, 2012 for a discussion). Given that the concept of motivation is being shaped by recent theories which seek to examine how learners consider who they are, their relationship with their social world and their goals for the future (Ushioda, 2011), it would seem that social technologies are in an important position to assist learners in achieving their language learning goals. Indeed, a lot has been written about the potential advantages of these social tools that enable learners to move their audience from beyond the relatively limited scope of their classroom or pre-determined groups to the wider community in general. Newer technologies such Facebook are thought to promote motivation through the interpersonal networks created through them, but there is still very little actual research available at this stage. In saying this, however, research from more established technologies suggest its potential as a language learning tool. Apart from the motivational increases which have been attributed to interacting with an authentic audience, blogs, for example, have been associated with improved autonomy. Pinkman (2005) found that Japanese learners of English were willing to post spontaneously to their blogs, and reply to comments from others, even when the comments were of a negative tone, while Bhattacharya and Chauhan (2010) concluded that through blog-writing learners became more able to take responsiblity for learning strategies and over time achieved a greater degree of independence from their teachers. Wikis have also had a favourable response from teachers and learners, with students taking the initiative to pay attention to form, making corrections not only on Wikis written by themselves, but also by other students in the class (Kessler, 2009). With this greater desire to take responsibility for producing and correcting language output, the potential of SNS such as Facebook would seem to be quite promising.

In addition to these types of sites, learners may also interact with one another in virtual worlds, otherwise known as multi-user virtual environments (MUVEs). Some of the benefits which have been associated with learning through MUVEs such as Second Life include the potential for anonymity, through hiding behind avatars, and increased participation (Deutschmann et al., 2009). While many learners experienced technical difficulties in the early stages (Peterson, 2010), learner perceptions of interactions through these environments have been very positive. Like other social technologies, participation in MUVEs has also been thought to contribute to learner autonomy. Collentine (2011) found that learners of Spanish involved in two murder-mystery tasks in a MUVE, called Unity, produced language of increased complexity and accuracy as a result of the decisions that they made during the tasks. It is important to bear in mind, however, that social technologies such as the ones listed here do not have any outcomes within themselves (see Stockwell & Tanaka-Ellis, 2012) and, if used specifically for educational purposes, depend on teachers to decide how learners interact with themselves or others. In the case of the study by Collentine, the virtual environment enabled learners to be put in situations that would normally not be possible in classroom settings and, as a result, learners were able to benefit from the variety of environments that can be created in MUVEs. If MUVEs are used independently of institutional learning contexts, however, learners may find that they gain for themselves extra opportunities for interactions with the people that they meet while online. This is particularly so for learners of English, where the default language in many of these social environments tends to be English, although there are, of course, pockets of users of other languages as well.

Mobile technologies

Mobile technologies have also become an everyday part of the lives of people around the world, and the reduction in costs and increasing functionalities of tools such as mobile phones make them a very attractive tool for language learning. So familiar have mobile technologies become these days that many people actually see them as an extension of themselves (Ros i Solé et al., 2010) and feel uncomfortable when they do not have immediate access to them. Mobile devices these days take many shapes and forms, ranging from mobile phones – including smart phones – to tablet computers, wireless laptops, PDAs and portable MP3 players. An important consideration of mobile learning, however, is that it takes place predominantly under unsupervised conditions, which means that if learners encounter difficulties there is a greater chance that they will reduce usage or even reject it altogether (see the discussion above regarding learner perspectives on motivation for language learning). One of the greatest attractions of mobile learning, particularly with mobile phones, is that, in most developed countries at least, almost all students already own these devices, making it easier to encourage learners to make the most of any spare time that they may have for their language learning.

A potential pitfall of mobile learning, however, is the concept of private and studying spaces (cf. Stockwell, 2008; see also Henry, this volume). While teachers may be enthusiastic about having their learners use their mobile phones or other devices for learning purposes, some learners have expressed resistance to having their own private space being used for educational purposes. When given a choice between using a mobile phone or a desktop computer for learning English vocabulary, Japanese students showed an overwhelming preference for using the desktop computers, indicating that the environments in which one would expect to use mobile phones (in transit, in a restaurant, etc.) were not conducive to learning. There has been, however, a slow increase in the number of learners who opt to use their mobile phones for learning (Stockwell, 2010). As the idea of the mobile phone as a universal tool becomes more acceptable, we would expect to see a gradual increase in the number of learners who actively embrace learning through their mobile devices.

Developments in technologies such as the three examples of technologies that have been provided here have done much to expand not only the times and places that learners can engage in learning a language, but also to alter who they interact with and how they do it. As teachers, it is important to be aware of what technologies learners are using and to consider how these could – and in some cases should – be applied to language learning contexts. This can only be achieved, however, through having a sufficient understanding of the various affordances and potential limitations of these technologies for learning a language, and selecting the appropriate technology for specific learning needs.

Local and global issues in teaching English with technology

Learning English has its own special considerations when compared with many other languages, such as Japanese, Indonesian or Arabic. While, of course, there are also individual characteristics of certain communities and regions in users of languages such as these, it is difficult to associate English with a specific target group. As Lamb (2004: 3) argues, 'English loses its association with particular Anglophone cultures and is instead identified with the powerful forces of globalisation', meaning that English is not learned specifically to converse with native speakers from Canada, New Zealand or England but, rather, it is used as a 'lingua franca between speakers from different language backgrounds' (Ushioda, 2006: 150). This means that the backgrounds of learners of English are exceptionally broad, from technologically highly developed countries such as France or South Korea, through to less-developed countries such as Vietnam or Bangladesh. At a societal level, there are great differences between the availability and costs of technologies (access to wireless Internet, Internet speed, etc.), the technological standards (SMS in Europe and the United States compared to mobile email in Japan), and access to relevant information and organisations (access to training in technology and links with academic organisations) (Stockwell, 2012). All of these aspects will have a large impact on the technological options that are available to both teachers and learners, as well as the individual views held towards technology for language learning.

While, of course, there are problems with the so-called 'digital divide', which refers to the 'troubling gaps between those who use computers and the [I]nternet and those who do not' (Mehra et al., 2004: 782), technology has also had a remarkable stabilising effect as well. Resources for teaching English, in particular those produced by commercial publishers, tend to be quite prohibitive in terms of cost for people in less-developed regions. Technology, then, means that through the Internet, resources in English are far more accessible to many. Computers have seen a reduction in price over time, but even lower-end machines are often beyond the reach of learners in some countries. However, the last few years in particular have seen a spread of smart phones, not only in developed countries, but also in other regions as well. This type of technology has the advantage of not requiring the cost of setting up expensive cabling which is needed for computers, as well as the fact that many people choose to own one even without consideration of educational purposes. In this way, the spread of technology has the potential to make English more accessible, and this in turn is likely to result in greater opportunities for learning. There is a large range of free resources for learning English available on the Internet, such as Randall's ESL Cyber Listening Lab (www.esl-lab.com) and BBC's Learning English site (www.bbc.co.uk/worldservice/learningenglish/), to name just two.

If these are utilised by both teachers and learners, despite the huge gap between the 'haves' and the 'have-nots', technology allows access to learning for a wider global audience with little extra financial outlay.

It is also natural that we would approach our different teaching environments in different regions in different ways. Even in countries where similar levels of technology are available, one would expect to see these technologies used in different ways, depending on the characteristics of both the learners and the teachers. Using technology to teach English (as a second language) in the United States, for example, would vary greatly from using similar technologies to teach English (as a foreign language) in Japan. Not only are there the obvious logistical differences between teaching in ESL and EFL contexts, but we also see large differences in the expectations of what technology is to be used for. In the United States, the primary SNS is Facebook, which eclipses any alternatives by an enormous margin. In Japan, in contrast, many young people prefer to use a Japanese-based system called Mixi, which has similar functionality to Facebook but allows for more interaction in closed communities. Using Facebook as a supplement to English classes in the EFL setting would be considered fairly normal, but to require learners in Japan to do so may at first meet with some resistance from learners who are more familiar with Mixi. Facebook is used by some learners in Japan, but typically this tends to revolve around those learners who either have experience living in an English-speaking country, or who are sufficiently motivated to try a different platform. There is no easy answer to the question of how to deal with these differences in concept but, at the very least, it requires teachers to have an understanding of the differences in learners' views towards technologies, and to make decisions based on what suits not only their pedagogical needs but also their individual and collective preferences.

Conclusion

The potential for technologies to enhance motivation of both teachers and learners of English is certainly powerful. Of course, it is important to be aware that technology use does not result in automatic motivational increases in teachers or learners, particularly where there is stress regarding availability of technology and skills in using them effectively. Learners are often more likely to adopt the latest personal-use technologies than are teachers, meaning that teachers are left with trying to bring themselves up to a comparable level with the learners, not infrequently within institutions that are reluctant to commit to the outlays required to not only update their technological resources, but also to train teachers to use them properly. Despite this, technologies have certainly become a more natural part of our everyday lives, and to that end to see their usage extended beyond daily uses to meeting our language learning needs is in one sense just a matter of time. When technologies do become the norm in our learning environments, however, it is possible to see that new challenges will be faced. For example, in a day and age when technologies are commonplace, in one sense it becomes more difficult to maintain learner curiosity (see Arnone et al., 2011), which will place a greater onus on teachers to think of innovative ways that will keep their learners engaged with the technologies that are available at the time. One of the most fundamental points to bear in mind, as Felix (2003) very rightly argues, is that technology should not be used as an alternative to good teaching practice. This leaves a great responsibility on the shoulders of teachers to consider how they can contribute to encouraging and maintaining learners' interest in learning the language. Given the speed of technological development and penetration into society, technology most certainly will have a role to play in accomplishing this, but it should not do so at the expense of the various goals held by both teachers and learners.

Engagement priorities

Technology has had an enormous impact on the teaching and learning environment, but there is still a good deal to consider regarding its effect on various aspects of motivation. Further discussion of the relationship between technology and motivation would need to consider: the ways in which tasks can be both designed and implemented, the motivation leading teachers and institutions to adopt technologies, the motivation for learners to choose to use technology to assist them in learning a language and the variation in views towards technologies on both regional and individual levels. While not exhaustive, some specific areas of discussion are as follows:

1. What features of technology-based tasks might be considered as contributing to enhancing learner motivation to use the technology? In other words, how can a task be created such that it promotes learners' sustained engagement with the technology?
2. Teachers' motivation to use technology for language teaching is a relatively under-researched area. Given that many students these days possess modern technologies, is it acceptable for teachers to refuse to use technology in their teaching environments?
3. Institutions often put pressure on both teachers and learners to use certain technologies. What steps should institutions take both before and after introduction of a technology to ensure greater usage?

4. Is it possible for a technology to enhance learners' motivation to learn a language? If not, why not? If so, how would the technology need to be used to achieve this?
5. Is it possible to have standard online resources for learners of English that would be applicable on a world scale? What features would be necessary to ensure that students of different backgrounds would be motivated to use them?

Suggested further reading

Chapelle, C. (2003). *English Language Learning and Technology.* Amsterdam: John Benjamins.

Although nearly a decade has passed since this book was published, it remains an important piece of work looking specifically at the way in which technology has affected the learning of English. While it does not have a specific section on motivation, Chapelle remains aware of its underlying importance, and as such makes reference to it at several points throughout the book.

Ushioda, E. (2011). Language learning motivation, self and identity: current theoretical perspectives. *Computer Assisted Language Learning,* 24(3): 199–210.

This article provides a discussion of the way in which motivation in learning a second language is being reconceptualised through contemporary theories of self and identity, and considers how digital technologies may play a role in shaping learners' motivation and their identities.

References

Appel, C. and Mullen, T. (2002). A new tool for teachers and researchers involved in e-mail tandem language learning. *ReCALL,* 14(2):195–208.

Arnone, M. P., Small, R. V., Chauncey, S. A. and McKenna, H. P. (2011). Curiosity, interest and engagement in technology-pervasive learning environments: a new research agenda. *Educational Technology, Research and Development,* 59(2): 181–98.

Atkinson, J. W. and Raynor, J. O. (eds) (1974). *Motivation and Achievement.* Washington, D.C.: Winston & Sons.

Baturay, M. H., Dalaglu, A. and Yildirim, S. (2010). Language practice with multimedia supported we-based grammar revision material. *ReCALL,* 22(3): 313–31.

Beauvois, M. H. (1995). E-talk: attitudes and motivation in computer-assisted classroom discussion. *Computers and the Humanities,* 28: 177–90.

Bennett, S., Maton, K. and Kervin, L. (2008). The 'digital natives' debate: a critical review of the evidence. *British Journal of Educational Technology,* 38(5): 775–86.

Bhattacharya, A. and Chauhan, K. (2010). Augmenting learner autonomy through blogging. *ELT Journal,* 64(4): 376–84.

Castellano, J., Mynard, J. and Rubesch, T. (2011). Student technology use in a self-access center. *Language Learning & Technology,* 15(3): 12–27.

Chen, C.-F. E. and Cheng, W.-Y. E. (2008). Beyond the design of automated writing evaluation: pedagogical practices and perceived learning effectiveness in EFL writing classes. *Language Learning & Technology,* 12(2): 94–112.

Collentine, K. (2011). Learner autonomy in a task-based 3D world and production. *Language Learning & Technology*, 15(3): 50–67.

Deutschmann, M., Panichi, L. and Molka-Danielsen, J. (2009). Designing oral participation in second life – a comparative study of two language proficiency courses. *ReCALL*, 21(2): 206–26.

Dörnyei, Z. (1999). Motivation. In B. Spolsky (ed.) *Concise Encyclopedia of Educational Linguistics*. Oxford: Elsevier, pp. 525–32.

Dörnyei, Z. and Ushioda, E. (eds) (2009). *Motivation, Language Identity and the L2 Self*. Bristol: Multilingual Matters.

Dörnyei, Z. and Ushioda, E. (2011). *Teaching and Researching Motivation* (Second Edition). Harlow: Pearson.

Ertmer, P. (2005). Teacher pedagogical beliefs: the final frontier in our quest for technology integration? *Educational Technology, Research and Development*, 53(4): 369–79.

Felix, U. (2003). Pedagogy on the line: identifying and closing the missing links. In U. Felix (ed.) *Language Learning Online: Towards Best Practice*. Lisse: Swets & Zeitlinger, pp. 147–70.

Fisher, L., Evans, M. and Esch, E. (2007). Computer-mediated communication: promoting autonomy and intercultural understanding at secondary level. *Language Learning Journal*, 30: 50–8.

Fox, M. (1988). *A Report on Studies of Motivation Teaching and Small Group Interaction with Special Reference to Computers and to the Teaching and Learning of Arithmetic*. Milton Keynes: The Open University, Institute of Educational Technology.

Gallardo del Puerto, F. and Gamboa, E. (2009). The evaluation of computer-mediated technology by second language teachers: collaboration and interaction in CALL. *Educational Media International*, 46(2): 137–52.

Hémard, D. (2006). Evaluating hypermedia structures as a means of improving language learning strategies and motivation. *ReCALL*, 18(1), 24–44.

Hoffman, R. (1994). The warm network: electronic mail, ESL learners and the personal touch. *On CALL*, 8(2): 10–13.

Hudson, J. M. and Bruckman, A. S. (2002): IRC Français: the creation of an internet-based SLA community. *Computer Assisted Language Learning*, 15(2): 109–34.

Jauregi, K., deGraff, R., van denBergh, H. and Kriz, M. (2012). Native/non-native speaker interactions through video-web communication: a clue for enhancing motivation? *Computer Assisted Language Learning*, 25(1): 1–19.

Jiang, W. and Ramsay, G. (2005). Rapport-building through CALL in teaching Chinese as a foreign language: an exploratory study. *Language Learning & Technology*, 9(2): 47–63.

Jung, I. (2011). The dimensions of e-learning quality: from the learner's perspective. *Educational Technology, Research and Development*, 59(4): 445–64.

Kelm, O. (1992). The use of synchronous computer networks in second language instruction: a preliminary report. *Foreign Language Annals*, 25: 441–54.

Kennedy, G. E., Judd, T. S., Churchwood, A., Gray, K. and Krause, K.-L. (2008). First year students' experiences with technology: are they really digital natives? *Australasian Journal of Educational Technology*, 24(1): 108–22.

Kessler, G. (2006). Assessing CALL teacher training: what are we doing and what could we do better? In P. Hubbard and M. Levy (eds) *Teacher Education in CALL*. Amsterdam: John Benjamins, pp. 23–42.

Kessler, G. (2009). Student-initiated attention to form in wiki-based collaborative writing. *Language Learning & Technology*, 13(1): 79–85.

Lai, C. and Gu, M. (2011). Self-regulated out-of-class learning with technology. *Language Learning & Technology*, 24(4): 317–35.

Lamb, M. (2004). Integrative motivation in a globalizing world. *System*, 32: 3–19.

Lee, L. (2009). Promoting intercultural exchanges with blogs and podcasting: a study of Spanish–American telecollaboration. *Computer Assisted Language Learning*, 22(5): 425–43.

Levy, M. and Stockwell, G. (2006). *CALL Dimensions: Options and Issues in Computer Assisted Language Learning*. Mahwah, NJ: Lawrence Erlbaum Associates.

Mehra, V., Merkel, C. and Bishop A. P. (2004). The internet for empowerment of minority and marginalized users. *New Media & Society*, 6(6): 781–802.

Murray, D. (1998). Language and society in cyberspace. *TESOL Matters*, 8(4): 9–21.

Murray, G., Gao, X. and Lamb, T. (eds) (2011). *Identity, Motivation and Autonomy in Language Learning*. Bristol: Multilingual Matters.

Pelgrum, W. J. (2001). Obstacles to the integration of ICT in education: results from a worldwide educational assessment. *Computers and Education*, 37: 163–78.

Peterson, M. (2010). Learner participation patterns and strategy use in Second Life: an exploratory case study. *ReCALL*, 22(3): 273–92.

Pinkman, K. (2005). Using blogs in the foreign language classroom: encouraging learner independence. *The JALT CALL Journal*, 1(1): 12–24.

Prensky, M. (2001). Digital natives, digital immigrants. *On the Horizon*, 9(5): 1–6.

Ros iSolé, C., Calic, J. and Neijmann, D. (2010). A social and self-reflective approach to MALL. *ReCALL*, 22(1): 39–52.

Sanprasert, N. (2010). The application of a course management system to enhance autonomy in learning English as a foreign language. *System*, 38: 109–23.

Shield, L. (2003). MOO as a language learning tool. In U. Felix (ed.) *Language Learning Online: Towards Best Practice*. Lisse: Swets and Zeitlinger, pp. 97–122.

Stockwell, G. (2008). Investigating learner preparedness for and usage patterns of mobile learning. *ReCALL*, 20 (3): 253–70.

Stockwell, G. (2009). Teacher education in CALL: teaching teachers to educate themselves. *Innovation in Language Learning and Teaching*, 3(1): 99–112.

Stockwell, G. (2010). Using mobile phones for vocabulary activities: examining the effect of the platform. *Language Learning & Technology*, 14(2): 95–110.

Stockwell, G. (2012). Conclusion. In G. Stockwell (ed.) *Computer Assisted Language Learning: Diversity in Research and Practice*. Cambridge: Cambridge University Press, pp. 164–73.

Stockwell, G. and Harrington, M. W. (2003). The incidental development of L2 proficiency in NS-NNS email interactions. *CALICO Journal*, 20(2): 337–59.

Stockwell, G. and Tanaka-Ellis, N. (2012). Diversity in environments. In G. Stockwell (ed.) *Computer Assisted Language Learning: Diversity in Research and Practice*. Cambridge: Cambridge University Press, pp. 71–89.

Strambi, A. and Bouvet, E. (2003). Flexibility and interaction at a distance: a mixed-mode environment for language learning. *Language Learning & Technology*, 7(3): 81–102.

Ushioda, E. (2006). Language motivation in a reconfigured Europe: access, identity, autonomy. *Journal of Multilingual and Multicultural Development*, 27(2): 148–61.

Ushioda, E. (2011). Language learning motivation, self and identity: current theoretical perspectives. *Computer Assisted Language Learning*, 24(3): 199–210.

Warschauer, M. (1995). *E-mail for English teaching*. Alexandria, VA: TESOL Publications.

Warschauer, M. (1996). Motivational aspects of using computers for writing and communication. In M. Warschauer (ed.) *Telecollaboration in Foreign Language Learning*. Honolulu, HI: University of Hawai'i Second Language Teaching and Curriculum Center, pp. 29–46.

Winke, P. and Goertler, S. (2008). Did we forget someone? Students' computer access and literacy for CALL. *CALICO Journal*, 25(3): 482–509.

10

Motivated by Visions: Stories from Chinese Contexts

Xuesong Gao

Introduction

The rise of English as an international language has always been a controversial issue. Its critics condemn the global dominance of English as a form of linguistic imperialism, in which hegemonic powers like Great Britain and the United States extend their influence and interests by promoting the teaching and learning of English (e.g., Phillipson, 1992). In contrast, others have observed that the ascension of English as an international language has been supported by individuals in various contexts who appropriate the language as a means to pursue their localised interests and agenda (e.g., Canagarajah, 2007). Research has also documented various ways in which individuals in many contexts are empowered by their English competence and see the language as an integral part of their identity (e.g., Lamb, 2007). These individuals' experiences raise intriguing questions for further research on the interplay between the individual creativity and contextual conditions under which English has spread as an international language. Such research helps reveal how individual learners motivate themselves and sustain their motivation in their autonomous efforts to develop English competence in particular contexts.

Language learning research has consistently demonstrated that autonomous language learners sustain their learning with a strong motivation, beliefs in what works in learning, and strategies that help them achieve their language learning objectives, all considered essential components of autonomous language learning (Oxford, 2003; 2008; Wenden, 1998; 2002; Yang, 1999; Zhang, 2003). In the light of this growing attention to individual learners' contextualised learning efforts, recent research has challenged the conceptualisation of motivation as an enduring psychological characteristic of the learner and begun to place greater emphasis than ever on its socially constructed, dynamic nature (e.g., Al-Shehri, 2009; Gao, 2006; 2007; 2010; Ushioda, 2011; Ushioda & Dörnyei, 2009). These studies have argued for the centrality of 'ideal self' as a motivating incentive in regulating language learners' efforts to learn English in particular contexts, as the globalisation process has made competence in English a highly valued asset for many in these contexts.

In this chapter, I draw on two empirical studies of autonomous learners' experiences in China – where real-life opportunities to use the language are scarce – and explore how these learners' visions of 'ideal self' operated with supportive social groups as powerful motivational forces underlying their autonomous language learning efforts. The first study (Gao, 2010) is about a physically disabled learner of English in the early 1980s, and the second (Gao, 2007) is about learners in the twenty-first century. Both studies documented how these learners transformed their engagement with a globalisation process into localised pursuit of 'ideal self' and English competence, which subsequently guided and sustained their autonomous learning efforts. Before I present these findings from the two studies, I shall first explore the shifting focus towards the 'ideal self', conceptualised as 'the representation of the attributes that someone would ideally like to possess – that is, a representation of personal hopes, aspirations or wishes' (Ushioda & Dörnyei, 2009: 3) – in research on language learners' autonomous learning.

The 'ideal self' in autonomy research

The shift towards the 'ideal self' in motivation research has been related to recent efforts to problematise the conceptualisation of learner attributes such as motivation and beliefs as 'static' features. As advanced by Ushioda (2011), such problematisation has led to a shift from a theoretical abstraction of learner attributes towards

> a focus on the agency of the individual person [...] with an identity, a personality, [...]; a person with goals, motives and intentions; a focus on the interaction between this self-reflective agent, and the fluid and complex web of social relations, activities, experiences and multiple micro- and macro-contexts ... (Ushioda, 2011: 12–13)

Recent studies, especially those endorsing socio-cultural perspectives that highlight the mediation of contextual conditions on language learning, have also supported this shift with views that perceive language learners' emerging motivation as associated with an interactive process between shifting contextual conditions and learners themselves (e.g., Gao, 2008; 2010; Lamb, 2007; Palfreyman, 2003). Socio-cultural perspectives on language learning 'view real-world situations as fundamental, not ancillary, to learning' (Zuengler & Miller, 2006: 37) and, as a result, language learning should be regarded not only as metacognitive and cognitive activities in individual brains but also as social acts that are meaningfully related to learners' identity formation. From this perspective, learning 'combines personal transformation with the evolution of social structures' through learners participating in those communities (Wenger, 2000: 227); it is also 'both a kind of action and a form of belonging' for learners (Wenger, 1998: 4). In the meantime, it can be argued that language learners' successful execution of these efforts to acquire linguistic competence hinges upon the visions of 'ideal self' to which they commit themselves (see Al-Shehri, 2009; Ushioda & Dörnyei, 2009).

Such emphasis on learners' visions of 'ideal self' as motivational forces underlines the critical role that learners' agency – their power of self-consciousness, reflexivity, intentionality, cognition, emotionality and so on (e.g., Giddens, 1984; Sealey & Carter, 2004) – has in the learning process. Individual learners reveal their agency through the exercise of their capacity and willpower to 'achieve desired and intended outcomes' in the language learning process (Giddens, 1984: 15). To facilitate their autonomous language learning, they also need to effect local changes and construct supportive social networks within their immediate learning settings as they pursue their visions and English competence 'within the constraints of reality' (Al-Shehri, 2009: 165). These 'constraints of reality' include contextual conditions, consisting of materials (artefacts) and discourses distributed through myriad social networks, which profoundly mediate language learners' learning efforts and pursuits of 'ideal self' (Oxford, 2003; Palfreyman, 2006). For instance, in the context of Chinese learners, this focus on language learners' pursuit of 'ideal self' may be seen as similar to the emphasis on individuals' 'efforts' and 'perseverance' in their pursuit of 'self-actualisation' and 'self-realisation', reflecting the profound influences of traditional Chinese cultural discourses and contemporary educational practices (Gu, 2003: 97; see also Gao, 2008; Jiang & Smith, 2009; Shi, 2006).Therefore, as language learners are seen as social agents who are able to 'reflect upon' and 'seek to alter or reinforce, the fitness of the social arrangements they encounter for the realisation of their own interests' (Sealey & Carter, 2004: 11), an examination of such efforts reveals how their visions of 'ideal self' work together with supportive social networks in mediating their autonomous language learning efforts.

In the coming sections, I shall draw on the data collected in the two studies I have undertaken with regards to autonomous language learners in the Chinese context (Gao, 2007; 2010). The first study (Gao, 2010) examined how a physically disabled Chinese learner imagined another self with whom she could engage in English conversations as she struggled to learn English in extremely deprived conditions because of her disability. The second study (Gao, 2007) explored how a group of learners came together to practise English and founded a community for self-assertion, which sustained their efforts to use English together.

A story of a disabled Chinese learner

The first study (Gao, 2010) examined the genesis of one legendary language learner's success in learning English by interpreting her published diaries, letters and autobiography. Zhang Haidi, the learner concerned in the inquiry, was promoted nationwide by the Chinese government as a role model on the Chinese mainland in the 1980s and influenced millions of Chinese of her time (Landsberger, 2001; Zhang, 1999). Born in 1955, she became a paraplegic at the age of five and survived 'four operations for the removal of tumours in her spine' (Landsberger, 2001: 554). Although she could not go to school because of her paralysis, she 'taught herself medicine, acupuncture, and classical literature' (Zhang, 1999: 115). Near the end of the Cultural Revolution (1966–76), she began to learn English and other foreign languages and reportedly had, by 1983, 'translated over 160,000 words in foreign books and reference materials' (Zhang, 1999). She later became a nationally famous author and because of her soaring success as language learner, translator and author, was appointed to be the chairperson for China's Disabled Federation. It must be noted that the source texts used in Gao (2010), mostly biographical accounts and diaries published by the propaganda departments in the 1980s, cannot be regarded as factual representations of Zhang Haidi and her language learning efforts. Most of the texts were published when Zhang was being promoted to be a role model nationwide on the Chinese mainland. Given this particular historical time, these texts included obvious ideological stances, such as calls for young people to work for a better socialist future. However, the essential elements of Zhang's language learning narratives were confirmed by her autobiography in 2004, after the Chinese mainland witnessed dramatic changes in terms of social, cultural and ideological conditions.

As identified in the analysis, narratives in the source texts were found to have consistently portrayed Zhang as a highly motivated language learner committed to socialist ideals and pursuit of 'ideal self'. Her commitment to the pursuit of 'ideal self' was seen to have sustained the unique ways that she used to overcome the contextual constraints and her physical disability in learning languages. It was also noted in the inquiry that she made tireless efforts to form supportive social networks facilitating her language learning efforts despite her physical predicament.

The importance of 'ideal self'

Due to her physical disability, Zhang needed unusually strong willpower to initiate and sustain her efforts to learn English. Her willpower, as reflected in her motivational discourses, was found in the analysis to be associated with a powerful vision of 'ideal self' in line with socialist ideals, the dominant political ideology in the 1980s.

According to her published diary, the catalytic event that made Zhang determined to learn English took place in a county hospital where she was a temporary medical worker in the acupuncture section. Because of her reputation for learning new things, 'an old comrade' approached her with a request regarding the English instructions on an imported medicine for cardiac problems:

> I took the medicine and looked at it. I had to apologize to my comrade: '[...] I have never learnt English'. This old comrade was very disappointed. [...] After she left, I felt really ashamed of myself. [...] I started thinking: [...] Why can't I learn English? If I learn English, I can have one more means to serve my people. [...] I must learn it. (Gao, 2010: 584)

In this particular extract, Zhang also expressed a strong desire to become a 'useful' member of society, which was closely associated with the ideological discourses of her time with an emphasis on serving the needs of 'our people' (Zhang, 1999). In spite of the obvious ideological imports, this desire to be 'useful' is also suggestive of her pursuit of an 'ideal self' underlying her language learning efforts (Ushioda & Dörnyei, 2009). In the meantime, her motivational discourses about learning English also include a pragmatic orientation as a crucial component since she saw the language as a means to acquire advanced technology for the benefit of the country. Due to her physical predicament, she considered translation one of the few means for her to make meaningful contributions. As a result, in her diaries and letters to her friends she made frequent references to her translation works:

> [...] my efforts to learn English continue. Now I can [...] translate the instructions for some of the imported medicines. I have sent the translation of The Encyclopaedia of Canine together with the English original to the Science Press through comrades. [...] I will be preparing to translate another book, an English novel called *'Surgery by the Sea'*. (Gao, 2010: 584)

By undertaking these translation efforts, Zhang began to see the learning of English as an additional means for her to prove herself as a competent member of society. Moreover, her visions of 'ideal self' were identified in the inquiry (Gao, 2010) to be a crucial motivational force sustaining her language learning efforts. From the very beginning, she projected another 'self' onto the confined world where she spent time learning English:

> I finally decided to find an English friend for myself. She is the me in the mirror. In order for me to practise English conversation with her, I wrote down two scripts, one for a girl from China and the other for the English girl. I began to talk to the me in the mirror [...] (Gao, 2010: 584)

This reference (in the biographical texts published in the 1980s) to another 'me' was presented as a strategy that Zhang adopted to overcome her physical disability and learn to speak English. In her recent memoirs in 2004, however, this 'me' has acquired more features and substance, revealing the critical play of her powerful imagination in the learning of English. First of all, this 'me' had an English name, as recorded in one of the imagined conversations as follows:

Who are you, please?
I am Mariana. (Gao, 2010: 584)

'Mariana' in due course has also more visual representations and 'she' is described in one of Zhang's diary entries as follows:

Perhaps you have read *Jane Eyre*. My home village is near the place the story occurred. Here it was winter. The sky was gray and the weather was cold. All tree leaves fell early before and the fields seemed vast and solitary under the cover of white snow. (Gao, 2010: 584)

The rich details Zhang added to this 'Mariana' in her autobiographical account suggest that she might be also another 'ideal self' that Zhang acquired through the process of learning English and might have been the 'self' with whom she identified for years. By creating and investing in this imagined self, Zhang sustained the motivational level necessary for her to overcome various difficulties in the process of learning English (see also Al-Shehri, 2009; Li, 2009; Ushioda & Dörnyei, 2009). It also helped her relate her language learning efforts to a process of 'self-cultivation' and 'self-realisation', which has been encouraged by traditional educational discourses (Gu, 2003: 97; Shi, 2006).

Supportive social networks

While Zhang's personal writings show how she committed herself to the learning of a language in pursuit of her visions of 'ideal self', I also showed in my analysis that she displayed an awareness of sustaining her committed learning efforts by creating supportive networks. Even though it was difficult for her to socialise with other language learners because of her medical condition, she still managed to create a social network of learners and teachers that supported her language learning. For instance, she solicited every possible help from any visitor who knew some English and who could help her learn English (however small their contribution), as follows:

Zhang keeps putting questions about learning English to anyone visiting her who happened to know some English. Many of them became her English teachers for one single letter or word. (Gao, 2010: 588)

She started to learn English at a time when China was still in political turmoil because of the ongoing Cultural Revolution, but she still managed to find an English teacher, one who had been exiled to a neighbouring village because of his overseas connections, considered then a sign of disloyalty to the nation. This teacher reportedly refused her requests at first but was finally moved by her insistence and decided to help her out secretly. Zhang conveyed her excitement about this achievement in a letter to a close friend, who was also learning English:

> I have improved my pronunciation because I am learning English from a teacher whose English was taught by an *English woman* (Zhang's original) in a church school in Beijing. He has also been to countries such as the US and the UK. He also helped me with my grammar. (Gao, 2010: 588)

The reference to the teacher's visit to 'countries such as the US and the UK' indicates that Zhang was also motivated to learn English as a means of enabling her to have global engagement. The 'English woman' in the extract not only gave the teacher the authority as an English teacher, but she was associated with the vision of 'ideal self' as embodied by 'Mariana', to whom Zhang wished to relate through the teacher's help.

Zhang continued her efforts to find social support for her learning of English. Her letters and diary entries record how she invested heavily in establishing a social network in relation to her language learning. In many of these letters, she made requests such as the following for help concerning English learning materials:

> I hope that you could do me three favours: 1) Could you lend the two books (about learning English, author's note) again after you finish learning them? 2) When you buy any English book, could you also buy me one? [...] 3) I hope that you can write to me regularly so that I can learn about your progress and learning methods. [...] (Gao, 2010: 588)

In fact, Zhang obtained almost all the learning materials through the help of her friends. She also returned their favours. As a result, she was able to create a supportive social network in the process of learning English. This group of 'friends' played an important role in sustaining Zhang's efforts to learn English and other foreign languages.

In summary, Gao's (2010) analysis revealed the importance of the 'ideal self' as a motivational incentive for Zhang to sustain her language learning efforts. Its findings also suggest that the 'ideal self' is associated with supportive social networks to aid her efforts to acquire linguistic competence and realise this 'ideal self'. The importance of such social networks also emerged to be a central theme in learners' autonomous learning as recorded in the second study, conducted among a group of learners who voluntarily gathered together to practise English on the Chinese mainland (Gao, 2007).

A tale of an English learners' community on the Chinese mainland

Gao (2007) documents and examines a creative way many Chinese learners address the lack of real-life opportunities to interact with English speakers in their pursuit of oral English competence. To overcome this contextual constraint on learning English, many learners ingeniously organise themselves into 'English corners', 'having as a defining characteristic non-native speakers' efforts to interact with each other in English' (Gao, 2007: 260). The study explored the discursive construction of an English club in a European-style café, called Blue Rain, in a medium-sized developed coastal city on the Chinese mainland by those who participated in it. In July 2005, when the English club decided to move its venue from Blue Rain Café to other locations, a participant posted a series of messages in an online discussion forum to commemorate the days that they had spent together in the café – messages which instantly attracted hundreds of responses from other participants who used to attend or were still attending the club's events. Narratives about the café became the focus of the analysis in Gao (2007), which revealed the importance of supportive social networks and visions of 'ideal self' in sustaining language learners' autonomous learning efforts.

The importance of community

As can be seen in the first message posted by the person who initiated this discussion, the club was seen as a crucial means for many individuals to pursue their 'ideal self' through socialising in English:

> I came to know that there was a place called 'Blue Rain Café' on the Internet by accident. A few months later, I [...] came upon a cafeteria on the roadside. It was Blue Rain Café. [...] I decided to walk in and met the legendary Steve and Mr. Chen and a group of people who are interested in English in this city. [...] While smiling and talking, hours passed away. And I never felt so much at ease. [...]. It seems that every person present and every discussion topic fitted in with décor as if they were all part of it. The place strengthened what we shared as individuals and pushed us together. [...] We had the same pursuit. And we also spoke Chinese, which gave us courage in communicating with each other, because we did not have to worry about whether we could be understood or not. Well, humans are gregarious creatures. [...] Before my eyes, they all appeared to be relaxed and were seriously discussing topics chosen at will, using their body language too. They all seemed to enjoy it very much. [...] Maybe English gave us a

sense of self-protection and security when using this non-mother tongue to communicate with others. [...] So I decided to stay on. I remember that I was a winner in virtual city building games like No. 9 City when I had little desire to talk to people. [...] But what I had before my eyes was totally different. This was real. [...] We all desire to be accepted and acknowledged by others. [...] There is nothing more interesting than actively displaying what is not well known to others in me before each new but unique individual while enjoying a cup of tea. (Gao, 2007: 262–63)

As constructed in this data extract, the English club at the café appears to have several attractions for those who are 'interested in English'. First of all, the club is full of individuals who worked together in pursuit of English competence in a supportive and relaxing manner. The ultimate aim of their efforts was to enjoy each other's presence and 'display what is not well known to others in me before each new but unique individual while enjoying a cup of tea'. The mutual support that members of the club gave to each other can be also sensed in the following extract, posted by a high school student who, when he first went there, was extremely nervous about his inadequate command of English:

In comparison with the others, my brothers and sisters, I am relatively a stranger and do not have many stories at Blue Rain Café. [...] When I came here for the first time, I was quite nervous and also excited. I thought that with my clumsy English I would make a spectacle of myself. I did! Haha. What I did not expect were your responses. You did not sneer at me or look down upon me. You responded to my poor performance with empathetic smiles and encouraging eyes. I made up my mind that I should be part of Blue Rain Café. By and by, I started feeling that I came to Blue Rain Café not only for practising oral English, but also to listen to your reflections on life (which can be surprisingly pleasant). As for me, I cannot learn all of those things from my textbooks (many thanks!!!) (Gao, 2007: 265)

Because of 'empathetic smiles and encouraging eyes' from other participants, the high school student found a friendly supportive group for his learning of English and a socialisation site in the club, where reflections on life experiences were safely shared. In such exchanges, whenever an individual's English fails to communicate the intended message, they are allowed to use Chinese as a backup so that they do not have to endure the stigma associated with these communication failures, as recalled by another participant:

Out of curiosity, I decided to find out what the English corner was. [...] Afterwards, I went there quite frequently and made quite a few friends.

[...] When I see new faces now, I start feeling that I am an old-timer. Blue Rain café, for me, is a place for relaxation. If I am in a good mood, I will talk non-stop. It is also a pleasure to sit there and listen to others when not in a talking mood. [...] If I want to speak English, I will speak English. If I do not, then I can use Chinese. There is no rule at Blue Rain café. (Gao, 2007: 266)

In the meantime, the participants felt emboldened to use English to communicate with each other. Indeed, they felt that English gave them 'a sense of self-protection and security' even if it was not their mother tongue. It can be argued that the quality of human relationships overrides the importance of providing language learning opportunities in the perceptions of individual participants at the club. As a result, the club became an important platform for the participants to use English, and a safe site for them to seek self-actualisation 'within the constraints of reality' (Al-Shehri, 2009: 165).

In pursuit of 'ideal' individuals

The supportive social network as identified in the analysis of the discussion posts relating to the Blue Rain Café encourages various participants to pursue the learning and use of English. It was also found in the analysis that the supportive learning community attracted participants because it has core members whose attributes reflect the visions of 'ideal self' that these participants had in learning English. In fact, it was noted that many discussants might have strongly identified themselves with the two coordinators of the club (Steve and Mr. Chen, pseudonyms). In spite of its extremely fluid membership, central figures such as Steve and Mr. Chen played an important role in maintaining community cohesion and guiding the participants to pursue the objective of making friends through using English together. They both had a 'perfect' command of English, which enabled them to undertake any conversation topics in English as recorded by the following participants' discussion posts:

Mr. Chen can talk about anything with you. He can make everything enjoyable for you. Everyone likes him and welcomes his participation. His experience and knowledge enable him to take on any topics with anybody. Every newcomer will stay with Mr. Chen for a few minutes so he is greeted by a lot of people each time. [...] (Gao, 2007: 264)

It was quite a dramatic experience to talk to Steve. The first time I came to Blue Rain Café, I was ill at ease in a corner, listening to others. There were [...] repeated references to Steve, which made me look forward to meeting him. [...] Then he appeared in the café. [...] I rushed to talk to him wondering whether this skinny man was the legendary Steve. [...] I asked him a question quite directly: 'So...you are Steve? What makes you so

famous?' He [...] laughed, 'Because I'm ugly!' I could not think of an immediate response (Gao, 2007: 265).

It is not difficult to detect signs of admiration that other club participants had
for the two coordinators in the above two extracts. One might see that the
two stood for the kind of 'ideal' self that other participants wanted to pursue
in their efforts to socialise with others in English. In many senses, Steve and
Mr. Chen represented the successful middle-class in the city, which increasingly benefits from China's deepened engagement with the world. They were
also found to have embodied a variety of competences, qualities and skills,
together with remarkable proficiency in English. In particular, they had valuable professional exposure and life experiences, which made them role models
for other aspiring participants. They also had attractive personal qualities and
were easy to get along with.

Participants in this club also found that this was a place for self-assertion. In
the club, the participants had many opportunities to assert what they wanted
to be before strangers in this new social group. They were susceptible to the
enticing prospect of having free conversations on anything without revealing
too much about themselves. Their portrayal of deep conversations with like-
minded people in the club is suggestive of the respondents' strong desire to
assert who they wanted to be as distinct from what they had already been
perceived as being in other arenas of life. Opportunities to satisfy such desires
in human exchanges were undoubtedly appealing to these participants, who
found it trivial to suffer boring questions related to their personal history
(what they were) in comparison with the gains in being what they wanted to
be, as can be seen in the following extracts:

> The purpose of going there for me is to find someone who I could have a
> deep talk with for sharing the same interests. [...] It's better on a dull rainy
> day, [a] few people sit opposite each other talking about films and music. I
> think it's better not to ask too much about private matters such as what do
> you do or what's your name in the forum. Just find something in common
> and exchange personal ideas. After leaving, you will recall this chat the
> whole week and you would expect to meet such a friend next time (Gao,
> 2007: 266).
>
> [I] agree with Mayflower for each time I went to EC (author's note: English
> corner). I was asked the same questions by different people, like name, occu-
> pation... I'm really sick of such questions but still wonder how can I be so
> patient to answer them again and again. But for compensation, I can always
> meet with different interesting people, have a nice and enlightening talk
> every time. That's the driving-force for me to put up with those boring ques-
> tions. But I didn't mean any offence here. (Gao, 2007: 266–67)

All these messages indicate that these participants were attracted to the community because they were given opportunities to become self-assertive individuals. As a result, this learning community had an inevitable impact upon the participants' self-perceptions and feelings of belonging, which in turn enhance the community's cohesion. As in the narrative of Emily, she even changed her English name to be identified with a group of participants with whom she continued to practise English beyond their participation in the club. The development of 'J-Group' in the following quote illustrates the way strangers of yesterday became members of today's English learning community in the English club:

> I found that I fell in love with it. I practised my oral English a lot and at the same time I made a great many good friends there. The first time I went there, I had a great time with Jett, Joy, Jason and Jane. It happened that four of us five had names that started with the letter J, so we came up with an idea to form a group, jokingly named J-Group. And I changed my original name Emily to Jemily and then became a member of the group. [...] We formed such a group to help us all practise English well. We had fun chatting in English. [...]. We not only chatted in the English corner but also on the internet. (Gao, 2007: 267)

As can be seen in the above-mentioned extracts, the learning community emerging from the English club not only allowed individual participants to pursue their visions of 'ideal self', they also had effects on their self-perceptions; this in turn might have helped sustain their desire to continue collaborating in English learning activities at and beyond the club, including forming English learning partnerships through online discussion and so on.

Discussion and conclusion

In this chapter, I have drawn on and re-examined two empirical studies on Chinese learners' experiences and re-examined the writing extracts related to how these learners were motivated to learn English autonomously in contexts in which real-life opportunities to use the language are scarce. The findings from the two studies illustrate how autonomous learners invest learning efforts when motivated by powerful visions of 'ideal self', and how they sustain their learning efforts through maintaining their access to supportive social networks (Al-Shehri, 2009; Ushioda & Dörnyei, 2009). Although the first study (Gao, 2010) is about a learner in the late 1970s and the second (Gao, 2007) about learners in the twenty-first century, both studies reveal that the learners' localised use of English enabled them to pursue their 'ideal self', which subsequently guided and sustained their autonomous learning efforts with new visions. It is noteworthy that in both studies language learners transformed their engagement with the global process into local constructions and maintenance of supportive communities, which profoundly mediated their pursuit of 'ideal self' when learning English.

In the first study (Gao, 2010), Zhang, as a disabled language learner, achieved language learning success almost impossible even for learners with no medical condition such as hers. It was noted that she projected different versions of her 'self' in sustaining her autonomous efforts to learn English. The narratives about her published in the 1980s portray her as someone who is physically disabled but wholeheartedly committed to serving the society and nation as a young socialist. Zhang, in her own accounts, also saw English competence as a crucial part of her pursuit of being a young socialist who could serve the society and nation in spite of her physical disabilities. Her more recent autobiographical account also includes an imagined self, embodied as 'Mariana', which appears to be much more private and less political. In addition to this resourcefulness, Zhang was also found to have persistently involved other language learners in forming supportive networks, which is indicative of the significance of these social networks for her pursuit of 'ideal self' and English competence. In the second study, learners were found to have come together to practise English, and in their efforts to use the language together they developed a strong sense of community in an English club. These learners were identified in the study to have also envisioned the use of English in their community as an important part of their 'middle-class' self identities. They have among themselves a few individuals embodying these desirable qualities of new individuals, such as the coordinators of the English club, who were both local and global in their outlook. In the community, the participants established a social space where they supported each other in creating new selves and pursuing such imagined selves. In other words, the club was a socialisation site where, in their perception, a sense of belonging brought and kept the participants together in a close-knit learning community. It was also a social community of English learners, where non-native speakers of English attempted to satisfy their inner needs for social exchanges and self-assertion in English (see also Chapter 8, this volume, for Henry's analysis of the digital game communities formed by Swedish learners of English).

Further reflections on the data also help show that these learners' visions of 'ideal self' emerge from their interactions with shifting contextual conditions. The highly politicised situation in the late 1970s imbued the learner's construction of 'ideal self' with socialist discourses, while language learners were imbued with a strong spirit of seeking pleasure and status in the relatively open Chinese society of the new century (Landsberger, 2001; Shi, 2006; Zhang, 1999). However, participants in both studies were found to have valued the importance of supportive networks in motivating and sustaining their efforts to learn English. These findings suggest that language learners need to believe in the localised use of English, the global language, to express their personal meanings and experiences so that they can continuously invest efforts in the learning of English. For these reasons, in such contexts I contend that language teachers can have a pivotal role to play in utilising language learners' visions of 'ideal self' and encouraging them to undertake efforts to construct local social networks in their learning efforts to pursue competence in English, the global language.

Engagement priorities

These findings suggest that critical examination of language learners' visions of 'ideal self' provides valuable opportunities for researchers to study how individuals see the language as a crucial part of their identity and how they can be empowered by their English competence. Further research into such engagement by learners will reveal the dynamic interaction of learners' visions and contextual mediation, which in turn can inform language teachers' pedagogical efforts to assist their pursuit of English competence as motivated by visions of 'ideal self'. The findings also provide a few priority issues for language teachers to address in their professional practice. In particular, they may get their learners to reflect on the following questions in order to help enhance their capacity for autonomous language learning:

1. How is English competence related to learners' visions of 'ideal self'? This may help them to identify what would motivate and sustain their learning efforts.
2. Which individuals closely resemble the 'ideal self' in their visions? The efforts to answer this question may help them realise that their visions are not fantasies. Critical engagement with this question also makes them appreciate the challenges that lie ahead in pursuit of their visions.
3. Who may share similar visions of 'ideal self' to theirs? The answer to this question decides whether it is possible for them to initiate and sustain supportive social networks for their language learning efforts.
4. What sorts of social networks are available in their learning context? With reference to Henry's (Chapter 8, this volume) analysis of digital game communities formed by Swedish learners of English, language teachers need to broaden their understanding of language learning beyond classrooms. With a better understanding of out-of-class learning, language teachers then can encourage language learners to find and form their own supportive learning networks.
5. How might these social networks be utilised to motivate their language learning? It is important that language teachers support language learners

with the language needed to enhance their participation in these networks. In other words, all the pedagogical efforts should focus on enabling language learners to use their imagination and foster social community so that using English could be made a meaningful and transformative experience that profoundly mediates their pursuit of 'ideal self'.

Suggested further reading

Dörnyei, Z. and Ushioda, E. (eds) (2009). *Motivation, Language Identity and the L2 Self.* Bristol: Multilingual Matters.
This is an excellent collection of studies that illustrate an entirely new direction in motivation research informed by self and identity perspectives.

Wenger, E. (2000). Communities of practice and social learning systems. *Organization,* 7(2): 225–46.
This article presents a concise but informative overview of the principles and procedures as to how we may develop social networks to support learning in general.

References

Al-Shehri, A. S. (2009). Motivation and vision: the relation between the ideal L2 self, imagination and visual style. In Z. Dörnyei and E. Ushioda (eds) *Motivation, Language Identity and the L2 Self.* Bristol: Multilingual Matters, pp. 164–71.

Canagarajah, S. (2007). Lingua Franca English, multilingual communities, and language acquisition. *Modern Language Journal,* 91(5): 921–37.

Gao, X. (2006). Understanding changes in Chinese students' uses of learning strategies in China and Britain: a socio-cultural re-interpretation. *System,* 34: 55–67.

Gao, X. (2007). A tale of Blue Rain Café: a study on the online narrative construction about a community of English learners on the Chinese mainland. *System,* 35: 259–70.

Gao, X. (2008). You had to work hard cause you didn't know whether you were going to wear shoes or straw sandals! *Journal of Language, Identity and Education,* 8(3): 169–87.

Gao, X. (2010). Autonomous language learning against all odds. *System,* 38: 580–90.

Giddens, A. (1984). *The Constitution of Society: Outline of the Theory of Structuration.* Berkeley, CA: University of California Press.

Gu, P. Y. (2003). Fine brush and freehand: the vocabulary-learning art of two successful Chinese EFL learners. *TESOL Quarterly,* 37(1): 73–104.

Jiang, X. and Smith, R. (2009). Chinese learners' strategy use in historical perspective: a cross-generational interview-based study. *System,* 37: 286–99.

Lamb, M. (2007). The impact of school on EFL learning motivation: an Indonesian case-study. *TESOL Quarterly,* 41(4): 757–80.

Landsberger, S. (2001). Learning by what example? educational propaganda in twenty-first century China. *Critical Asian Studies,* 33(4): 541–71.

Li, Z. (2009). Beautiful English vs. Multilingual self. In J. Lo Bianco, J. Orton, J. and Y. Gao (eds) *China and English: Globalization and the Dilemmas of Identity.* Bristol: Multilingual Matters, pp. 125–36.

Oxford, R. (2003). Towards a more systematic model of L2 learner autonomy. In D. Palfreyman and R. C. Smith (eds) *Learner Autonomy across Cultures: Language Education Perspectives.* Basingstoke: Palgrave Macmillan, pp. 75–92.

Oxford, R. (2008). Hero with a thousand faces: learner autonomy, learning strategies and learning tactics in independent language learning. In S. Hurd and T. Lewis (eds) *Language Learning Strategies in Independent Settings*. Bristol: Multilingual Matters, pp. 41–63.

Palfreyman, D. (2003). Expanding the discourse on learner development: a reply to Anita Wenden. *Applied Linguistics*, 24: 243–48.

Palfreyman, D. (2006). Social context and resources for language learning. *System*, 34: 352–70.

Phillipson, R. (1992). *Linguistic Imperialism*. Oxford: Oxford University Press.

Sealey, A. and Carter, B. (2004). *Applied Linguistics as Social Science*. London: Continuum.

Shi, L. J. (2006). The successors to Confucianism or a new generation? A question-naire study on Chinese students' culture of learning English. *Language, Culture and Curriculum*, 19(1): 122–47.

Ushioda, E. (2011). Motivating learners to speak as themselves. In G. Murray, X. Gao and T. Lamb (eds) *Identity, Motivation and Autonomy in Language Learning*. Bristol: Multilingual Matters, pp. 11–24.

Ushioda, E. and Dörnyei, Z. (2009). Motivation, language identities and the L2 self: a theoretical overview. In Z. Dörnyei and E. Ushioda (eds) *Motivation, Language Identity and the L2 Self*. Bristol: Multilingual Matters, pp. 1–8.

Wenden, A. (1998). Metacognitive knowledge and language learning. *Applied Linguistics*, 19: 515–37.

Wenden, A. (2002). Learner development in language learning. *Applied Linguistics*, 23: 32–55.

Wenger, E. (1998). *Communities of Practice: Learning, Meaning, and Identity*. New York: Cambridge University Press.

Wenger, E. (2000). Communities of practice and social learning systems. *Organization*, 7(2): 225–46.

Yang, N. (1999). The relationship between EFL learners' beliefs and learning strategy use. *System*, 27: 515–35.

Zhang, J. L. (2003). Research into Chinese EFL learner strategies: methods, findings and instructional issues. *RELC Journal*, 34: 284–322.

Zhang, M. (1999). From Lei Feng to Zhang Haidi: changing media images of model youth in the post-Mao reform era. In R. Kluver and J. Powers (eds) *Civic Discourse, Civil Society, and Chinese Communities*. Stamford, CT: Ablex Publishing Corporation, pp. 111–23.

Zuengler, J. and Miller, E. R. (2006). Cognitive and sociocultural perspectives: two parallel SLA worlds. *TESOL Quarterly*, 40(1): 35–58.

11
Social Identity and Language Learning Motivation: Exploring the Connection and Activating Learning

Lane Igoudin

Immigrant pathways to the language classroom are manifold. Some may have arrived in their new homeland as children and now need additional training to enhance the quality of their language. Others may have come later in life with some rudimentary exposure to their second language, but with an educational degree, a career in their native country and the presence of learning skills and strategies they entail. Still others might have come without much prior schooling and are now building their strength in their second language from the ground up.

Teaching in a large, urban English as a Second Language (ESL) programme in Southern California, I see all these types of students. These learners have mastered enough English to survive, but still come back to school to study, filling up our evening ESL classes after long hours at work, some still in their nursing scrubs and checked restaurant kitchen trousers. What drives them? What makes them commit to the challenges of learning despite, or on top of, the pressures of earning a living, taking care of children and elderly parents, and supporting extended families in their countries of origin? Why are they in my class?

Social context of motivation for language learning

To fully understand the social framework of adult language learning, we have to reach across the disciplinary boundaries into the fields of behavioural and educational psychology as well as sociology.

Research in educational psychology postulates that adults' engagement in learning activities is tied directly to their view of themselves and their place in the society. Due to important physical and psychological developments in adult life, factors that have direct bearing on adult learning include: possession of reasons for learning, the adult concept of the self, timing of learning experience to life events, need for application of knowledge to real-life situations, and the internal origin of the desire to learn (Knowles, 1990). Motivation, here, is the impulse, the energy that under the right circumstances may translate into an effort to learn. Adult education is fundamentally a choice and, thus, my preferred definition of motivation is: 'the choices people make as to what experiences or goals they will approach or avoid, and the degree of effort they will exert in that respect' (Keller, 1983: 389).

Adult participation in learning may arise from a variety of reasons originating in their social lives. To identify and classify those reasons, in one well-known research project, an Education Participation Scale (a 40-item interview instrument) was administered to more than 12,000 participants around the world (Bolshier & Collins, 1983). Based on the participants' responses, the researchers proposed six fundamental psychosocial motivational orientations guiding adult participation in educational activities:

- *cognitive interest* (enjoyment of learning for its own sake);
- *community service* (advancement of one's family and community);
- *external expectations* (participation due to a requirement, professional or otherwise);
- *professional advancement* (employment/career-oriented reasons);
- *social contact* (interest in group activities and relationship-building);
- *social stimulation* (education as an escape from boredom or frustration).

From the behavioural psychology standpoint, motivation, like other learning-associated behaviours, is an expression of two general tendencies: to master and to belong (Jones, 1968; MacKeracher, 1989). The tendency to master moves a person to achieve the central, powerful status in his/her social context, to organise it and control his/her actions and interactions within it 'in order to enhance survival and self-esteem' (MacKeracher, 1989: 191). Being informed and skilled reduces the uncertainty of new experiences and assures the individual's identity and integrity. The tendency to belong moves the individual to join a social unit in order to enhance security and the sense of connectedness with others. This sense of connection is desired both at the temporal (past and future) and social levels, as in successful interpersonal relationships and inclusion in activities and membership in self-selected groups.

This notion clearly applies to immigrant language learners, who as newcomers standing outside of the dominant language society have to make an effort to *master* their social situation, in part by acquiring the language that allows them to access power in the L2 society, and to integrate into it, that is, to *belong*.

As seen above, learning is inseparable from the socio-cultural context in which it takes place. Jarvis (1987) and Mezirow (1981) suggested a correlation between the adults' potential to learn and the harmony between them and the environment in which they function. 'When there is disharmony or discontinuity – both subsumed under the idea of *disjuncture* – then people have to seek to adjust (learn), so that harmony can be re-established' (Jarvis, 1987: 79). Learning activity may occur as a proactive, relevant, and meaningful response of the adult to the conflict generated by disjuncture.

Lastly, it is important to keep in mind that motivation for learning is not a stable condition. Keller (1983) pointed out the *relevance* of the learning situation as a prerequisite to sustaining motivation over time. Failure in a learning situation dissolves a student's motivation, causing *learned helplessness* (Bandura, 1982; DeCharms, 1984; Weiner, 1984), or *amotivation*. Relating this condition to the adult self, Crookes (2003) asserted that a student who has experienced such failure in language learning would likely attribute it to his/her own shortcomings, rather than to problems with the course content or materials. Relevance extends beyond the learner's goals in the classroom to include the fulfilment sought from the learning process for the psychological needs of achievement, affiliation, and, ultimately, power.

Observing motivation in the language classroom

In the classroom context, motivation is a cyclical, interactive process between the learner and the learning environment. Motivation initiates the student's actions in the class and is influenced by the feedback and behaviours of others in the classroom. 'In directing and coordinating various operations towards an object or goal, motivation transforms a number of separate reactions into significant action' (Julkunen, 2001: 30; see also Crookes & Schmidt, 1991; Pintrich & Schunk, 1996). The interaction between the learner and his or her peers also affects their motivation, in that being in a positive group encourages enthusiasm for learning, while being in a negative group inhibits it (Chang, 2010: 149).

When observed in a classroom, the learner's actions signifying interest and engagement in the learning process can be used as evidence of motivation. A motivated learner, for example, may employ meta-cognitive *learning strategies* that make learning more effective, such as asking for help or practising with a friend (Dörnyei, 2005). Crookes (2003: 129) defines temporal manifestations of motivation as *persistence*, which occurs when a person focuses action on the same thing for an extended period of time.

Recently, qualitative methodologies for motivation research have begun to emerge, employing interviews and observation in the study of language learning motivation (Guilloteaux & Dörnyei, 2008; Song, 2006; Syed, 2001;

Ushioda, 2001). These methods support a vision of language learning motivation as a dynamic, longitudinal process in which the learners' cognitions and beliefs, social context, and the relevance of the curriculum to the learners' interests directly affect involvement in learning. Syed's study, in particular, showed that student motivation is affected by classroom atmosphere, turn-taking practices, teacher-student interaction, and learning activities used in the course, while Song's study of failure in a community college ESL course showed socially derived factors, such as family and job responsibilities, contributing significantly to students' failure in the course.

The socio-educational model of second language acquisition focusing on the integrative/instrumental dichotomy (Gardner and Lambert, 1972) laid the groundwork for contemporary research on language learning motivation and, despite considerable criticism (Au, 1988; Canagarajah, 2006; Peirce, 1995), continues to influence the field. The last 20 years saw a surge of interest in language learning motivation, following Crookes and Schmidt's (1991) article 'Motivation: Reopening the research agenda' in *Language Learning*. Only recently, however, did linguists begin to distinguish between second and foreign language learners in the study of motivation, and to suggest that 'the dynamics involved in learning these two different types of language may be quite different' (Gardner, 2001 in Dörnyei & Schmidt, 2001: 11). So far, however, most research done in the field – including an array of important volumes that summarise current research in language learning motivation (e.g., Dörnyei, 2003; Dörnyei & Schmidt, 2001; Ushioda & Dörnyei, 2009) – has focused overwhelmingly on foreign, rather than second language learning.

This is quite unfortunate, as ESL students – the bulk of whom are immigrants learning English in an English-speaking (L2) society – find themselves in a very different learning situation from EFL learners, with the social context, realities, and pressures of living in an L2 society directly affecting their motivation and the ways in which language educators can address it. That is to say, an adult immigrant from Mexico will be learning English in Kansas City under vastly different social circumstances than a language student taking an English class in Mexico.

Compared to other adult students, ESL students have an additional challenge in not only learning the language, but also socialising into the L2 society's culture (Florez & Burt, 2001). The ESL programmes, curricula, and teaching styles may sometimes be a difficult fit with the immigrant's cultural experience and expectations. Resistance, failure, and disengagement are not uncommon results of the interaction between an English learner and the educational process. From the academic point of view, L2 proficiency for ESL students does not stop at the language alone, but affects other skills necessary to succeed in the college environment, such as math, reading, writing, and learning skills (Fulks & Alancraig, 2008). Knowing how to address the underlying student motivation issues is, therefore, crucial to providing quality education to ESL students.

The need for more research into motivational processes within the ESL population is clear, and some studies of L2-learning immigrants in English-speaking countries such as Australia, Canada, and the United States have begun to appear (Bernat, 2004; Noels et al., 1999; Paper, 1990; Reynoso, 2008; Skilton-Sylvester, 2002; Song, 2006; Waterman, 2008).

Driven by my own interest in adult student motivation – both as a linguist interested in psychological and social factors affecting L2 acquisition, and as a classroom practitioner – I conducted a research project (Igoudin, 2008) that looked into why adult immigrants choose to take an advanced L2 course, and what are the factors that foster or inhibit their desire to learn. Conducted in one semester-length advanced ESL reading course taught by another instructor at a Southern California community college, the project investigated motivational processes among ten adult immigrants who were enrolled. The study employed a combination of qualitative and quantitative methods, including individual interviews that elicited in-depth descriptive data on student beliefs and attitudes, and an attitude motivation test battery (AMTB), which tested the strength of various components within the participants' motivation for language learning. Interview and survey results were triangulated with 15 hours of classroom observation that highlighted students' motivational behaviours in real-time classroom, and relevant, socio-cultural data, including participant demographics and projected goals, as well as analysis of course documents (syllabus, attendance records, and grades). Some findings from the study are cited throughout the chapter.

Adult ESL pathways to formal language learning in California

The learning landscape an adult immigrant enters in California requires considerable knowledge. While the state's public policy supports the integration of immigrants into the mainstream society, the educational tracks that lead to formal language acquisition are hardly straightforward; they frequently overlap or show gaps, mostly due to the discordant priorities and funding sources of English-teaching programmes.

Historically, adult education schemes have tied the learning of English as a second language to the importance of the immigrant's employment attainment and career development. Note, for example, the central position of employability in the California Department of Education (CDE) definition of ESL in its *Adult Education Handbook for California* (1997): 'education for adults whose inability to speak, read, or write the English language constitutes a substantial impairment of their ability to get or retain employment and to function in society' (*AEHC*, 1997: 203).

Since its beginning in the mid-nineteenth century, adult education in California (and in the United States at large) has been divided into two pathways, vocational and academic, 'in recognition of [their] distinctive purposes, ethos, policies, organisation, and forms of provision' (Titmus, 1989: 93). Today, state-sponsored adult ESL education is delivered primarily through a system of adult schools, as well as credit and non-credit programmes at the state's 112 community colleges, the largest college system in the world. While the ESL statistics are hard to separate from remedial English and math in the state's basic skills data (one reason being that many ESL students take remedial math as well), the magnitude of this population is staggering: In the academic year 2006–07 alone, 719,482 students in the California Community College system took at least one basic skills and/or ESL course (*Board of Governors of the California Community Colleges*, 2008: 7).

In a real-life application of such division, ESL educational schemes at community colleges are often separated into two programmes. Vocational ESL programmes primarily offer L2 education at lower levels as part of basic adult education and citizenship preparation. Its courses are usually free and non-credited, funded by local and state budgets, as well as by federal grants. Academic ESL programmes, on the other hand, are geared towards higher levels of language proficiency, in particular to college writing and reading. Language education, here, serves as the first step on the education ladder leading to academic degrees (Associate, Bachelor and graduate) or certificated vocational education. The ESL courses in this track offer college credit, including some that are transferable for university credit. Nor are they free, although many students, particularly in poorer districts (which are also those with higher concentrations of immigrant populations) qualify for financial aid. The funding of these programmes comes primarily from the state.

The system is anything but uniform and is often confusing to the language learner. Whether a particular community college offers credit and/or non-credit ESL classes, their organisation, number, curricular content, and the unit credit they earn vary widely from one district to the next. In some programmes, ESL courses are dual-listed as credit and non-credit, drawing both groups of students. Moreover, since assessment procedures vary between 72 community college districts, placement is district-specific, and transfer between ESL programmes of (and sometimes within) different districts is limited. The point of exit out of ESL and into the mainstream English programmes is also decided by an individual community college district and, sometimes, a particular college within the district as well.

In recent years, the need for more college graduates to sustain California's economy, compounded by unprecedented cuts to the state budget, have led to reconsideration of educational priorities in the state's community college system. Whereas these colleges had traditionally served multiple types of student populations, the high-school graduate population, college-bound and requiring minimum remediation, appears to be the one favoured by the state policymakers. As a result, funding for adult education and non-credit ESL programmes has been significantly reduced, and the remaining ESL programmes (as well as the colleges at large) are under pressure to produce data that shows student persistence, programme completion, and increased transfer rates to four-year colleges and universities (*SSTF*, 2012: 7–9).

Viewed as a remedial service, college ESL has been under unprecedented attack. A recent legislative proposal grouped ESL with remedial English and math and called for 'a clear strategy [...] to move students from educational basic skills to career and college readiness' (*SSTF*, 2011: 44), leaving it in the hands of the state government to determine where these programmes should be placed (p. 46), and opening the door to cutting credit ESL courses at the college level. After considerable protests from the students, faculty, and unions throughout the state (see, for instance, *ASCCC*, 2011), this recommendation was removed, for the time being, from the final reform proposal, but the overall political climate remains unfriendly to ESL.

Into this complex language education landscape steps an immigrant learner with his/her own multifaceted set of needs, desires, and aspirations.

Student self-concept in second-language acquisition

> Who am I?
> Why am I taking this class?
> Why do I need to be here?
> Who will I be after I finish this course?

These questions are at the centre of the adult students' engagement in a learning process and are often mirrored by the teachers' wondering:

> Why are they in my class?
> They seem to want to learn the language, but why aren't they interested?
> Why do they take it all so personally?

As we will learn in this chapter, answering these questions, which are rarely made explicit, is crucial to understanding student motivation and success in the language classroom. Furthermore, what we know about our students' ideas of themselves can help us activate important motivational processes within them.

Origin of motivation and the self

Self-concepts are 'individuals' mental images of themselves' (Reeve, 1997: 240). In ongoing interaction with others, humans receive feedback which they process in relation to their view of their selves. Often this communicative loop concerns language skills, a sensitive issue with the second language learner. Consider these observations made in class by my students:

- Yesterday, I had to repeat my words twice at work because my customers could not understand my accent.
- Today I had to ask my nephew to help me write a letter to the landlord because my writing skills are limited.
- My neighbour only says hello to me, but talks more to my wife because her English is better.

While the recollection of each experience may be lost, the experiences themselves solidify, over time, into conclusions people have about themselves. For example, an adult relates these generalisations to the important aspects of his or her life: academic competence, intellectual ability, friendships, romantic relationships, and moral conduct (Harter, 1990). Studies show that once an acceptable view of oneself in a particular domain is established, the self is very resistant to contradictory information that challenges it (Markus, 1983). The contradiction produces emotional tension and the motivational energy to resolve it.

Let's look more closely at how the processes within the self generate motivation. According to Reeve (1997), the self produces motivational energy in two ways:

1. To direct the individual to behave in the ways that ensure the positive relationship between the self-view and the social feedback it receives. The contradictory feedback, for example, a person's generalisation that his or her particular language skill is inadequate, will motivate the adult to restore the harmony.
2. To achieve a different, or desired self-concept. In a similar vein, Ushioda & Dörnyei (2009) reconceptualised language learning motivation as a part of an internally driven move from the current, deficient self-concept to the *ideal self* whose desirable attributes include second language proficiency.

It should be noted that while we can sense a motivational potential in these contexts, it may not necessarily lead to the act of engagement in learning, which depends on other factors and circumstances.

My study (Igoudin, 2008) shed light on one particular place in which the social context and motivation for language learning intersected. Prompted by the question, 'Has anything happened in your personal life that sparked your interest in studying English?', participants often produced narratives illustrating how their motivation originated in specific instances of disjuncture between their L2 proficiency and the needs arising from the social context of their lives. Here, again, motivation moves an individual to restore harmony between the self and his/her environment. Let us consider the following excerpts from the interviews with five out of ten study participants.

In the first example, Tomas, who had completed his university education and worked as an engineer in Mexico, wanted to recapture his academic success in the United States: 'If I want to get a master's degree, I need English. If I want to keep studying here, I need to speak good English to understand and write and listen'. His English language proficiency, however, stood in the way of his achieving his goal.

Another student, Lucia, felt isolated in her social circle. Her friends spoke fluent English and had to switch to Spanish when addressing her. The sense of separation and embarrassment motivated her to resume her English studies:

> Lucia: I've been meeting people; they are from Central America or South America. They are here living probably 15–20 years already, so they speak English very well. So, one of them, we are friends, but sometimes I feel like we cannot be together, we cannot be friends because I'm not at the level she is. Sometimes, that push me down, really down, because I feel like we are the same age, we love each other, but I feel like, I have a big, big difference because she speak English very well and Spanish, and I don't. [...] That happened, like, 6 months ago that I decided to come to college. I had started already another school, I finished 3 years and then I stopped.
> Interviewer: Why did you start again?
> Lucia: Because of her and other friends. Sometimes when I go out with her and her friends, all of them speak English. and she has to sometime translate to me something, and I feel embarrassed, so embarrassed.

Poor job prospects in her native El Salvador led Blanca to planning an education and a career in the United States. English was an integral step on her way to achieving that goal:

> Blanca: In my country, there are many professionals, many engineers and many people that have their careers, but they can't find any jobs. So I said, what are you going to study here? If one day I have my degrees, where am I going to work? So I said, I better go another place to study and then maybe find a better job.
> Interviewer: How would you describe your reasons for learning English?
> Blanca: Because I'm in a different country, not in my country, I have to learn English.

Anabel's poor English skills were detrimental to her career growth. To her, learning the language and moving up the employment ladder has since gone hand in hand:

> Anabel: First thing I want to know the language, everything that is English – all the pronunciation, I want it get better because my work. I get this right, speak with everybody, and I want to be able to understand, sometimes I don't understand some words. That is why I'm here and I want to get my degree, administrative assistant. [...] I'm moving up because my English and my school.
> Interviewer: Because your English is better?
> Anabel: Yes, because before I start in the warehouse and then I jumped to the QC [quality control], then went to the clerk, and now I'm revenue auditor.

Chibith, a Cambodian who was born in the United States and grew up bilingual, also felt a disconnect when assessing her command of English. Fluent orally, Chibith was nonetheless unsatisfied with her communicative, writing, reading, and listening skills. At the time of the study, she was attending her fourth ESL class and preparing to transfer into the mainstream English curriculum. Her gains in language education proved to her that she could fill the gaps.

> I have a problem communicating. Now that I'm in class and learning, I have a better communication style. [...] I have listening problems too, like retaining information. I always have to ask people 2–3 times what they say for me to know what they're saying. I got better reading too. Before I had to read the text 2–3 times to understand the information. Now I read it one time and understand the whole thing. And with writing – I used to hate writing. But ever since I took my ESL 56 class in the summer, I think I have a better writing style and I enjoy it.

Social identity and language learning

The interview excerpts above highlight specific instances of misalignment between an individual's language proficiency and his/her social environment, which eventually led towards language learning. Further exploration revealed the student's *social identity* – a person's definition of his or her 'meaning in the world' and value to others (Eckert, 2000) – to be an important factor shaping his/her motivation. Both identity formation and learning originate and develop in interaction with the learner's social context, but also with each other, making their relationship a shared, dialogical process (Ligorio, 2010).

Recent studies have exposed additional links between language learning and the learners' changing perspectives of themselves in a new language environment. Applying Pierre Bourdieu's socio-economical paradigm (1991) to language learning, Peirce (1995: 17) introduced the concept of *investment* in learning a dominant language as a means to 'acquire a wider range of symbolic and material resources [and] increase the value of [the learners'] cultural capital'. Two recent qualitative studies, of six Dominican and four Cambodian adult students (Reynoso, 2008; Skilton-Sylvester, 2002, respectively), confirmed the interconnectedness of the social and cultural identities, on one hand, and the investment and persistence in taking adult ESL courses on the other. Meanwhile, Sfard and Prusak (2005) suggested language learning itself to be the closing of a gap between the learners' actual and designated, or desired, identities.

Similarly, a strong correlation emerged in my 2008 study between a participant's inclusion of L2 culture in their social identity and high integrative content in their motivation for language learning. Indeed I found it difficult to separate the study of the participants' integrative motives from the study of their changing identity. Advanced language learning clearly served a dual purpose to these students: as a means to improve mastery of a language (which is what the educators are traditionally concerned with), and as a transitional step on the path towards achieving their social goals, including integration into L2 society and attainment of a desired, integrative identity.

The interviews, in particular, highlighted the relationship between the 'designated identity' (Sfard & Prusak, 2005) or the 'ideal L2 self' (Ushioda & Dörnyei, 2009) – an internal perception of one's anticipated self as a speaker of L2 – and language learning as a path towards it.

For example, Tomas who said he wanted to talk as if he 'were like an American', produced a high score (83 per cent) in his attitudes towards the L2 speakers and culture and the highest overall score for the (integrative) section of the survey (91 per cent). He also showed 2:1 weighting of integrative versus instrumental motives. This is how he explained it:

> Tomas: I like English, the language, and I like to read most of the articles in the magazines, everything. And I like to meet people, I like to understand them, I like to learn, but good English... I'd like to talk like if I were like an American.
> Interviewer: That makes sense. But do you have reasons like you want to get a job?
> Tomas: Yeah, but if I speak good English, of course, I will get a job.

Likewise, Lucia, who scored high (84 per cent) on the integrative motives overall, showed a strong pull towards the new culture. She wanted to function actively in it, certainly not as an outsider, saying: 'I want to be part of this culture. If you don't learn English, it's like I'm not here. It's not just about work, it's not just about school, I wanna be part of this culture, and without English it is not gonna happen'.

On the other hand, Chibith, concerned with retaining her Cambodian identity, scored only 60 per cent in her integrative orientation. Her attitude was in no way negative, and she appreciated the benefits language proficiency would bring her, yet she was keen on keeping an equilibrium between her 'Americanised' and Cambodian selves. The fact that she was born in the United States was a likely factor in her identity struggle.

> I'd like to be seen as Cambodian. [...] All these new generations coming up, they don't understand, they don't know who they are. And that thing pisses me off, you know? All they know how to speak is English, and they should, because...They forget themselves, and I don't want to be like them. So I'm trying to learn English, at the same time, remember my own culture and who I am. [...] I want to advance as far as I can and try to be Americanized, and, at the same time, know who I am, and what culture my parents came from.

As socially constructed identities change, balancing first and second language identities becomes more complicated. The surveyed students' socio-cultural context of learning was markedly bilingual. Though it was possible for most study participants, as Spanish speakers residing in greater Los Angeles, to function entirely in their native language, the cumulative picture which emerged from the surveys and interviews showed that most students commonly used both languages off-campus while use of their native languages was limited primarily to their family networks.

Furthermore, the subjects' desired workplace language environments have shown the move from bilingual to English-only. Of the eight employed students, four worked in bilingual environments. Two were employed in English-only and two in Spanish-only workplaces. At the same time, six projected their long-term careers in English-only environments and three others in bilingual workplaces. In one such example, the young, entrepreneurial Daniel sought both integration in the English-speaking culture and respect for his roots. There is a tinge of stigma about his perception of Spanish speakers, something he clearly wants to overcome:

> Daniel: Actually, you speak like everybody thinks [you are] like. If you speak Spanish, it's gonna be like, 'Oh, you're Mexican or something.' So I'm in America, so I have to speak a little bit of English. And speaking English, just like the teacher say, changes yourself. So if you start speaking English, you start understanding Americans living here, you get into the culture.

Interviewer: How do you want to be seen?

Daniel: I'd like to be seen like...a Mexican who made it in America! [laughs]

A brief theoretical analysis

Adult second language learning is inherently a voluntary process, in particular, at the more advanced, post-survival stages of language acquisition. Set in a social context, thus, adult learning is not simply a process of passive acquisition of knowledge, but also one of externalisation of experience. The desire to be in the classroom may originate within the adults' vision of who they are and who they want to be. Psychologically, the student is continuously engaged in defining and redefining his or her self, relating it to the society at large, and discovering, developing, and fulfilling personal potential.

Applying these generalisations to the adult immigrant experience, it seems likely that fundamental life changes brought about by immersion in a society communicating in an unfamiliar language, compounded by the necessity to function in it, may cause disjuncture in these adults' lives and prompt them to seek language education in order to adjust to these changes. Some immigrants may seek language education immediately upon arrival, whereas for others the language disjuncture may occur later in their lives when higher levels of language proficiency (i.e., beyond the survival skills) may be desired. Deficiency of knowledge combined with an evolved self-concept set in a specific socio-cultural milieu may then generate a new need – a need to learn.

Applying the understanding of motivation to pedagogical practice

The purpose of the previous sections of this chapter has been to briefly outline the multifaceted interaction between the student's self and the social context in which adult ESL learning takes place. The following section is dedicated to turning this *applicable* (that is relevant to the classroom practice) knowledge into *actionable* knowledge (Argyris & Schön, 1974), in this case, sound strategies for working with student motivation based on the scholarship above. In

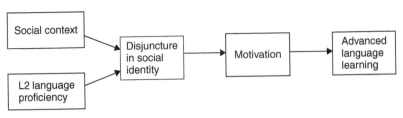

Figure 11.1   Socially situated model of adult language learning motivation

both practical and theoretical terms, our goal is to use the power of student motivation to foster second language learning through both:

1. changing our classroom practices as teachers;
2. changing our students' beliefs and behaviours that affect their learning.

Supporting this idea, a recent study of language teachers' use of motivational strategies in the classroom linked such practices with the increased levels of student motivation and the improvement in the observable classroom behaviours, such as higher participation, volunteering, and attentiveness in class (Guilloteaux & Dörnyei, 2008).

With so much already known about adult motivation for language learning, how can we intervene pedagogically to address its complexities in a way that is both logical and effective?

Core values in motivating the adult self

Understanding the processes within our students' selves is a good first step towards engaging adult students in learning. Applying this knowledge to teaching practices, we should capitalise on those motivational techniques that positively reaffirm adults' ideas of their selves and help them restore harmony through learning. To do so, I propose the following core values that should guide our teaching strategies and actions:

- respect
- fairness
- responsibility

Respect

Adult students expect to be treated with respect and, in turn, offer respect to their instructors. A rude, condescending, or paternalising treatment in a voluntary learning situation will, at least, decrease adults' motivation to learn and, at worst, make them abandon language learning altogether.

How can we signal respect to our students? First of all, we can do this by assuming that the instructor is an integral part of the group of adults participating in the learning process, even if our roles in it are different. It is sometimes easy to forget that the instructor functions within, not above, the social milieu of the adult classroom. Sharing some information about us – and, in particular, about how our backgrounds led to teaching language – will communicate to students their worth as an equal audience while not undermining our authority.

Meanwhile, making an effort to learn about our students will signal interest in their backgrounds as well. 'English language learners' abilities, experiences, and expectations can affect learning. Get to know their backgrounds and goals as well as proficiency levels and skill needs' (Florez & Burt, 2001). This can be done, for example, as part of a first-day writing diagnostic or through initial introductions in an oral skills class.

Furthermore, an encounter between unfamiliar adults usually begins with formal greetings and small talk which establish the friendly, mutually respectful atmosphere for the subsequent communication. While we cannot always greet our students individually, we can certainly welcome students as a group at the beginning of any class session. Povlacs (1987) also suggests personalising it on the crucial first day of class by greeting students at the classroom door.

Much research has been done on the importance of the use of names in the learning process. ESL students' names, however, can be often hard to pronounce to a native English speaker. Asking a student informally about the correct way to say his or her name, and apologising in advance for mispronouncing it, can defuse a potentially demotivating situation.

During the course, it is also important to use the name preferred by the student, be that his or her native, English, middle, married, maiden, or double name, or a nickname. I once had a student in a writing course who liked to be called '89', a nickname referring to his birth year. While it generated a few laughs at first, after a while '89' was just another name in the class, but using it showed my respect for his unconventional name choice. Finally, once a student's name is learned, other students should be encouraged to learn it and use it as well.

Fairness

Few things can signal lack of respect to an adult student as being treated unfairly or unequally. Perceived preferential treatment communicates a variation in the value of the adult students in the eyes of the teacher. 'If teachers are unfair, they will be negative factor [in student motivation],' wrote one of my students. 'ESL students will feel dispirited and leave ESL class' (Igoudin, 2009).

Additionally, adjusting grading or other class expectations to the individual student's needs or abilities actually erodes the instructor's authority and makes the students take him or her less seriously, lessening their enthusiasm for the class itself. On the other hand, instructors who are clear and consistent in their classroom policies send the message of respecting their students and having a firm control over the course of the class. Measured by the same standard, students are led to believe that their problems in the class are caused by their own deficiencies in their learning, not by the instructor's subjective opinion of them.

Classroom equity (Armstrong, 2009) can be further supported by the following course management strategies that emphasise transparency:

- Posting class policies such as grading, absences, late work, testing procedures, and general decorum in the syllabus. Equally essential is to adhere to these policies later.
- Including grading criteria into the task description, for example, in an essay or a presentation assignment.
- Using content management software which provides ongoing student access to current grades, or printing out and distributing to students their grades throughout the course, to take the mystery out of the final grade.

Responsibility

Who is responsible for student learning? The simple answer is students. But while the responsibility is ultimately the students' own, there is quite a lot we can do to support their efforts. On a larger scale, we need to work consciously to change the teaching paradigm to one that increases the learner's independence, rather than reliance on the teacher, both in and out class. The more adult learners are involved in a course, the more they see themselves as being in control. According to Hallberg and Hallberg (2011), a strong sense of responsibility is a top factor for student success in college. A learner-centred course helps students to take more control of their education by engaging them in the following types of learning (Doyle, 2008):

- first-hand learning;
- collaborative learning;
- practising;
- reflecting and self-evaluating;
- teaching of others;
- developing skills for lifelong learning;
- developing meta-cognitive skills.

Assigning students from different L1 backgrounds to work together – for example on a group presentation for a speaking class – will require them to use L2 to mediate the desired communicative meaning, apply L2-specific standards of politeness, and practise the L2 vocabulary – knowledge and skills that will come in handy in future academic subject classes and work situations.

This learner-driven shift in student behaviours and learning activities may clash with the students' anticipation of how they should learn and act in the classroom. This contradiction is culture-based in that ESL students and teachers may perceive the appropriateness of classroom behaviours in the context of their native cultures:

> If the American adult ideal is to be self-reliant, at ease in expressing and defending personal opinions, and interested in personal advancement, teachers will expect to provide instruction addressed to these goals and may unconsciously attribute these same goals to their students. (McGroarty, 1993: 1)

The first step to helping students adjust to learner-centred teaching is *to explain* why this approach is the best possible way to not only acquire language in interactive, deeper ways, but also to enhance academic success. Adults need to know why they are asked to do a task, especially when they are expected to do more. The explanation could include references to available research and evidence of peer success in learner-based settings, or examples from past classes.

Another way to motivate the student's sense of responsibility is to use a *self-assessment* which engages students in reflection on their involvement with the learning process. Quick and efficient, such assessment can be completed at the beginning of a course and be followed by a class discussion. *The Basic Skills Handbook* (Fulks & Alancraig, 2008), which focuses on teaching practices that promote student success, offers an interesting example of such assessment developed at Crafton Hills College in California. The assessment rubric statements cited below are designed to highlight behaviours and attitudes that lead to college success:

Responsibility

- I realise that ultimately, I am responsible for my own success in college.
- I make decisions and take timely action to advance my own educational goals.
- When I make mistakes or bad choices, I take time to learn from these experiences.

Motivation

- I am determined to graduate from college and be successful. I have personally important reasons to succeed.
- I am motivated to do my best in classes, and I have strategies that work for me.
- My desire to be successful helps me to overcome any obstacles I encounter.

A similar 'college success' self-assessment given to ESL (and other students) at Cypress College uses a five-point Likert scale to engage the student in the evaluation of their college study effort, goals, and practices (Hallberg & Hallberg, 2011). This 100-statement self-survey, which also can be completed online, includes statements like: I am the one who drives myself, and I try to be very involved in my school/college activities.

Emphasising continuous assessment and monitoring of student motivation, *On Course*, written by Skip Downing, a fellow U.S. community college instructor, has been a bestseller with community college faculty and counsellors alike. Now in its sixth edition, *On Course* (2010) takes a direct approach to student motivation, appealing to students' instrumental motives and focussing on hands-on activities designed to boost student motivation throughout a course.

Putting these ideas into practice, the adult ESL education programme at Santa Barbara City College began to offer a special 'student success' course in which ESL students practise goal-setting, study skills, learning strategies, and time management, and learn about peer success and role models. In addition, students are encouraged to sign contracts committing to attending the ESL class they are enrolling in. These new approaches, along with curriculum changes, are believed to be the reason for the 18 per cent improvement in retention and 14 per cent improvement in attendance (Lavigne & Bailey, 2008).

Nobody rises to low expectations. Rising to high expectations, however, communicates to students the educator's belief in their potential, regardless of their backgrounds, and refocuses the expectation on their effort:

> The first factor that affects a student's motivation in ESL is that the class is too easy. If a student thinks a class is too easy, they would not study hard. As a result, for them not studying hard, they might fail a test because they take it for granted that the test would be too easy and think they don't need to study for it. (Hyun, a student, in Igoudin, 2009)

The 2007 Community College Survey of Student Engagement, which surveyed more than 330,000 community college students in the United States and Canada, identified *setting and communicating high expectations* among several strategies that motivate students in educational settings (*CCSSE*, 2007). With high expectations, the study found, students who need developmental education (which includes English language learners) 'start to believe, some of them for the first time, that they are capable of college-level work' (*CCSSE*, 2007: 3).

High expectations are meant for both the students and the teachers: while we expect students to maximise their own effort in class, including their attendance, completion of assignments, preparation, and participation, students expect us to offer an academically rigorous curriculum, demand high-level understanding and skills, maintain high grading standards, and be available to help students outside of class (*CCSSE*, 2008).

Summary of motivational strategies

1. Review course content for the opportunities to include or expand learner-centred teaching techniques.
2. Where possible, include the teaching of skills and strategies that support the student's responsibility, such as goal-setting and time management into ESL curriculum.
3. Explain why student-centred learning is important, especially if some students in class resist it.
4. Support fairness and transparency in grading and other policies by including them in the syllabus and course assignments.
5. Introduce yourself to your students and explain the reasons how and why you decided to become a language teacher.
6. Make an effort to learn about your students in writing or orally.
7. Learn the proper pronunciation of students' first names and use them throughout the course.
8. Set high academic expectations for the course and be passionate about students' achieving them.
9. Keep students apprised of their progress throughout the course.
10. Use self-assessment to encourage students to evaluate their responsibility for learning.

Engagement priorities

Implications of social identity for language learning motivation are plentiful. Acquisition of a second language can arise as a need, and later be developed, abandoned, or ignored – all in relation to the processes within the student's self-concept. From the tension within the self rises the motivational energy which may ultimately direct and shape the resulting behaviour. Appropriate pedagogical interventions, including those listed in this chapter, can support the second language students' desire to learn and turn their motivational energy into effort and accomplishment. Still, just as many areas remain open to exploration. Among these are:

1. Much research on motivation is tied to task, course, and/or programme completion, and overall student success. Can it be that this viewpoint of motivation is driven primarily by the needs of the educational system itself, rather than the learner's?
2. Individual success seems to be at the core of current motivational research. How much of what we know of motivation is derived from the cultural, specifically, Western point of view?

3. The social scene upon which the learner acts does not end at the class-room door. How can the social context of the classroom itself affect student motivation?

4. Going back to the student's reporting her feeling of embarrassment as part of her drive to take L2 classes (Lucia in Igoudin, 2008), what is the role of emotive factors in student motivation?

5. It is not uncommon for ESL students to change or discover their career interests while taking ESL courses. How does student motivation evolve in response to the evolution of the learner's goals during the learning process?

6. Few ESL students, especially at advanced levels, take only ESL courses. How does engagement in non-ESL curriculum affect their motivation for language learning?

Suggested further reading

Downing, S. (2010). *On Course: Strategies for Creating Success in College and in Life* (Sixth Edition). Orlando, FL: Houghton Mifflin.

The author engages student motivation hands-on to solve challenges in academic courses. Though his largely instrumental approach may not work for all language learning populations, the book, supported by professional workshops, has been very influential in U.S. academia. For more information and an extensive database of student success strategies, visit www.oncourseworkshop.com.

Florez, M. and Burt, M. (2001). *Beginning to Work with Adult English Language Learners: Some Considerations.* Washington, D.C.: Center for Applied Linguistics (CAELA). Available at: http://www.cal.org/caela/esl_resources/digests/beginQA.html [Accessed 08/30/12].

The Center for Adult English Language Acquisition (CAELA), affiliated with the U.S. Department of Education, presents an easily accessible digest of ideas and strategies that apply relevant adult psychology research to effective second language instruction.

Reeve, J. (2008). *Understanding Motivation and Emotion* (Fifth Edition). Orlando, FL: Harcourt Brace.

This comprehensive textbook goes deep into the psychological underpinnings of human motivation and relates it to the environment and culture.

References

Academic Senate for California Community Colleges (ASCCC) (2011). Resolution 05.01: Oppose Student Success Task Force (SSTF) Recommendation on Basic Skills Funding; Resolution 06.04 Removal of ESL Students from SSTF Recommendations. Available at: http://asccc.org/resources/resolutions [Accessed 30/01/12].

Adult Education Handbook for California (AEHC) (1997). Compiled by T. Bauer. Sacramento, CA: Adult Education Policy and Placing Unit, California Department of Education.

Argyris, C. and Schön, D. A. (1974). *Theory in Practice: Increasing Professional Effectiveness*. San Franciso, CA: Jossey Bass.

Armstrong, M. (2009). Eight lessons: becoming the great teachers you already are. *Thought and Action*, 25: 7–14.

Au, S. Y. (1988). A critical appraisal of Gardner's social psychological theory of second-language learning. *Language Learning*, 38: 75–100.

Bandura, A. (1982). Self-efficacy mechanism in human agency. *American Psychologist*, 37: 747–55.

Bernat, E. (2004). Investigating Vietnamese ESL learners' beliefs about language learning. *English Australia Journal*, 21(2): 40–54.

Board of Governors of the California Community Colleges (2008). Report on the system's current programs in English as a second language (ESL) and basic skills. Available at: http://www.cccco.edu/Portals/4/Executive/Board/2008 _agendas/january/7-1_ Basic%20skills%20report%2012–19–07%20(3).pdf [Accessed 23/09/08].

Bolshier, R. and Collins, J. B. (1983). Education participation scale factor structure and correlates for twelve thousand learners. *International Journal of Lifelong Education*, 2(2): 163–77.

Bourdieu, P. (1991). *Language and Symbolic Power*. Cambridge, MA: Harvard University Press.

Canagarajah, A. (2006). TESOL at forty: what are the issues? *TESOL Quarterly*, 40(1): 9–34.

Chang, L. (2010). Group processes and EFL learners' motivation: a study of group dynamics in EFL classrooms. *TESOL Quarterly*, 44(1): 129–54.

Community College Survey of Student Engagement (CCSSE) (2007). *Findings: Executive Summary*. Austin, Texas: The University of Texas at Austin, Community College Leadership Program.

Community College Survey of Student Engagement (CCSSE) (2008). *High Expectations and High Support*. Austin, Texas: The University of Texas at Austin, Community College Leadership Program.

Crookes, G. (2003). *A Practicum in TESOL*. New York: Cambridge University Press.

Crookes, G. and Schmidt, R. (1991). Motivation: reopening the research agenda. *Language Learning*, 41: 469–512.

DeCharms, R. (1984). Motivation enhancement in educational settings. In R. E. Ames and C. Ames (eds) *Research on Motivation in Education* (Volume 1). New York: Academic Press, pp. 275–310.

Dörnyei, Z. (ed.) (2003). *Attitudes, Orientations, and Motivations in Language Learning: Advances in Theory, Research, and Applications*, Hoboken, NJ: Wiley-Blackwell.

Dörnyei, Z. (2005). *Motivational Strategies in the Language Classroom*. Cambridge: Cambridge University Press.

Dörnyei, Z. and Schmidt, R. (eds) (2001). *Motivation and Second Language Acquisition*. Honolulu, HI: Second Language Teaching and Curriculum Center, University of Hawaii at Manoa.

Doyle, T. (2008). A clear rationale for learner-centered teaching. *NEA Higher Education Advocate*, 26(1): 6–7.

Downing, S. (2010). *On Course: Strategies for Creating Success in College and in Life* (Sixth Edition). Orlando, FL: Houghton Mifflin.

Eckert. P. (2000). *Linguistic Variation as Social Practice*. Malden, MA: Blackwell Publishers.

Florez, M. and Burt, M. (2001). *Beginning to Work with Adult English Language Learners: Some Considerations*. Washington, D.C.: Center for Applied Linguistics (CAELA).

Available at: http://www.cal.org/caela/esl_resources/digests/beginQA.html [Accessed 08/30/12].

Fulks, J. and Alancraig, M. (eds) (2008). *Constructing a Framework for Success: A Holistic Approach to Basic Skills.* Sacramento, CA: Academic Senate for California Community Colleges. Available at: http://www.cccbsi.org/basic-skills-handbook [Accessed 03/12/09].

Gardner, R. C. (2001). Integrative motivation and second language acquisition. In Z. Dörnyei and R. Schmidt (eds) *Motivation and Second Language Acquisition.* Honolulu, HI: Second Language Teaching and Curriculum Center, University of Hawaii at Manoa, pp. 1–20.

Gardner, R. C. and Lambert, W. E. (1972). *Attitudes and Motivation in Second Language.* Rowley, MA: Newbury House.

Guilloteaux, M. and Dörnyei, Z. (2008). Motivating language learners: a classroom-oriented investigation of the effects of motivational strategies on student motivation. *TESOL Quarterly,* 42(1): 55–77.

Hallberg, E. and Hallberg, K. (2011). *College Success Factors Index (CSFI) 2.0* (Second Edition). Stamford, CT: Cengage Learning.

Harter, S. (1990). Causes, correlates, and the functional role of global self-worth: a life-span perspective. In R. Sternberg and J. Kolligian, Jr. (eds) *Competence Considered.* New Haven, CT: Yale University Press, pp. 67–97.

Igoudin, A. L. (2008). Adult ESL student motivation for participation in advanced language learning. *The CATESOL Journal,* 19(1): 27–48.

Igoudin, A. L. (2009). *In their Own Words: What ESL Students Write About Language Learning Motivation.* Paper presented at 2009 CATESOL Statewide Conference. Pasadena. 16–19 April 2009.

Jarvis, P. (1987). *Adult Learning in the Social Context.* New York: Croom Helm.

Jones, R. (1968). *Fantasy and Feeling in Education.* New York: New York University Press.

Julkunen, K. (2001). Situation- and task-specific motivation in foreign language learning. In Z. Dörnyei and R. Schmidt (eds) *Motivation and Second Language Acquisition.* Honolulu, HI: Second Language Teaching and Curriculum Center, University of Hawaii at Manoa, pp. 29–42.

Keller, J. M. (1983). Motivational design of instruction. In C. M. Reigeluth (ed.) *Instructional Design Theories and Models.* Hillsdale, NJ: Erlbaum, pp. 386–433.

Knowles, M. (1990). *The Adult Learner: A Neglected Species* (Fourth Edition). Houston, TX: Gulf Publishing Company.

Lavigne, P. and Bailey, J. (2008). SBCC changes boost ESL class attendance, retention. *CATESOL News,* 40(2): 1–4.

Ligorio, M. B. (2010). Dialogical relationship between identity and learning. *Culture and Psychology,* 16(1): 93–107.

MacKeracher, D. (1989). Lifespan learning: implications for educators. In C. J. Titmus (ed.) *Lifelong Education for Adults: An International Handbook.* New York: Pergamon, pp. 189–92.

Markus, H. (1983). Self-knowledge: an expected view. *Journal of Personality,* 51: 543–65.

McGroarty, M. (1993). *Cross-Cultural Issues in Adult ESL Classrooms.* Washington, D.C.: Center for Applied Linguistics (CAELA).

Mezirow, J. (1981). A critical theory of adult learning and education. *Adult Education,* 32(1): 3–27.

Noels, K. A., Adrian-Taylor, S. and Johns, K. (1999). *Motivation for Language Learning and Communication Style of Significant Others: An Examination of Learners in Three Contexts*. Paper presented at the Meeting of the National Communication Association, Chicago, November 1999.

Paper, L. C. (1990). An ESL motivations assessment for a community-based ESL programme. *TESL Canada Journal/Revue TESL du Canada*, 7(2): 31–44.

Peirce, B. Norton. (1995). Social identity, investment, and language learning. *TESOL Quarterly*, 29: 9–32.

Pintrich, P. and Schunk, D. (1996). *Motivation in Education: Theory, Research, and Applications*. Englewood Cliffs, NJ: Prentice Hall.

Povlacs, J. (1987). *101 Things You Can Do the First Three Weeks of Class*. CTL Idea Paper, No. 2. Center for Teaching and Learning, Ball State University, Muncie, Indiana.

Reeve, J. (1997). *Understanding Motivation and Emotion* (Second Edition). Orlando, FL: Harcourt Brace.

Reynoso, N. A. (2008). Academic resiliency among Dominican English-language learners. *Community College Journal of Research and Practice*, 32(4): 391–434.

Sfard, A. and Prusak, A. (2005). Telling identities: in search of an analytic tool for investigating learning as a culturally shaped activity. *Educational Researcher*, 34(4): 14–22.

Skilton-Sylvester, E. (2002). Should I stay or should I go? investigating Cambodian women's participation and investment in adult ESL programs. *Adult Education Quarterly*, 53(1): 9–26.

Song, B. (2006). Failure in a college ESL course: perspectives of instructors and students. *Community College Journal of Research and Practice*, 30(5/6): 417–31.

Student Success Task Force (SSTF) (2011). *Refocusing California Community Colleges Toward Student Success: Draft Recommendations*. California Community Colleges. Available at: http://californiacommunitycolleges.cccco.edu/Portals/0/DocDownloads/PressReleases/SEP2011/PDF_%20Student_Success_Task_Force_Draft_Recommendations_Sept_2011.pdf [Accessed 30/01/12].

Student Success Task Force (SSTF) (2012). *Advancing Student Success in California Community Colleges: Recommendations*. California Community Colleges. Available at: http://californiacommunitycolleges.cccco.edu/Portals/0/Executive/StudentSuccessTaskForce/SSTF_Final_Report_1-17-12_Print.pdf [Accessed 30/01/12].

Syed, Z. (2001). Notions of self in foreign language learning: a qualitative analysis. In Z. Dörnyei and R. Schmidt (eds) *Motivation and Second Language Acquisition*. Honolulu, HI: Second Language Teaching and Curriculum Center, University of Hawaii at Manoa, pp. 127–48.

Titmus, C. J. (1989). Adult education for employment. In C. J. Titmus (ed.) *Lifelong Education for Adults: An International Handbook*. New York: Pergamon, pp. 93–9.

Ushioda, E. (2001). Language learning at university: exploring the role of motivational thinking. In Z. Dörnyei and R. Schmidt (eds) *Motivation and Second Language Acquisition*. Honolulu, HI: Second Language Teaching and Curriculum Center, University of Hawaii at Manoa, pp. 93–126.

Ushioda, E. and Dörnyei, Z. (2009). Motivation, language identities, and the L2 self: a theoretical overview. In Dörnyei, Z., and E. Ushioda (eds) *Motivation, Language Identity and the L2 Self*. Bristol: Multilingual Matters, pp. 1–8.

Waterman, R. A. (2008). Strength behind the sociolinguistic wall: the dreams, commitments, and capacities of Mexican mothers. *Journal of Latinos and Education*, 7(2): 144–62.

Weiner, B. (1984). Principles for a theory of student motivation and their application within an attributional framework. In R. E. Ames and C. Ames (eds) *Research on Motivation in Education* (Volume 1). New York: Academic Press, pp. 15–38.

12

'Native Speaker' English Language Teachers: Disengaged from the Changing International Landscape of their Profession

Pamela Aboshiha

Introduction

Traditionally, the field of English language teaching has conceptualised the 'native speaker' English language teacher as an ideal speaker, teacher, trainer and expert. In fact, the label 'native speaker' teacher communicates much more than simple information about linguistic ability in the field of English language teaching. In the opinions of several scholars (for example, Canagarajah, 1999; Holliday, 2005; 2006; Kubota, 2002; Pennycook, 1994; Phillipson, 1992), the label and its associated discourse reflect, not just the language proficiency of the 'native speaker' English language teacher, but a litany of opinions, practices and prejudices which have developed into a deep-rooted and extensively referred to ELT ideology. Indeed, Nayar (2002), in his analysis of hundreds of English language teacher comments posted on a website, concludes that the 'native speaker' is identified as a teacher who is in control, with all the answers, an authority on both grammar and universal acceptability, a representative of correct language, of sound thinking and, Nayar opines, even proper social behaviour in English. This same theme is continued by Holliday, who sees 'native-speakerism' as being so deeply embedded in TESOL that people are 'standardly unaware of its presence and its impact' (2005: 10). Indeed, 'native speaker' English language teachers have traditionally obtained employment and much influence in international educational institutions, with the discourse of their training becoming not only their own dominant professional paradigm, but also the dominant professional paradigm for many 'non-native speaker' English language teachers worldwide. Indeed, it seems the 'native speaker' teacher has 'remained as a central part of the conventional wisdom of the English Language Teaching profession' (Phillipson, 1992: 199).

Problematising the 'status quo'

However, globalisation has created a need for an international lingua franca, and it has adopted English to fill the role, with Graddol predicting that 'those who speak English alongside other languages will outnumber first language speakers and, increasingly, will decide the global future of the language' (1997: 11). Crystal notes as well that 'it is plain that no one can now claim sole owner-ship [of English]' (1997: 139) and adds poignantly, 'The loss of ownership is of course uncomfortable to those, especially in Britain, who feel that the language is theirs by historical right; but they have no alternative' (Crystal, 1997: 130).

Within this landscape, forward thinking academics in Applied Linguistics (such as Llurda, 2004; Holliday, 2005; Jenkins, 2000; Kirkpatrick, 2007; McKay, 2002; Rajagopalan, 2004; Seidlhofer, 2001) insist that this changing ownership of English is already upon us and suggest that we are now in the process of moving away from a position in which learners aspire to the norms of the 'native speaker' English language teacher in the areas of phonology and culture.

Specifically, there have been debates over the appropriateness of the language teaching methodology currently practised by 'native speaker' English language teachers (for example, Bax, 2003; Brown, 2002; Canagarajah, 2002; Holliday, 1994; Prabhu, 1990), and these challenges are added to by Jenkins' (2000) belief that a less 'native speaker' related English is what should be taught to learners who need to communicate internationally. She theorises that the growth in English as an international tool of communication points to a need for a change in learners' pronunciation needs and goals, calling for 'a radical re-think in terms of the role of pronunciation norms and models for classes aiming to prepare learners for interaction in (international) contexts' (Jenkins, 1998: 119).

Furthermore, as English becomes an economic commodity and a passport for entrance to the global world, the language can no longer be viewed as a particular symbol of identity or nationality. Seeing English as an instrumental tool for communication seems also to affect people's need to be taught any specific 'native speaker' culture which arises from a particular speech commu-nity. Consequently, in terms of cultural awareness (the knowledge people have acquired as members of their social group), McKay (2002) suggests that the users of English internationally no longer need to internalise the cultural norms of, for example, the United Kingdom, the United States, or Australasia, in order to use the language effectively.

These academic predictions of increasingly dominant 'non-native speaker' interaction in English and the handing over of the language from 'native speaker' to international proprietors thus serve to highlight the importance of problematising the traditional role and practices of the 'native speaker' English language teacher. If English is now used and owned internationally, the hitherto celebrated professional status of the 'native speaker' teacher, and what and how they teach, is inevitably open to critique.

However, these are scholarly predictions about the current and possible future landscape of ELT, made by Applied Linguists or English Language Teaching academics usually working in universities, and classroom teachers have a history of scepticism regarding the role of theoreticians in enabling the development of the practice of English language instruction (Kinginger, 2002). Thus, whatever might be written about in academia may well find little resonance in the world of the 'native speaker' practitioner. For this reason I now give a brief overview of the relationship between English language teachers and their academic counterparts.

English language teachers and academia

First, there has been substantial discussion regarding the existence of an unequal relationship between practitioners and academics involved in English language teaching and the extent to which this relationship 'emphasises the primacy of theory and theoreticians' (Kinginger, 2002: 193). On one side of the hierarchical dichotomy are the scholars, producing codified knowledge in the form of academic papers and texts about English language teaching and, as we have seen above in relation to globalisation, the thinking which underpins, problematises and moves the profession forward. However, these academics do not practise language teaching themselves. On the other hand, there are the English language teachers in classrooms who, it is expected, read scholars' work as part of preparation for the profession, but who do not themselves generally produce codified knowledge. Moreover, these practitioners appear to uphold a set of priorities different to that of scholars in their professional lives (Freeman & Johnson, 1998). This habit of the profession of demoting teachers to consumers of knowledge, rather than co-constructors of theory, has caused Clarke (1994: 9–10) to surmise: 'Because the individuals involved in developing theory are seldom full-time language teachers themselves, the theory/practice distinction creates a strata of expertise in which teachers are considered less expert than theorists'. At the same time he somewhat radically suggests that 'the only real solution [to this problem] would be to turn the hierarchy on its head, putting teachers on the top and arraying others – pundits, professors, administrators, researchers, and so forth – below them' (Clarke, 1994: 18). Sharkey & Johnson (2003: x) illustrate this reversal in an incident that occurred as they (English language teachers) were working towards their doctorates:

> However, the professor told us that if we wanted to make it in higher education, we had to stop talking about teaching. The professor drew a triangle on the board, with theorists at the top and practitioners, including black

feminist writer, bell hooks, on the bottom. If we wanted to do theory, according to this model, we had to leave teaching, and our teacher identities behind. Several of us, all women, did not accept either the hierarchy or the theory practice split. Were the two not always present? Were we not theorising our practice through analysis of our classrooms? Further, the discussion on issues of knowledge and power were situated in the traditional rigid academic hierarchy of professor as knower and student as lump of clay.

The sidelining of teachers in knowledge creation is also taken up by Crookes (1997: 96) when he bemoans the fact that teachers' voices are, on the whole, 'absent from the published record [and] should indicate its weakness [...] the words of teachers rarely appear in academic journals related to teaching or learning – a conspicuous silence with obvious implications'. Johnson and Golombek (2002: 1) complain of the same positioning:

> Teachers have been viewed as objects of study rather than as knowing professionals or agents of change. Teachers have been marginalized in that they are told what they should know and how they should use that knowledge.

This understanding that teachers must learn from academic theory 'what they should know and how they should use that knowledge' seems to derive from the widespread societal concept that one aspect of a profession is a body of codified knowledge, that is the expert, legitimate, received knowledge of a particular field. Access to such powerful and influential codified discourses which, according to the discourse itself, inevitably influence and define pedagogy, seems therefore imperative for teachers. However, much 'professionalism' in teaching is seen as based on experience and 'knowing-in-action' (Szesztay, 2004). Teacher knowledge, rather than something which is codified, is normally tacit and hard to articulate, and is in a dialectical relationship with the teachers' world of practice. It is often told in stories which are disseminated along mainly oral channels and, generally, 'teachers are primarily concerned with developing insights for the practice of language instruction' (Kinginger, 2002: 193).

Thus, teacher knowledge remains majorly unrecorded, with few teachers participating in the codification of their understandings based on practical insights, or pushing forward their own research agendas, or creating new knowledge – despite the recognised gap and an avowed aim of developing 'a systematic and rigorous body of knowledge about teaching' (Cochran-Smith & Lytle, 1990: 2). Moreover, the claim by Freeman and Johnson (1998) that priorities and values of the powerful, codified knowledge of academics are not necessarily shared by teachers has the potential to further damage the already prickly interface between academics and practitioners. Certainly, then, the 'native speaker' English language teachers described at the beginning of this chapter may well fail to appreciate, or empathise with, academic views of a changing English language teaching scenario.

Thus, when reading what academics write about practitioners, it seems that there exists a stratified profession in which academia relishes superior status yet recognises a need for teacher knowledge grounded in practice. There is also little willingness on the part of academia to upturn the 'status quo' in order to accommodate teacher contribution, and there is the continued expectation that teachers consume and implement scholarly 'dicta'. That teachers are considered consumers of received knowledge but are mainly engaged in acquiring practical perspectives, consequently leads to a thorny question with regard to the recounted academic challenges. What are the implications for the future of English language teaching if the prediction of a shifting paradigm, away from the supremacy of 'native speakers', is not seen by teachers to 'articulate easily or cogently into classroom practice' (Freeman & Johnson, 1998: 413)?

A study with some 'native speaker' teachers

The questions

Thus, as the literature reveals an uneasy academic/practitioner relationship, and and extensive debate among academics continues to problematise the role of the 'native speaker' English language teacher, it seems timely to investigate the extent to which such teachers are conversant with the arguments that their status, methodological, phonological and cultural norms are being queried. It also seems appropriate to investigate the extent to which the 'native speaker' teachers are prepared to reflect on, and possibly implement, changes to their roles and practices if they are to play a less dominant role in the future of ELT. In Aboshiha (2008) these questions are posed, alongside an attempt to explore the answers of a group of such experienced 'native speaker' English language teachers working in a variety of international institutions. The earlier part of the study focussed on what the teachers thought about specific academic predictions, such as Jenkins's notion of teaching a 'core lingua franca'. However, as the research unfolded it became apparent that the small group of teachers I was interviewing and e-mailing experienced an unhealthy, unproductive relationship with academia. They were not motivated to read academic products, or interested in whether academia had the ability to guide teachers in their daily practices or to help them understand their professional identities. Far from following the 'dicta' of academic work, the 'native speaker' teachers in the study seemed disinclined to read, were furtive in acknowledging that they either failed to read or to implement what they had read, and were dismissive of the codified knowledge of their profession and the challenges this knowledge was laying down. In fact, the teachers seemed almost completely focussed on their own teacher knowledge, derived from classroom practice. I now describe part of this study.

The respondents and data-gathering tools

The aim of the study was to explore the reactions of 'native speaker' EFL teachers towards the academic views of the current landscape of English language teaching, as outlined at the beginning of this chapter. In order to do this, I interviewed and then undertook e-mail correspondence with eight experienced 'native speaker' practitioners who, at the time of the interviews, were teaching English in Portugal, France, Abu Dhabi, Japan, Saudi Arabia and the United Kingdom. These teachers had also taught English in Turkey, Poland, Italy, Libya, Ecuador, Egypt, Romania and Cyprus, and each had a minimum of eight years' experience in the profession. Three further teachers were later added to this core group. All had recognised British EFL qualifications, such as Cambridge ESOL DELTA (Diploma in English Language Teaching to Adults) or a Trinity Diploma, and most had an MA TESOL. This group was typical of a large number of British-trained teachers who have made EFL or ESOL their careers and who spend their professional lives teaching English internationally, gaining employment readily in worldwide institutions because of the considerable longstanding opportunities afforded them by their 'native speaker-ness'. Besides their general English language teaching, two of the teachers had experience of teacher training, one had taught business English, one young learners, one had co-authored a book about teacher training, and one had a Postgraduate Certificate of Education. I interviewed them all in the United Kingdom during their summer holidays and continued sporadic e-mail correspondence with them when they returned to their places of work.

As a practising EFL teacher, with an MA TESOL and international teaching experience myself, I also became part of the group of interviewees in the study, and I kept field notes in my English language teaching institution over the research period. Then, with the collected data from the 11 teacher interviews, their e-mails and my own field notes, I was able eventually to piece together some understanding of the relationship between these 'native speaker' English language teachers and the specific predictions of academics about the future of ELT, and also their relationship with academia in general.

The 'native speaker' teachers' views

Reactions to the specific pedagogical implications for change

Initially, when questioned as to whether the 'native speaker' teacher might adapt his/her teaching of certain aspects of phonology in order to allow greater intelligibility between speakers of English internationally, the teachers were not just dismissive of this idea of Jenkins, but they expressed irritation with the academic as well. For example, the teachers used language such as 'a crackpot idea', 'ludicrous', 'unworkable', revealing that they had little respect for both the idea and for the academic who had made the proposal. They also indicated that that they did not wish to be 'dictated to' in terms of implementing such phonological alternatives in EFL classes and, with such comments, positioning themselves as inferior to academics, whom they saw as doing 'the dictating'. In other words, not only was the idea of adapting to alternative phonological norms uncomfortable for the teachers but the academic voices through which this idea was disseminated also appeared unpopular. Moreover, this initial unease with the specific arguments being put forward by academics about the role and practices of 'native speaker' EFL teachers in a globalising world was seen to be only the 'tip of the iceberg', as the research began to uncover a substantial rift between these classroom teachers and the codified knowledge of English language teaching.

Reading is not useful

The teachers claimed, quite defiantly, that they knew nothing about the literature of the field or what ELT academics had written, and they also stated that the work of academics was of no particular interest or relevance to their professional lives and daily practice. What is more, none of the teachers admitted to reading about what was happening in their field in connection with future developments (in which their own role might be less secure). In fact, there were comments to indicate that they actively disliked reading about issues to do with their profession, and that what they read was not practical enough. One interviewee, Basil, exemplifies this when he says: 'I'm not a book reader – not an EFL book reader. I wouldn't read Applied Linguistics'. He continued: 'We're pretty bad about tuning in to what's going on' Aboshiha, 2008: 163 [Basil]. Another, Rosa, said, 'I haven't read anything professionally for ages and I don't want to' (Aboshiha, 2008: 163 [Rosa]). She also stated:

> ...when I was trying to sort of learn, but even then, it wasn't the theory so much as the actual practical tuition on how to teach, you know the methodology in practical terms rather than what came out of books. So I don't know. I'm a bit sceptical when it comes to books. (Aboshiha, 2008: 163 [Rosa])

The teachers determinedly identified themselves as people who 'practised', almost deliberately uninfluenced by academia and its literature and, during the interviews, there was no indication that the literature of the field served to heighten or deepen their understanding of what was happening internationally in their profession of EFL and how this might impact on their practice. The teachers seemed to perceive reading about professional matters as an activity they would do, or had done, only to get further qualifications, like a master's degree, or such reading as an activity they had undertaken or begun to undertake on their pre-service courses, when they were completely inexperienced practitioners. But even that initial reading did not appear to be particularly highly valued unless it was 'practical', that is, unless it told them how to do something in the classroom.

Academics are disconnected from classroom reality

These 'native speaker' teachers, focused on their daily classroom practice, dismissed academics and their writing as unconcerned with the everyday classroom realities. They positioned themselves in another classificatory system with, this time, they themselves, the teachers, as practical people able to work at the 'chalk face' of language classrooms and not connected with those who, to their mind, could not cope with the real world of language teaching, but who still wrote about it. When talking about academics no longer working in a language classroom, the comments were made disparagingly; for example: 'Academia bubble, babble, sounds good but doesn't actually work' (Aboshiha, 2008: 161 [Vera]); 'Academics have to justify their salaries' (Aboshiha, 2008: 161 [Jane]); 'Can't they say things simply, it's just meaningless stuff for the sake of it. I've read the paper. There are a lot of words and paragraphs but it doesn't really say much. When would I ever use this? Why can't we have something that is useful in the classroom' (Aboshiha, 2008: 161 [Field Notes]); 'You know, I think these people, they lose touch with teaching EFL [...] they tell us how you should do this, this and this. And you think, how many years ago did you do this?' (Aboshiha, 2008: 161 [Nuala]). Alex also related the reasons for his lack of respect for academics:

> This…this is probably going to get me slayed or slain. I tend to think a lot of academics have run from the classroom because they can't cope in the classroom. And they don't relate their experiences in the classrooms to their theories. People I've worked with, they write well. I don't necessarily agree with their ideas but then I also find out that a lot of these people are not teaching because they can't do it. So, if they can't do it in the classroom, why should I be listening to what they write? It's very broad and a generalisation…. Of course there'll be some people who are absolutely brilliant in the classroom and have the energy and insight to go and write brilliant stuff. But there are an awful lot of second rate people who want to be academics who can't hack it in the classroom, so why should I listen to them outside the classroom? (Aboshiha, 2008: 161 [Alex])

He also commented:

> But I do think it [the literature] is all based on the fact that you are going to be walking in and have 14, 15 really dedicated, motivated students. I have never had a class like that. I've always had one or two, three or four, or

five or six, or seven or eight who really don't want to be there. (Aboshiha, 2008: 165 [Alex])

Rob also described in detail the 'reluctant learners' of his particular context. He felt these learners and the reality of their social context were 'not considered' by academics in their work:

> There are 2 levels of resentment: a) Social Engineering – unemployed youth are coerced into training situations that they do not want to be in – by the government, to avoid social and civil unrest, by their fathers to help provide for the family, by their peers. Result – reluctant learners. We have trainee aircraft technicians not at all interested in aircraft. Therefore, course materials, specifically designed to meet their needs, do not meet their interests or desires.
>
> b) Anti-foreignness – This second level of resentment refers to the fact that some of them may genuinely be interested in aircraft but, possibly quite legitimately, question the need for this training to be done in English. Result – reluctant learners. (Aboshiha, 2008: 165 [Rob])

Also, I recorded an incident in my research diary about 'real world' teaching, and what I perceived as the impossibility of reading or thinking in any way about my new role in teaching English in a world in which English had become a 'lingua franca', when all I was doing was what I termed 'fire-fighting' just to stay afloat in my daily life:

> Back after the summer break
> My first day back after a summer break. Today, the list of students supposed to be in my class did not resemble the students sitting in the class. My Director of Studies said that this class has used every book on the shelf in their previous classes and I'd be hard pressed to find something! As for the afternoon examination class, nobody seems to have a clue about which books they have used or what they can move on to or who will be in the class. The worst thing is the materials and what I can do. I spent the break and my lunch-hour, without a drink or food, literally running all over the place to try to find a working photocopier to copy pages. Chaotic and exhausting!!! How can one manage to think about wider issues in ELT when this is going on? I was shattered and angry when I got home and quite ready to walk out. (Aboshiha, 2008: 166 [Field Notes])

Another teacher, Nuala, complained about her desire to find application in theoretical work, yet at the same time she is wary of anything being 'too theoretical':

> Sometimes, especially after writing my MA dissertation I really feel practice and theory, there is a huge gap between those two. But at times, you

read certain kinds of journals and you think 'Ah, this is a bit more down to earth and, maybe, I can apply this to my class.' But when you start reading those books and you think 'How is this going to help me?' I think we should still be doing some reading. I think we all need theory. But I think at the same time it is something that isn't too theoretical...something that can be applied to the class (Aboshiha, 2008: 166-167 [Nuala]).

Another teacher, Ned, complained of the 'intellectualisation' of the subject matter in a practical profession:

There was some new information on the Dip [Postgraduate Diploma TESOL course] as well and many of those things were useful for me but I also started to encounter a lot of information which I thought was just people being academic for the sake of that in itself. This is a very practical thing we do and there's only so far you can go with the theory, you know if you are trying to break it down into a science, there's not really that much to it, in my opinion (Aboshiha, 2008: 167 [Ned]).

This same point was further illustrated by one of my colleagues, standing by the photocopier, chatting about the field of EFL in general. He said: 'Well, there's not that much really to know[;] it's not rocket science – I mean there's just so much to uncover, and it seems like we've pretty much done as much as we can' (Aboshiha, 2008: 167 [Field Notes]).

Perceptions of academic discourse from literature and daily comment

Moreover, the teachers seemed to see the production of papers, texts and the giving of conference papers as a way of maintaining status and power for the academics, rather than, in their opinion, any genuine attempt to develop and explore ideas for the benefit of practitioners in the field of English Language teaching. Ken and Rosa viewed it in the following ways:

But perhaps there is something wrong in academic culture, not with specific academics but the general culture is not pushing forward new theory, pushing forward boundaries, it's more looking after themselves in a community. It's being done to maintain their position and maintain the community as a whole, I mean, everybody going to each other's talks. It doesn't matter if it's a good talk but they've written a book and they came to your talk so you go to theirs. That's what I see. (Aboshiha, 2008: 163 [Ken])

I don't believe for a moment that academics write for the sake of teachers; they write for themselves, to get published and look good on the CV. (Aboshiha, 2008: 163 [Rosa])

Mike declared, too: 'If someone writes an article it's going to be for other people in their positions in other universities round the world'. (Aboshiha, 2008: 164 [Mike])

Such comments by these 'native speaker' teachers reflected a general feeling of disillusionment about academia and a feeling of marginalisation for the teachers. In my field notes, I recorded an incident which revealed my own feelings of inadequacy when confronted by an academic who also seemed preoccupied with maintaining status vis-à-vis a classroom teacher:

> Academic discourse at work
>
> Jon, a new academic colleague came to see me working with some trainee EFL teachers on a pre-service course. It was perhaps the worst day he could have come. Two trainees were facing failure on the very intensive course and everyone was tired. What's more I had needed to reduce the seminar to about 50 minutes, an impossibly short time for the work I needed to cover.
>
> As a teacher, though, I felt if I refused it would 'look bad' and Jon would either think I had something to hide or believed I wasn't doing my job properly.
>
> Jon came to the session and did not sit quietly at the back, watching, as I would have expected (and hoped for) but sometimes, when the trainees were working together, walked around and chatted and commented. Once, when a trainee made a comment that Jon disagreed with, Jon started a discussion to 'correct' the trainee. I felt my space and working relationship with the trainees had been rudely invaded and that Jon was attempting to 'position' himself as an expert, although he knew nothing of the course or its requirements or anything about the trainees' successes and failures.
>
> After the 'observation' Jon commented 'that must be so difficult, weaving discourse, teaching methodology and new knowledge into a session'. Jon then paused and added, quite pointedly: 'Of course, I'm working at Master's level'. (Aboshiha, 2008: 164-165 [Field Notes])

Here, as an EFL teacher and trainer, I believed I observed a deliberate attempt by an academic to assert power when sharing a classroom with a practitioner. The invasion of the classroom and learner's space, the interrogation and criticism of the learner, while my 'practitioner' lesson was supposed to be going on, were all evidence of this.

Also, still acknowledging the discourse of power in the literature, some reading was seen as 'not accessible to the average reader' (Aboshiha, 2008: 163 [Ken]). Another teacher commented:

> I remember thinking how difficult the reading was, after I came into the field from my original degree, history. It is often difficult to read and I think

the academics who are easy to read, like Thornbury, are people who've moved out of teaching. (Aboshiha, 2008: 163 [Jenny email])

Thus, academics were seen by this group of 'native speaker' teachers as attempting to exert a superior status in the field of EFL, both through the discourse of academic papers and, as well, in everyday discourse. The academics, at least through the teachers' eyes, used publications to assert power, saying that when they, the teachers, experience the codified discourse of academic English, they view the genre as a way for theoreticians to assert a more dominant identity over them. High social distance seemed to be created, as Ken said, 'to maintain the community' and cement the academics' own dominant identity. In this way the teachers felt they were seen to be a subordinate group and 'inferior' to the academics, despite contrarily asserting their own 'status' as practitioners who could cope with the real world of the classroom.

Comments

Almost exclusively, this small group of 'native speaker' English language teachers failed to engage with the academic arguments problematising the traditional status and role of 'native speaker teachers'. More concerningly, these experienced, qualified 'native speaker' teachers of English not only failed to engage with the arguments, they evidenced much disenchantment with the work of academics and showed no motivation to read scholarly works about such topics as these current challenges to their position and practice as English language teachers. The teachers seemed to perceive academics as using the legitimate, codified discourse in publications to maintain status over classroom practitioners, writing about topics which, to the teachers' minds, did not address their everyday realities and pedagogical concerns. Thus, a major finding from the study (Aboshiha, 2008) was a worrying gap between academic problematising of changes to the traditional supremacy of 'native speaker' teachers in ELT and the same teachers' lack of interest (and ignorance) that this was being written about. A second finding was that the 'native speaker' EFL teachers exhibited a disquieting relationship with academia, academics, and their literature. The experienced teachers in the study hardly valued the codified knowledge of the profession as having the potential for guiding teachers' practice and understanding of their role as English language teachers in the wider world. On the contrary, it appeared the teachers very much viewed their identity as 'practical practitioners', capable of, or needing to be capable only of, dealing with everyday realities and also not finding that academic insight aided this in any constructive manner. The teachers also attempted to position academics as out of touch with the real world of the EFL classroom, both specifically in the case of academic predictions, such as Jenkins' ideas about a 'core lingua franca', and generally with regard to academic understanding as a whole.

One unfortunate conclusion that may be drawn from the study is that these 'native speaker' EFL teachers appear to read the literature of their profession only when they undertake study to obtain advanced qualifications, and then they promptly forget what they have read or consign it to a 'useless for the classroom' pile. The motivation to read further in order to enhance or think about practice, or to view reading academic articles or texts as valuable in updating knowledge and perspectives on ELT was, in this study, conspicuously and worryingly absent. This seems to leave the work of ELT academics and the world of ELT practitioners as two separate endeavours, with the codified academic genre failing to inform the practices and roles of teachers in any meaningful, substantial or consistent manner. Also, the study raised the issue of the lack of codified teacher knowledge, which may, as noted by Freeman and Johnson (1998), resonate with teachers more than does academic work because it would more harmoniously encompass the priorities they relate to. Finally, this lack of motivation to read scholarly works related to the ELT profession occurred, despite the warning to teachers by Kinginger (2002: 94) that 'to deny access to these genres would be as disempowering as to demand unconditional reverence and subservience to them'.

Suggestions for teacher training and teacher education

What then could be done to smooth this rough and unhappy interface between such teachers of the English language and the academics writing about the profession, especially in view of the current changing paradigm? How might teachers see codified knowledge as contributing more to their daily lives and teaching roles? How might the teachers be more motivated to read and keep abreast of scholarly thinking? And how might teachers be encouraged to record their own knowledge?

One starting point could be on initial pre-service teacher training courses for 'native speaker' teachers such as Cambridge CELTA (Certificate in English Language Teaching to Adults), a recognised and valued preparatory course for an overwhelming majority of 'native speaker' English language teachers. Perhaps on this course, teachers need to start out by being more encouraged to read about their profession, with this reading viewed as intrinsic to learning about teaching, and where reflection on the role and position of 'native speaker' English language teachers' methodological and phonological norms becomes core to the course. On CELTA, pre-service teachers have the opportunity to obtain excellent classroom skills, basic information about lesson types and some teaching practice, but the focus remains almost exclusively practical and unquestioning of the power and influence of the 'native speaker' teacher, or of the pedagogical approach enshrined in the course. This prioritising of practice over theory at the outset of a teacher's career sends a clear message that it is acceptable not to engage with the thinking of the profession. It is interpreted as 'practice is the only thing that matters' in EFL. I contend that unless such neophyte 'native speaker' teachers are introduced to the relevance and importance of thinking about ELT and its wide and changing role in the world, the profession runs the risk of relegating its teachers to narrow-minded, unthinking implementers of classroom tasks and activities.

Secondly, when teachers have begun to practise, they often attend in-service workshops set up by local or national institutions. These workshops inevitably focus on the practical – extending and refining teachers' existing repertoire of, for example, vocabulary teaching, or ideas for using IT in the classroom. While these practical workshops undoubtedly add to the range and richness of teachers' classroom techniques, they might well be profitably balanced with academic papers to read. These would encourage intelligent discussion of wider issues and, in the longer term, replenish English language teachers intellectually, rather than allowing them to stagnate some years after a severely restricted diet of in-service 'practical teaching tips'.

Thirdly, directors of studies, or others in academic management roles who normally direct such 'in-service' workshops, need to be convinced of the importance and relevance of the developmental aspects of reading what is being written about by the profession. They, too, need intelligent and stimulating updating, not one more new idea for 'teaching the present perfect' to disseminate to teachers.

Finally, academics, aware of this unproductive divide, need to make some genuine attempt to engage with practitioners. They might find ways of writing themselves, or of co-authoring work with teachers, which could make scholarly papers more palatable and relevant to classroom teachers. This, of course, is if at the end of the day academics are convinced that their work should be relevant to practitioners on a consistent and meaningful basis.

Engagement priorities

This small study raised some provocative and interesting issues regarding the interface between academia and practitioners involved in TEFL, and with which it seems the profession needs to engage. The 'native speaker' study problematised whether, and to what extent, the published work of academia resonates in the daily lives of practitioners and, indeed, whether there is motivation for academics to design work which has practical implication. The former revelation led, I believe, to the imperative need for some investigation into genres of academic publication which might resonate productively with EFL practitioners. An equally important further need is for research into how practitioners might best be motivated to engage with academic theory about the profession of ELT. The following questions may be useful starting points for such engagement.

1. Is a central concern of teacher education the transfer of knowledge from one domain to another, or is teaching English an endeavour different to writing about issues related to the profession?
2. Is the lack of motivation towards reading academic papers and texts a phenomenon related solely to 'native speaker' teachers, or to all EFL teachers?
3. What suggestions that have been made in this chapter might motivate EFL teachers to engage more with academic papers?
4. What other strategies might motivate teachers to engage more with academic publications?
5. How could teachers themselves be motivated to write more articles which are not just concerned with 'classroom tips'?

Suggested further reading

Borg, S. (2006). *Teacher Cognition and Language Education* London: Continuum.

This book explores what pre-service and in-service teachers think, know and believe. It also gives ideas about how teachers could research this cognition, and this might inspire teachers to investigate and write about their own 'theories'.

Fenton-Smith, B. and Stillwell, C. (2010). Reading discussion groups for teachers: connecting theory to practice. *English Language Teaching Journal,* 65(3): 251–59.

This article describes one practical way, a reading discussion group, which could help teachers engage with ideas.

References

Aboshiha, P. (2008). *Identity and Dilemma: The 'Native Speaker' English Language Teacher in a Globalising World.* Unpublished PhD Dissertation, University of Kent, Canterbury.

Bax, S. (2003). The end of CLT: a context approach to language teaching. *English Language Teaching Journal,* 57(3): 278–87.

Brown, H. (2002). English language teaching in the 'post method' era: towards better diagnosis, treatment and assessment.' In J. Richards and W. Renandya (eds) *Methodology in Language Teaching: An Anthology of Current Practice.* Cambridge: Cambridge University Press, pp. 9–18

Canagarajah, S. (1999). Interrogating the 'native speaker fallacy': non-linguistic roots, non-pedagogical results. In G. Braine (ed.) *Non-Native Educators in English Language Teaching.* Mahwah, NJ: Lawrence Erlbaum Associates, pp. 77–92.

Canagarajah, S. (2002). Method and practice in periphery classrooms. In D. Block and D. Cameron (eds) *Globalization and Language Teaching*. London: Routledge, pp. 134–50.

Clarke, M. (1994). The dysfunctions of the theory practice discourse. *TESOL Quarterly*, 28(1): 9–25.

Cochran-Smith, M. and Lytle, S. (1990). Research on teaching and teacher research: the issues that divide. *Educational Researcher*, 19(2): 2–11.

Crookes, G. (1997). SLA and second language pedagogy. *Studies in Second Language Acquisition*, 19(1): 93–116.

Crystal, D. (1997). *English as a Global Language*. Cambridge: Cambridge University Press.

Freeman, D. and Johnson, K. (1998). Reconceptualising the knowledge base of teacher education. *TESOL Quarterly*, 32(3): 397–417.

Graddol, D. (1997). *The Future of English*. The British Council.

Holliday, A. (1994). *Appropriate Methodology and Social Context*. Cambridge: Cambridge University Press.

Holliday, A. (2005). *The Struggle to Teach English as an International Language*. Oxford: Oxford University Press.

Holliday, A. (2006). Native-speakerism. *English Language Teaching Journal*, 60(4): 385–87.

Jenkins, J. (1998). Which pronunciation norms and models for English as an International language? *English Language Teaching Journal*, 52(2): 119–26.

Jenkins, J. (2000). *The Phonology of English as an International Language*. Oxford: Oxford University Press.

Johnson, K. and Golombek, P. (2002). Inquiry into experience: teachers' personal and professional growth. In K. Johnson and P. Golombek (eds) *Teachers' Narrative Inquiry as Professional Development*. Cambridge: Cambridge University Press, pp. 1–14.

Kinginger, C. (2002). Genres of power in language teacher education: interpreting the 'experts'. In S. Savignon (ed.), *Interpreting Communicative Language Teaching*. New Haven, CT: Yale University Press, pp. 193–207.

Kirkpatrick, A. (2007). *World Englishes: Implications for International Communication and English Language Teaching*. Cambridge: Cambridge University Press.

Kubota, R. (2002). The impact of globalization on language teaching in Japan. In D. Block and D. Cameron (eds) *Globalization and Language Teaching*. London: Routledge, pp. 13–28.

Llurda, E. (2004). Non-native speaker teachers and English as an international language. *International Journal of Applied Linguistics*, 14(3): 314–23.

McKay, S. (2002). *Teaching English as an International Language*. Oxford: Oxford University Press.

Nayar, B. (2002). Ideological binarism in the identities of native and non-native English speakers. In A. Duszac (ed.) *Us and Others: Social Identities Across Languages, Discourse and Cultures*. Amsterdam: John Benjamins, pp. 463–80.

Pennycook, A. (1994). *The Cultural Politics of English as an International Language*. Harlow: Longman.

Phillipson, R. (1992). *Linguistic Imperialism*. Oxford: Oxford University Press.

Prabhu, N. (1990). There is no best method – why?' *TESOL Quarterly*, 24(2): 161–76.

Rajagopalan, K. (2004). The concept of 'World English' and its implications for ELT. *English Language Teaching Journal*, 58(2): 111–17.

Seidlhofer, B. (2001). Closing a conceptual gap: the case for a description of English as a lingua franca' *International Journal of Applied Linguistics*, 11(2): 133–58.

Sharkey, J. and Johnson, K. (eds) (2003). *The TESOL Quarterly Dialogues*. Alexandria, VA: TESOL Inc.

Szesztay, M. (2004). Teachers' ways of knowing. *English Language Teaching Journal*, 58(2): 129–36.

13
Motivation and ELT: Looking Ahead to the Future

Ema Ushioda

Global trends, motivational dissonances

At a 2012 conference in Austria hosted by the International Association of Teachers of English as a Foreign Language (IATEFL) Learner Autonomy Special Interest Group, I presented a paper in which I drew together emergent issues and insights from the draft chapters of this volume and explored their resonance with English language teachers and educators working in various European contexts (Ushioda, 2012a). According to the European Commission (2006), English is the most widely used lingua franca across the countries of the European Union, and dominates foreign language curricula in mainstream education in Europe (Eurydice, 2005). Yet, as several contributors to this volume have highlighted, the unquestioned importance ascribed to English in global, national and educational policy terms does not simply translate into unquestioned positive motivation for learners of English, and this dissonance presents significant challenges for teachers at a local level.

Indeed, at the conference in Austria I heard numerous accounts from teachers that many students seem to dislike studying English or invest little effort in their formal English lessons, even if they may engage with English informally outside school. This clearly echoes the arguments put forward by Henry (Chapter 8) and Taylor (Chapter 3) regarding motivational dissonances between students' in-class and out-of-class contexts of encounters with English. These dissonances represent a significant critical challenge for teachers working in settings in which English has become a major medium of youth culture, entertainment and recreational activity. As teachers from several European countries (e.g., Austria, Denmark, Germany, Slovenia) remarked at the conference, in addition to a general sense of boredom with school English lessons, a motivational by-product of young people's engagement in English-mediated entertainment and leisure-time activity is an assumed comfortable fluency in English and concomitant lack of motivation to focus on developing higher levels of grammatical control and accuracy.

Furthermore, in some countries, such as Finland, where attainment of high levels of English proficiency is increasingly the norm, teachers speak of a growing motivational divide between those who peak at such 'normal' high levels of proficiency and those few who succeed in achieving superlative degrees of mastery at the upper reaches of C2 (highest proficiency level) in the Common European Framework of Reference (CEFR) levels of language proficiency (Council of Europe, 2001). In such contexts, the bar is being raised where optimal levels of English proficiency are concerned, affecting access to the more elite academic and professional career pathways and impacting on the motivation of otherwise competent English users who find the bar, nevertheless, beyond their reach. In short, even in contexts where high levels of English proficiency are very much standard, we see English continuing to exercise a significant gatekeeping role in determining academic, career and social progression, just as in other local, national and international settings in which the English language bar may be comparatively lower. As illustrated in this volume, such settings include, for example, the context of ESL for adult immigrants in the United States (Igoudin, Chapter 11), English for medical purposes in the Arab Gulf region (Malcolm, Chapter 6), or English for academic purposes in Australia (Woodrow, Chapter 7).

Professional challenges

Broadly speaking, then, the challenges for teachers are to find ways of addressing such motivational dissonances between young people's informal engagement with English outside school and the formal English lessons they experience in school; between their personal goals and interests, and the goals and demands of the curriculum; between their developing fluency in English and the effort needed to achieve accurate control over form; and between their existing levels of proficiency and the exacting standards required for access to desired academic, social and career pathways. Of course, as evidenced in Gao's stories of autonomous and self-motivated learners of English in China (Chapter 10), there are initiatives that learners themselves can take to deal with some of these dissonances and to find ways of enhancing their motivation and learning opportunities outside the classroom. Inside the classroom, however, the pedagogical responsibility clearly lies with teachers to engage students' interest and work with them to address these motivational dissonances in constructive ways. As the arguments put forward by Banegas (Chapter 5), Henry (Chapter 8), Igoudin (Chapter 11) and Taylor (Chapter 3) suggest, valuable steps in this regard would seem to include giving students voice in expressing their interests and identities, facilitating their autonomy in negotiating ideas and preferences, and encouraging them to build their own personally relevant connections between what they do in class, their lives outside class, and their aspirations and desired identities for the future (for further discussion on the pedagogical interactions among motivation, autonomy and identity, see Ushioda, 2011a; 2011b).

However, it is not my purpose in this concluding chapter to present a consolidated set of pedagogical recommendations gleaned from the various contributions to this volume. After all, a key message in this collection is that the global ELT landscape is complex and diverse and that contexts of learning are both localised and fluid, rendering it increasingly difficult to characterise the interactions among motivation, context and pedagogy in a generalised sense. Rather, the value of a collection of this kind is that it opens windows onto different contexts, experiences and practices and raises locally produced insights and questions which may resonate in various ways with ELT practitioners in other contexts, as was the case with the teachers I addressed at the conference in Austria.

Yet, ultimately, if there is a generalisable implication to be drawn from the various chapters in this collection, it is perhaps the rather simple and unsurprising one that teachers can have a significant impact on students' motivation. This is clearly a double-edged sword, since our impact as teachers can be negative as well as positive, as evidenced by the growing body of research on demotivation in language learning in which teachers and their instructional practices emerge as significant negative factors (for an overview of L2 demotivation studies, see Dörnyei & Ushioda, 2011). Obviously the professional challenge we face is to make our impact on students' motivation as positive as we can. How we achieve this will depend very much on our professional skills and experience, as well as on our understanding of our learners, of the contexts we work in and of the resources at our disposal, including the motivational and language learning potential of various technologies (see Stockwell, Chapter 9).

While highlighting the impact of teachers and instructional practices on student motivation might seem like stating the obvious, the issue of real significance here is the emphasis this brings to the local micro-contextual dynamics of teacher–student interactions, relations and classroom practices where motivation is concerned. In other words, whatever generalised prominence learning and using English may have in the prevailing discourses of globalisation and global education, in national or regional curriculum policy or across society at large, at a fundamental level it is what happens (or does not happen) in each individual classroom, as orchestrated by the teacher, that will have a critical bearing on how students are motivated (or not) to invest effort in learning English. This seems to be a common insight across many of the chapters in this volume, as highlighted for example in Kuchah's analysis (Chapter 4) of Francophone children's and parents' motivation to opt for English-medium schooling in Cameroon. As he shows, it is the rich quality of children's day-to-day learning experiences with Anglophone teachers that has a pivotal role to play in influencing motivation to choose English-medium education this regard. Similarly, the classroom vignettes portrayed by Lamb and Budiyanto (Chapter 2) and their analysis point to the significance of this localised level of teacher-orchestrated activities, interactions and experiences in shaping students' affective engagement with English in a provincial Indonesian ELT setting in which English language communication opportunities outside class are limited.

As I outlined in Chapter 1, with the changing global landscape of ELT and the increasing diversity of settings in which learning English is situated, local contexts of learning assume particular importance for discussions of motivation. In light of the concluding analysis in the current chapter, I think it is important to amplify this argument by emphasising the point that, by local contexts of learning, we mean more than just the physical, social or virtual setting, however defined. Local contexts of learning embrace also the microlevel of dynamic interactions, relations, practices and shared histories and experiences in particular classrooms as shaped and orchestrated by particular teachers. As illustrated in many of the chapters in this volume, it is at this very localised level of students' learning experience that the real potential for engaging (or disengaging) their motivation may lie. This places a premium on the teacher's skills, understanding and readiness to respond to the challenge.

Future lines of research inquiry

From a theoretical and research perspective, these arguments also place a premium on teacher- and classroom-focused empirical studies to investigate how teachers' instructional and interactional practices contribute to shaping processes of motivation in their classrooms. As I have discussed elsewhere (Ushioda, 2012b), richly detailed analyses of motivation grounded in actual classroom events and interactions remain very rare in a field where methods of inquiry have typically relied on self-report instruments such as questionnaires and interviews. While qualitative research interviews may allow for richer individual perspectives to emerge than questionnaire methods, the interview context is necessarily different from the classroom context under focus in terms of interactants, purpose, temporal perspective and (more often than not) physical setting. Our understanding of how motivation is experienced and engaged through specific classroom events, interactions and practices is limited to what teacher or student participants can usefully tell us and rationalise retrospectively in response to our probing questions.

There is clearly scope here for developing a more richly grounded and multidimensional *in situ* analysis of how processes of motivation evolve through particular classroom events, interactions and practices. As I have suggested (Ushioda, 2012b), this could entail capturing (i.e., through video and audio recording as well as observational field notes) the events under focus, such as students' interactions in a group work task, processes of teacher feedback on student performance, or critical episodes in a lesson. Through a detailed multimodal analysis of the event (taking into account, for example, aspects of classroom discourse, non-verbal interactions, off-task behaviours), we can develop our interpretative perspective as informed by our theoretical and analytical insights in relation to processes of motivation. Our interpretative perspective might then be triangulated with teacher and student participants' own retrospective accounts through stimulated recall interviews (Gass & Mackey, 2000), enabling us to build an integrated analysis of motivational processes and practices at work in the classroom from multiple perspectives.

Another important line of research inquiry lies with teachers themselves, since they are ideally positioned to understand their learners and have a vested interest in knowing how best to engage their motivation. Surprisingly, perhaps, teacher research on motivation in relation to their own classroom practice remains rather scarce in the field. Among the contributors in this collection, for example, only Banegas (Chapter 5) reports on a practitioner research study grounded in his own classroom experiences and practices as well as those of his colleagues participating in collaborative action research.

Aside from more general practical and ideological reasons why language teachers may be reluctant to engage in or with academic research (for detailed discussion, see Borg, 2010; see also Aboshiha, Chapter 12), there may be more specific perceived barriers to teacher research on motivation in relation to their own classroom practice. In particular, teachers gathering self-report data on classroom motivation from their own students may feel that the reliability of such data is questionable. After all, students may refrain from voicing their true opinions out of respect for (or fear of) the teacher, or because of unclear evaluative consequences. Teachers may also feel concerned that the methods they use to investigate motivation in their classrooms may unduly influence students' motivation itself (thereby raising the vexed issue of data validity or contamination), or that such research processes may interfere with the teaching process and their pedagogical priorities and responsibilities (see, for example, Li, 2006).

One way forward for teacher-researchers in this regard may be to consider an integration rather than separation of their teaching and researching objectives. Accordingly, the tools they use to 'investigate' their students' motivation might be regarded as functioning simultaneously (and primarily) as pedagogical tools designed to enhance students' voice and involvement in learning and thus to engage their motivation. One example would be the practices reported by Banegas (Chapter 5) to involve students in suggesting and negotiating lesson topics and, subsequently, to invite their personal evaluation of these lesson experiences. Another example might be the use of students' language learning stories or histories in class. These can function on the one hand as pedagogical tools to engage students in communicating in English while encouraging reflection on language learning processes, and on the other as investigative tools for the teacher to enable better understanding of individual students' experiences and motivation (for discussion of language learner stories from pedagogical and research perspectives see, for example, Benson & Nunan, 2005; also Kalaja et al., 2008). After all, if engaging our students' motivation is a key professional challenge and priority, then all aspects of our classroom practice that can contribute to this have pedagogical value and validity, including the (research) opportunities we create to listen to what students have to say.

As this concluding chapter has emphasised, across the changing global landscape of ELT, the localised practices and skills of teachers working in particular classrooms with particular learners seem pivotal in shaping processes of motivation. As a field of inquiry, research on motivation in language learning will be significantly enriched through a sharper empirical focus on these classrooms, practices and teacher–student interactions, and such empirical insights, in turn, can undoubtedly contribute to informing future theory and local practice.

References

Benson, P. and Nunan, D. (eds) (2005). *Learners' Stories: Difference and Diversity in Language Learning.* Cambridge: Cambridge University Press.

Borg, S. (2010). Language teacher research engagement. *Language Teaching,* 43(4): 391–429.

Council of Europe (2001). *Common European Framework of Reference for Languages: Learning, Teaching, Assessment.* Cambridge: Cambridge University Press.

Dörnyei, Z. and Ushioda, E. (2011). *Teaching and Researching Motivation* (Second Edition). Harlow: Pearson.

European Commission (2006). *Europeans and their Languages.* Special Eurobarometer 243. Available at: http://ec.europa.eu/public_opinion/archives/ebs/ebs_243_en.pdf [Accessed 18/06/12].

Eurydice (2005). *Key Data on Teaching Languages at School in Europe.* Brussels: Eurydice European Unit.

Gass, S. and Mackey, A. (2000). *Stimulated Recall Methodology in Second Language Research.* Mahwah, NJ: Lawrence Erlbaum.

Kalaja, P., Menezes, V. and Barcelos, A. M. F. (eds) (2008). *Narratives of Learning and Teaching EFL.* Basingstoke: Palgrave Macmillan.

Li, N. (2006). Researching and experiencing motivation: a plea for balanced research. *Language Teaching Research,* 10(4): 437–56.

Ushioda, E. (2011a). Language learning motivation, self and identity: current theoretical perspectives. *Computer Assisted Language Learning,* 24(3): 199–210.

Ushioda, E. (2011b). Motivating learners to speak as themselves. In G. Murray, X. Gao and T. Lamb (eds) *Identity, Motivation and Autonomy in Language Learning*. Bristol: Multilingual Matters, 11–24.

Ushioda, E. (2012a). *Learner Autonomy as the Answer to Motivation in the Era of Global English*. Plenary paper presented at IATEFL LA SIG Conference, University of Graz, 1–2 June 2012.

Ushioda, E. (2012b). Motivation: L2 learning as a special case? In S. Mercer, S. Ryan and M. Williams (eds) *Psychology for Language Learning: Insights from Research, Theory and Practice*. Basingstoke: Palgrave Macmillan, pp. 58–73.

Index

Printed and bound in Great Britain by
CPI Antony Rowe, Chippenham and Eastbourne